My Search
for Ancient Wisdom

My Search for Ancient Wisdom: One Prisoner's Journey of Transformation
Copyright © 2022, Mary E. Mitchell and Michael J. Nichols

Park Point Press
An imprint of Centers for Spiritual Living
573 Park Point Drive
Golden, CO 80401-7402
720-496-1370

www.csl.org/publications/books
www.scienceofmind.com/publish-your-book

Printed in the United States of America
Published March 2022

Editor: Julie Mierau, JM Wordsmith
Design/Layout: Maria Robinson, Designs On You, LLC
Illustrations copyright © Charles Patrick Smith

ISBN paperback: 978-1-956198-13-3
ISBN ebook: 978-1-956198-14-0

My Search
for Ancient Wisdom

One Prisoner's Journey of Transformation

MICHAEL J.
NICHOLS

&

MARY E.
MITCHELL

Park Point
PRESS

Park Point Press is an imprint of Centers for Spiritual Living
573 Park Point Drive | Golden CO 80401

DEDICATION

For many people, prison is just a chapter in their lives. But for me, it is the whole book. Pertaining to the idea and concept of a book, as I embark on this task, I want my world comprehended by my valor and my pain recognized, my misdeeds conceptualized. I want you to be able to understand my truths and my deceptions, the source of my generosities as well as my cruelties. Few would ever know the magnitude and dynamics of mastery that have come from surviving prison.

— DR. MICHAEL J. NICHOLS

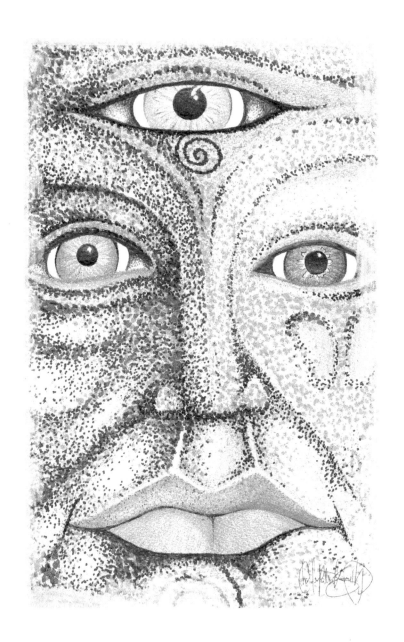

PRAISE FOR
My Search for Ancient Wisdom

Among the most poignant and humbling exchanges of my life over the last twenty years have been my interactions and correspondence with incarcerated men. Forever students and teachers of each other, mutual spiritual mentorship within the context of prison is a relationship rarely experienced. Dr. Michael J. Nichols and Rev. Dr. Mary Mitchell have truly taken us "inside," in every sense of the word, to a powerful place of insight and compassion. Intriguing and inspirational, their journey together into practical spirituality is an invitation to us all.

REV. DEBORAH L. JOHNSON
Author of *The Sacred Yes* and *Your Deepest Intent*

This book is a testament to the ways we can reach beyond the walls of our Centers for Spiritual Living, whereby we bring the teachings of Science of Mind to those who want and in some cases desperately hunger for the "emancipation from every discord of every nature." Having had family members who were incarcerated, I know all too well the desire for lasting change. The interaction, as shared in this book, demonstrates ways we can be a beneficial presence in the world. In fact, this is a demonstration of what it means to manifest "a world that works for all," including those who are often forgotten and denied access to a spiritual path of liberation, authenticity, forgiveness, and the awakening of their spiritual magnificence to such a degree that even if they are behind prison walls for the remainder of their lives, they are free.

REV. RAYMONT L. ANDERSON, D.D., PH.D., MSC.D.
Senior Minister, The Center for Spiritual Living Greater Baltimore

I have often wondered how the philosophy of Science of Mind would hold up under seriously bad circumstances, especially prolonged ones. Reading *My Search for Ancient Wisdom* gave me an inspiring and heart-touching answer to my question. Yes, the principles work if you *work* them, even in the worst of conditions, and surely that is what Dr. Nichols experienced.

Nichols walks the reader through his journey to a higher form of thought and action. He avoids the many grim details of life as a prisoner in the United States, although he does refer to them. He mainly focuses on what he is learning as he corresponds with Rev. Dr.

Mary Mitchell and reads many of the books that relate to the philosophy she shares with him. His thirst for knowledge leads him to study the Science of Mind history, the people like Ernest Holmes, founder of the Science of Mind philosophy, and more. Watching Nichols's learning and epiphanies bloom was both inspiring and illuminating. He not only describes what he is learning but how he applies it and the results as well.

Having studied some of the same books as Nichols and being steeped in the Science of Mind philosophy, I found myself seeing things with a new and deeper perspective. His authentic determination to learn, apply the learning, and use what he was learning to help others lead better lives motivated me to do better in my own life. I so admire his willingness to delve into this unique spiritual philosophy. I also admire his willingness to take a strong look at himself and the beliefs that drove him for so long—beliefs that did not make his life better—and embrace different beliefs even when that made things hard for him in prison. Over time, he gained the respect of fellow inmates and apparently even the guards.

This book is worth reading by the general public because so few know the dehumanizing conditions of our prison system and so many have an unforgiving detachment when it comes to those who have been incarcerated. It would especially benefit Science of Mind adherents to learn about Nichols's struggle and triumph over terrible circumstances using the Science of Mind principles.

REVEREND PAMELAGRACE BEATTY

Author of *Dancing in the Light of Possibilities*

My Search for Ancient Wisdom is a fascinating and inspiring publication of the correspondence between two spiritual co-travelers. Michael, an inmate serving a life sentence, and Mary, a minister of Centers for Spiritual Living, share their letters, poems, and journal writings, giving us, the readers, an intimate view into their lives, challenges, and spiritual evolution. The dialogue is raw, compelling, eye-opening, and, above all, a confirmation of the power of loving-kindness, inquiry, and spiritual study.

REV. EDWARD VILJOEN, D.D.

Author of *The Bhagavad Gita: The Song of God Retold in Simplified English,*
The Power of Meditation: An Ancient Technique to Access Your Inner Power,
and *Ordinary Goodness: The Surprisingly Effortless Path to Creating a Life of Meaning and Beauty.*
Senior Minister, Center for Spiritual Living, Santa Rosa, California,
and Spiritual Leader for the international organization Centers for Spiritual Living

I was inspired by the book *My Search for Ancient Wisdom*. Anyone reading this book will encounter a story of transformation in the midst of a challenging circumstance.

REV. GAYLON MCDOWELL
Christ Universal Temple in Chicago and host of the podcast
Truth Transforms on Unity Online Radio

Some of the great writings of the ages were written by people who were incarcerated. While in a Roman prison, the Apostle Paul wrote many of his letters to various churches that became New Testament books. Viktor Frankl envisioned his amazing book, *Man's Search for Meaning,* while in a Nazi concentration camp, and Nelson Mandela's *Long Walk to Freedom* emerged similarly from his time in a South African prison. In *My Search for Ancient Wisdom,* Rev. Mitchell facilitates extraordinary correspondence with Michael as he faces a sentence of life without parole. Their exchanges are substantive, powerful, and revealing. Read it—and let your mind be free.

REV. DR. JOHN B. WATERHOUSE
Co-Founding Minister, Center for Spiritual Living, Asheville,
and former President of Centers for Spiritual Living

You cannot help but be inspired by *My Search for Ancient Wisdom*. This is an incredible story of a friendship and mentorship that unfolded after Rev. Mary responded to a request from a prison inmate. Michael is a remarkable intellect and his journey in the prison system is enlightening, as well as frustrating. The hunger he has for learning New Thought teachings and the depth to which he studies them are remarkable. This book also serves as a lesson in the teachings of Ernest Holmes and many other authors. It is a class in metaphysics. The continuing story is beautifully written and an inspirational read. I highly recommend it.

REV. BONNIE ANDERSON
Ordained Minister, Centers for Spiritual Living

Wow—what a journey! These letters between Michael and Mary are a profound revelation of spirituality in relationship to the plight of the over-incarceration of African-American men in the United States today. Exploring spirituality, the Science of Mind, institutionalized racism, and the criminal incarceration system is an eye-opening study of the human spirit reaching for a higher Self. Eloquent, insightful, challenging, and deep.

Be prepared to go on a journey in which your own spirituality may be confronted, inspired, and strengthened. A powerful read.

REV. DR. PETRA WELDES
Co-Spiritual Director, CSL Dallas, a Center for Spiritual Living

We all have relationships that profoundly affect us. Mary shares with us an incredible journey of growth, forgiveness, and love with an inmate, a "lifer." We are fortunate to be passive participants in this journey of change centered in the Divine. As Michael struggles to survive within the confines of prison, Rev. Mary offers acceptance, encouragement, kindness, and a teaching that unfolds new truth and knowledge. Michael's poetry gives us further insight into his intellect, artistry, and search for knowledge. Mary's acceptance and willingness to include him in her classes from afar creates a relationship that will touch your heart and speak to your soul.

REV. EILEEN O. BROWNELL, M.S.
Staff Minister, Center for Spiritual Living, Chico, California

I, too, have had the extreme honor and pleasure of getting to know Dr. Michael J. Nichols for the past twelve years. Dr. Michael's writings give us a glimpse into his inner-most thoughts as he processes not only the deprivation and cruelty of living in prison for more than thirty years (since the age of nineteen) and having a life sentence but also the plight of growing up Black in America. He shares with us his spiritual journey as he devours and studies from the greats. He has used this bleak, abnormally unhealthy environment as a classroom to master himself and achieve one of the highest levels of spiritual awareness I have ever seen. Like Viktor Frankl in *Man's Search for Meaning,* everything has been taken from him but his power to choose how to think and feel. Today, he is a free man, inside. I am so proud of him. Thank you, Dr. Mary, for diligently walking by his side and being there for him with your words of wisdom and love.

CATH DEPALMA
New Thought Minister, Author, and Motivational Speaker

This book is a living chronicle of the intersection of two lives and the miracles that arose between them. Through letters spanning more than a decade, Dr. Michael J. Nichols, a convicted felon, and Rev. Dr. Mary Mitchell, a New Thought teacher and minister, enable readers to experience firsthand an extraordinary journey of awakening consciousness amidst the harsh realities of hardcore prison life.

Dr. Mary is a gentle, gifted teacher, and Dr. Michael is a superlatively articulate student who holds nothing back and has everything on the line. At times I found this book so painful I could barely read on; however, in each reading I, too, expanded and grew through the stirring lived experience that is Dr. Michael's world and Dr. Mary's steady tutelage to see beyond appearances. If ever two people answered a soul assignment, it is Dr. Michael and Dr. Mary.

Dr. Michael and Dr. Mary rip away the veil of our cultural naïveté about our national penal system. Readers are witness to his discovery of a deeper freedom through revelation after revelation. James Baldwin wrote, "If I love you, I have to make you conscious of the things you don't see." I yearn to know that this raw, real documentary of spiritual awakening reverberates far and wide, a tough-love wake-up note to those of us who are honored to read it.

REV. MARY BETH SPEER
Secretary and Membership Chair, Affiliated New Thought Network

There is hope for millions of prisoners to lift themselves from the depths of despair when they begin to ask questions like, "Is there any good that can come from me being here?"

In 2009, I received a letter from Michael, a murderer in prison sentenced to life without parole who sought my help in understanding spirituality and metaphysics. As a minister, I was happy to respond. He was studying the world's religions and African history, seeking a greater understanding of his life. His goal was to find Truth both spiritually and through his ancestry to determine if it was possible that there was a larger purpose for being in prison for life.

Entering prison in 1991 at the age of nineteen, he wrote that there was a time when he hurt people to the point of death. Today, after more than three decades in prison, he has purged his gangster influence through spiritual and historical studies, discipline, and mental strength. When we began corresponding, he wrote about prison as a terrestrial hell, a land of madness with walls of ignorance and morbid ideologies.

He experienced sensory deprivation, repression, harassment, mental stagnation, and blatant racism. He observed other prisoners filled with rage, hate, and despair. He watched day-to-day rules destroy social bonds and increase distrust among inmates, leaving them feeling worthless and lifeless. His early letters were full of hate and anger at the system, the guards, the rules, and frustration with finding himself in "the hole" of solitary confinement for his hostile behavior.

Over time and through study, Michael began to realize and understand that there is a power for good in the universe—and his beliefs began to shift. He was able to prove to himself that it's true: What goes around comes around, what you give you receive, the Law of Cause and Effect is a universal law always in operation, often called karma. As he began to see things from this broader perspective of how life works and the science

CONTINUED

behind the power of his mind, he began to lift himself up out of the dungeon of hell. His genuine understanding of the power of positive thinking and how directing the energetic power of his mind in a positive and life-affirming way could and did bring him liberation.

Today, he meets confrontation and anger with a different spirit and a humane smile. He is able to be what he has been fated to become, what I think of as a prison buddha, one who reaches out to help others to show them there is another way.

If you have a loved one, young or old, who is on a self-destructive path or already incarcerated, I believe reading about Michael's journey can help save their lives. Within these pages, you and they may find morsels of wisdom from Michael's transformative journey to uplift, to inspire, to help inform you and them about the journey ahead.

Through my correspondence over the years with four prisoners, I have come to recognize when true transformation occurs. Yes, it can happen even within the walls of a prison cell. When that occurs and becomes embedded in their personality, I believe it is time for more mercy and grace within the system to give them a second chance.

— REV. DR. MARY E. MITCHELL
Engaging Grace prison ministry, author, teacher, and speaker

For many, many moons, while living in the realm of the 9th Dominion, I needed to understand truths. I needed to understand reality. I was raised in America, yet I am an African and a descendant of those who were kidnapped and brought to this land from Africa. Everything I was taught in American schools was designed to perpetuate deceptions that would keep my mind confined in such a way that prison would be inevitable, sooner or later.

Entering the 9th Dominion straight after graduating high school, I entered a world of unrestrained realities. No more illusions about the truth of the world. But this world only provided a small piece of a reality. I sought help from those in the free world. I moved past barriers that inhibit most convicts. And I met a mentor and friend, Rev. Dr. Mary E. Mitchell. The letters contained within this book I wrote to her over a period of thirteen years. The letters reflect the process of my mind.

Rev. Mary recognized my suffering and decided to apply her knowledge of Science of Mind to aid me in my healing and provide me the knowledge necessary to transform completely without the need to continue to carry negative baggage.

In a universe of practically infinite possibilities, we can have orderly perceptions. They need not be chaotic. Having the ability to know how to use your mind in just such a way came from my search for ancient wisdom. Deep in all people lies the latent ability of our awareness to focus itself on unusual aspects and concepts of the world, or on the unknown that we do not recognize to even exist.

Science of Mind taught me that we have the ability to summon events without ever suspecting the obsessiveness of our attention on things—objects, situations, or people—through fear, attachment, desire, or curiosity. We unconsciously summon events and experiences into our lives.

A problem is only a statement of certain conditions of life through which a principle of truth can be applied to produce a desired result as a means of growth

CONTINUED

for the individual who may face it. Conditions in life that seem opposed to an individual's highest good are but points of practice until they can attain that strength of character to see and manifest only the truth of Universal Mind. When we can focus on the reality of truth, we will see the world with clarity. All unpleasantness vanishes and everything we exhibit is a good that can show forth in our character and within our sphere.

Nature is in harmony and is working under the influence of Higher Purpose. Any inharmonious condition in the nature of our being is evidence that we are out of harmony with the natural order of things. So, we must approach every condition in tune with our quiddity.

Nature is eternally attuned to the good, for we are the offspring of God and God is good.

— DR. MICHAEL J. NICHOLS

by Dr. Michael J. Nichols

> *To study esoteric science is to consider consciousness a function of Mental Energy and recognize that everything in the universe has its own consciousness, making everything related; the study and teaching of mechanistic aspects of control, limitation, projection, and focusing this Mental Energy to make progression in the world.*

For me, understanding esoteric science meant understanding ancient African science and then understanding the spiritual philosophy, Science of Mind. These teachings taught me to develop an essential reality within in order to produce an essential reality without.

I know myself as Mind—as God As Man, In Man, Is Man. I forever more control my experiences through thought and not through the manipulation of events. I no longer have to ask what the obscurations are. What will lift the veils of obscurations and what will perpetuate them? My quest for the wisdom that derived from antiquity, from African heritage, ancestry, and science, was the discovery of the laws of nature. This not only disclosed the subtle forces at work in the physical realm, but also equally revealed to me the Science of Mind and how laws of thought were taught by Jesus Christ.

Metaphysics is an extension of physics and psychology, which uncover the invisible cause of many physical ailments and teach me the broader laws of Mind, the laws that govern all human activity. The wisdom attained from the ancient elders has shown me how to develop the calm to remain in an undisturbed state no matter what happens within my sphere of influence.

Change is always taking place within the changeless. This may seem to be a paradoxical statement. Is it not oxymoronic to consider the stability of change with changelessness? Or is it just a reminder that nothing, no matter how it may seem to

CONTINUED

our myopic vision, lasts forever in its present form? Whether something is deemed positive or negative, enlightened or devastating, eventually the current things in a person's life will give way to other things—and these may not be simply physical situations but also ideas, beliefs, or behaviors.

How do we reestablish a firmness once believed immovable? The depths of my spirituality have never been based on monuments of form. Essential Spirit is centered everywhere and excludes nothing and no one. From my ancestry, I see the understanding of self-knowledge as the basis of all true knowledge. The mastery of passions is required as the first step. It is the taming of the hyena, as it is known by many African scholars, putting this being, this Djab, under control of my Higher Being.

The psyche is where any passion would run wild if left untamed and allowed to rule. The Higher Power gains control when you know how to use what It has given for you to maintain dominion over your entire existence. Come to know the Divine Form that inhabits the vessel of intricate design.

The word "education" comes from ancient Kemet belief in "educo" and is based on the understanding that all you need to know is inside the self. This African civilization viewed education as the structuring of each individual to bring out their higher potential. From the past comes the truth of things that have been changed, corrupted, and distorted in the present.

I am a huntersman. A man must hunt himself, seek out his own truth, no matter the peril, for only then will he be at peace. Many within the realm in which I dwell fear finding themselves, for the imagination sometimes makes demands the mind cannot accept. Some people can fool others some of the time, but they cannot fake vibration, and ultimately it is our vibration that others respond to.

A strong and stable mind is the greatest asset a person can possess. We must make our minds steady enough so that they are never disturbed by any and everything that happens or by the words others say. Whatever the mind believes is experienced in some degree as reality. Some of the knowledge I attained was at first elusive, but that aspect of esotericism must exist for its own reason. Yet, no matter, nothing should be blindly accepted—but neither should anything be blindly rejected.

Take time to teach yourself. Learn how to heal yourself. My growth took years. I still grow. I still learn, but now I am much wiser and much healthier as a result of all I have learned so far.

May God bless you all in your endeavors.

by Rev. Dr. Mary E. Mitchell

In 2009, I received a letter from Dr. Michael J. Nichols about his search for ancient wisdom and his curiosity about an article I had written in *Creative Thought* magazine. He wondered if the philosophy I described, called Science of Mind, would help him adjust to a prison sentence of life without parole for murder in 1991 when he was nineteen.

At the time, besides my full-time work in the field of environmental restoration, I was a licensed minister teaching metaphysics at what is now called the Center for Spiritual Living in Redding, California. Metaphysics is a philosophy that invites students to see the connection between ourselves and reality, understand the power of our minds, and explore how interacting within the energy field in the environment helps us understand what our life in this world is all about and how we can use it to shape our experiences for the better.

Dr. Nichols's eloquent writing style and his heartfelt desire impressed me, so I responded. And here we are, still corresponding in 2021. Over time, there was a monumental shift away from his initial gangster attitude of anger and hatred, to a deep personal reflection of life as he put the Science of Mind principles to use with the guards and other prisoners. This, along with the dozens of classes he has taken, has made a dramatic shift in his personality, and today he believes this teaching has unequivocally saved his life. Now I often refer to him as a prison buddha, a teacher, listener, and peacemaker. Some examples from his letters:

- Prison for many has been a laboratory, a learning institution, an asylum, a necropolis, a zoo, and much more. But it also allows one to either make use of or forge the opportunities that do exist to attain moral values that a difficult situation may afford him.

- There is something greater than me at work and it takes incredible faith to see the spiritual perspective of a challenge.

CONTINUED

- I've become calm in the measure that I understand myself as a thought-evolved being and even though there are many things that happen in this land that I do not agree with, I have ceased to fuss and fume and worry.

- Each one, teach one. That is how we get to survive in these isolated death camps. We reach out to one another, teach each other, lift each other up, work together, strive together, collaborate, and conglomerate.

- In my awareness, I have acknowledged the great mystery and it is that in this life I have been perfectly placed in exactly the right position to make all the difference in the world.

Is it possible that Dr. Nichols will ever be released on parole due to his dramatic transformation? I continue to have faith that he will. In the past few years, states are examining the staggering cost of keeping one person in prison. It costs an average of $50,000 to $60,000/ year, but in some states, like California, it costs $81,000. Since those serving life without parole are expected to spend the rest of their life in prison, it's a significant part of every state and city budget.

In a recent Vera Institute of Justice report, the number of individuals incarcerated in the United States in 2020 was 1,818,700. One in seven or about 260,000 are in for life. Three years ago, the State of Missouri began discussions about legislation that would open up parole for prisoners who have served 25 years with a good record. When I heard this, I wrote a letter to the governor of Missouri and included some of Michael's letters. The governor's assistant responded and invited me to monitor the state's progress with this legislation, but to date nothing has been passed. In my opinion, a focus on true rehabilitation should be a major focal point in every prison facility, and I believe the practical spirituality found in *The Science of Mind* textbook offers a blueprint that would save lives, if it were made available. Regarding any spiritual texts, most prisons only recognize the Bible and the Koran.

Of course, there is a difference of opinion about this topic. Recent research by The Sentencing Project found that "people age out of criminal behavior, producing diminishing returns for public safety. The financial and moral costs to communities is very high and diverts funds from crime prevention and social intervention programs." The report proposes a crime policy based on research and mercy.

Dr. Nichols can apply for parole every three years, which he does, and continually updates his portfolio showing the classes he has taken and work he does in the prison. Every day I visualize him as a free man back at home with his family.

ACKNOWLEDGMENTS

from Dr. Michael J. Nichols:

I would like to acknowledge my mentor and spiritual advisor, Rev. Dr. Mary E. Mitchell. I also acknowledge my mentor and spiritual advisor, Rev. Cath Depalma, and her backbone, Mr. John. I acknowledge some of the first contacts I made with Rev. Mary Beth Speer, who told me that the vision of Science of Mind was the awakening of humanity to its spiritual magnificence. And Rev. Mary Jo, who enlightened me to Phineas Parkhurst Quimby.

I have a special acknowledgement to Mr. Paul, the mountain that is supportive of my mentor Rev. Mary Mitchell's endeavors.

To Almighty Bondye, thank you for your blessings. Reler (amen).

from Rev. Dr. Mary E. Mitchell:

It is with deep gratitude that I acknowledge Dr. Nichols for contacting me in 2009, asking for more information on metaphysics and the philosophy I've been teaching for years called the Science of Mind. His hope was that it might be something that could make his life in prison easier to bear. It's fascinating to look back through our letters and see the seeds of enlightenment that led to his amazing transformation. Our connection also accelerated my spiritual growth, as I responded to the many questions and observations in his inquisitive and intellectual mind.

A special bouquet of gratitude to my husband, Paul, for his relentless support of the time it takes to have an effective prison ministry. And to our two cats, Amazing Graze and Mama Mia, who parade across my desk while I write, thank you for making sure I take appropriate breaks to give you my loving attention.

CONTINUED

Heartfelt thanks to Charles Patrick Smith, another prison correspondent, for his insight, intuition, and personal communication with God in creating the compelling artwork in this book.

A big hug and three cheers to Stephanie Finne, Julie Mierau, and Maria Robinson, the Park Point Press team, for acknowledging the power in this book of letters and bringing your amazing talents together, resulting in such an inspiring publication.

And finally, I am deeply grateful to the many people who took time to read the draft manuscript and write the many rich endorsements that say it all. Thank you!

EDITOR'S NOTE

The letters in this book stand as written by the correspondents. The original letters from Dr. Nichols were handwritten and are transcribed here as accurately as possible. In some cases, letters were slightly edited for clarity. The collection of letters, curated by Rev. Dr. Mary Mitchell, delves into the essence of her correspondence with Dr. Nichols and is not intended to include each letter over the course of their correspondence.

Many names for God appear in this book—Source, Mind, Creative Intelligence, Spirit, Truth, among others. All synonyms for God are set off with initial capital letters.

Throughout this work are references to Science of Mind (or the Science of Mind), referring to a philosophy and belief system, founded by Ernest Holmes more than 100 years ago, that today operates under the auspices of Centers for Spiritual Living (CSL). The textbook and magazine of the same name are set off in italics.

The correspondents use terms that may be unfamiliar to readers to describe both the prison setting and Science of Mind, New Thought, and other spiritual precepts. To assist you in understanding these terms, we include a glossary at the end of this book.

TABLE OF CONTENTS

Examining different theological schools of thought — Looking for wisdom — Studying Science of Mind — Why am I here? — What is desire? — Life without parole — Seeking truth, wisdom, knowledge — This realm, this terrestrial hell, this land of madness — The primary object is to survive — With truth, wisdom, and understanding as catalysts, a complete change in thinking flows — Walking a more truthful path — Trying to make sense of things — Cultivating my mind, exercising it, strengthening it, sharpening it — Who is really crazy?

God offers to every mind a choice between truth and repose — In prison, kindness and compassion are outlawed — Man cannot imprison consciousness — The prison staff set one group against another — Is violence the only answer? — How can one combat injustice with those who only believe in hate and more hate? — Liberation is gained from education — How can one be of this world and not a part of it? — Shedding the skin of my old ways — Anything accepted as truth makes a subconscious impression — I've been given a precious understanding so unexpectedly that has changed me forever and for the better.

A higher order structure emerges in my conscious, each more complex until there is only unity in all directions — My search for absolute Truth — Concrete walls, razor wire, electric fences can never hold down the thoughts of a prisoner — Malevolent influences imposed morbid teachings, manipulating the present by eliminating the past, rewriting history to accommodate its plans for the future — The world in which I existed ensured I would not succeed — In this world, darkness of the mind, corruption, wickedness, and hatred pay out with generous interest — A social disorder infused fear, doubt, confusion, and self-loathing into me — Learning my true history and searching for hidden truths — If I hold no goal higher than unraveling the secrets of the Universe, I must let the Truth into my soul.

Every year, month, week, and day is the facsimile of the last year, month, week, and day — Humans encased in concrete cannot truly grow, development is arrested, the being regresses and becomes the living dead — The future is a non-reality, taken before it has been touched — Lifelessness, unnecessary victimization, the dark forest, coercive controls, self-loathing, manufactured criminality — Developing immunity, courage — Discovering the purpose of my existence — The hole — Denying myself freedom — The death of my son — Elimination of hope — The prison of my own mind — My ancestors — Coming to terms with who I am — The power of a committed mind erased negative emotions — Ancient African Science, esoteric studies — Grandmother and Mother, library card, trombone, marching band, ROTC, Uncle Jr. — The warrior's way of life — Prison, an opportunity to learn my rich African heritage and culture.

The Law of Cause and Effect — New Thought research and religions — Teleology of the Universe — Science of Mind stepped into my true Spirit — In Potosi Prison, more reverence for man than their own God — The mind has a way of punishing itself for destroying life with no remorse — No story is a straight line — The madness that engulfed me — Curiosity, one of my strongest virtues — All along the answers were within me — Guided to my roots — There is grace, if one pays close attention — Only individual opinions are fixed and dogmatic; Truth is more dynamic — When a man changes his mind, he changes the world — See Truth only — I can endure and survive; this, for me, is a source of pride — How I value these lands in which I have evolved — I discover how truly necessary my life and another's life are to each other . . . Exploring new horizons.

Working toward the possibility of greater wholeness, of positive thought, as well as a consistency of right thinking — Since studying Science of Mind, I haven't had an assault in almost ten years — Realizing my behavior hurt others left me crushed, knowing my choices produced lasting harm in the world — Coming into accountability, I realized how demented and domineering I had become, all derived from fear — As a criminal thinker, my excessive reactions to small events often reveal a negative sociopathic issue — Letting go of old ideas, old habits, and even old lives allows for a new one to grow — I am dedicated to work for the good of others, to eliminate my destructive habits and weaknesses — Divinity has brought me to this point, to be who I truly am.

Adversity teaches patience, compassion, and tolerance, bringing a new perception of the world — Overcoming ignorance, anger, and greed and turning toward happiness and good fortune stems from our own positive actions and thoughts — Working as a Daily Living Assistant, helping handicapped inmates — Many staff members believe a lifer doesn't need to be rehabilitated, which is erroneous thinking — I've encountered another world within this one, a world of illness, dementia, paranoia, illogical fears, chronic maladies, and blatant madness — None of these patients has any religious services, which saddened my heart — How does one introduce spirituality to the refused? — Science of Mind teaches that anger and malice cannot breathe the same atmosphere as goodness and purity — Within this realm, pretty much everyone is angry about something — I gave up the last remaining vestiges of anger a couple of years ago — Intelligence is the power of choice, while anger cripples rational thought.

Appearing in "Open Doors," a youth intervention video, speaking on the pitfalls of living and glo-rifying the gangster lifestyle — As a DLA, witnessing an overwhelming excess of elder abuse — In the hole for a dangerous contraband infraction, keeping a weapon close at hand — Before a dream is realized, I have to purge a habit born out of fear, preparing my Spirit and my will — For the first time in two decades, I really want to be a free man again — When a person really desires something, all the Universe conspires to help him to realize his dream — You took my thoughts out of the grave and gave me a chance to breathe and think in a brighter way.

Pressed by poverty and corruption, I dream of better things, of retirement, of grace, of beauty — This 9th Dominion can no longer hold me — Years from now I am a successful author, film maker, spiritual speaker, a master of certain forces of the mind — Arrested development has limited my ability. I have never paid a utility bill or owned a car or gone grocery shopping — I now prepare for this major transition — No situation is hopeless — *Regarding COVID-19:* The world has been given an opportunity for great reflection, a chance to change course for the betterment of all beings — I refrain from violence — The prison system evolved to create a realm of absolute compliance — The number one enemy of progress is questions — In the past, I relied on violence — I cannot return to the free world with this type of mind state — I keep myself humble and continue in my studies — I continue my pursuit of liberation.

The riot, the whole, the situation — Understanding and surviving in ad-seg — Scarecrows, straw men without vision, living lives filled with fear — Moving forward in expression to help others — The Creator is the author — Maintaining a peaceful state of mind — Living by God's mercy and grace — Decades spent searching for Ancient Wisdom.

ILLUSTRATIONS

My Search
for Ancient Wisdom

CHAPTER 1

2009

Is There a Larger
Purpose for
Being in Prison for Life?

Examining different theological schools of thought — Looking for wisdom — Studying Science of Mind — Why am I here? — What is desire? — Life without parole — Seeking truth, wisdom, knowledge — This Realm, this terrestrial hell, this land of madness — The primary object is to survive — With truth, wisdom, and understanding as catalysts, a complete change in thinking flows — Walking a more truthful path —Trying to make sense of things — Cultivating my mind, exercising it, strengthening it, sharpening it — Who is really crazy?

3/2 0/09

DEAR REV. MARY,

I came across your writings in a *Creative Thought* magazine and what was written compelled me to write to you. I know this may seem somewhat unorthodox, but at the moment my search engine is in a void and perhaps Science of Mind is the verity that will allow my long journey to finally come to an end.

I have no knowledge of Religious Science, nor am I familiar with Science of Mind teachings of Dr. Ernest Holmes, yet this is something I am earnestly intent on learning about.

Currently, I am in prison, which inhibits my access to resources, and under these present conditions I cannot receive any bound books. But if you are willing and you deem it feasible to reach back out to me and enlighten me, I can receive periodicals, photocopies of tomes, computer printouts of literature, and tracts pertaining to any information that will allow me to grasp the philosophy of Religious Science and Science of Mind.

I have become refined in many different theological schools of thought and disciplines. I am an apt student. I know there exist detractors who will and would remonstrate anyone reaching out to the incarcerated, but I pray this missive and my humble request does not fall upon deaf ears.

As a token of future fellowship, I offer to you the gesture of a poem that I entered in a contest I did not win. Hopefully you enjoy it.

HE DREAMS

Three hundred men sleep under the state's blankets
I am one, in the hour of the dream
We are all free men, citizens
Of a world that, even in nightmare
Mocks this asylum put together from
Concrete, razor wire, hatred, greed and corruption.
The exact pressure of my daughter's weight
Her light one-year-old body on my chest
Tells me what causes that perfect bliss

More distinct than decades of this other life.
This other life where three hundred slaves are resurrected
From their slumber and the state's blanket
Grey corpses yawning like caskets grave worn.
Some have dreamed of riches and women
While I held Mikaela, who was never born.

4/2/09

DEAR MICHAEL,

Thank you for your letter inquiring about the philosophy known as Religious Science as described in the text *The Science of Mind* written by Dr. Ernest Holmes. It may be just what you are looking for or not, but I am very happy to share with you what I have learned and you can let me know if it is helpful. I've been writing down my understanding of Holmes and metaphysics that I hope someday to put into a book of lessons, so I'm happy to share these with you. If it's not your "cup of tea," just let me know. If it is of interest, then I welcome the dialogue and will send you a couple of books to read.

Many people come to this teaching hoping to get something or find an easy way to avoid life's problems and think if they could only be more spiritual that life would surely be blissful. What does becoming more "spiritual" mean? I had to dig around in Webster's to find a definition that seemed appropriate. The definition of spirituality is "the quality or state of being spiritual." Looking up spiritual, it says, "relating to, consisting of, or affecting the spirit." I finally got to the core of this by looking up spirit, which in my dictionary has fourteen definitions, but the one most appropriate for our topic is "an animating or vital principle held to give life to physical organisms." Now we're getting somewhere.

In the definition of spirit, it was refreshing not to find the word supernatural, but instead to see it defined as "departing from what is usual or normal so as to appear to transcend the laws of nature." Why? Because spirituality does not transcend the law; it is the law of nature. This is the vital principle which gives us life. It is natural; there is nothing supernatural about it. Holmes and others discovered this life is as spiritual as it's going to get. We already are spiritual beings and everything in our life is spiritual. It doesn't take years of study to "get it." Our task, which we call the spiritual journey, is to consciously recognize it or, as Holmes called it, The Thing Itself.

When you begin studying Science of Mind, you will find out that the spiritual path is the consciousness we hold every moment in every activity. Living the Science of Mind is not something to be done whenever we have time. It is a moment-by-moment lifelong practice, a journey where we have the choice of experiencing peace, security, and happiness.

In a yoga class, I heard a mantra that struck me as profound: I am the creator; I am the destroyer. After saying it a few times, the meaning begins to sink in and I can see how true it is. At any moment, I can create a more loving atmosphere or, in the blink of an eye, I can destroy it. The challenge is no one can make the choice for us: We must make the great discovery for ourselves. This is not a course with tests or things to memorize. It is a process of opening our hearts and minds to our true nature, our real potential.

The lessons I created are tools for our personal journey. Along the way, you will more fully understand how to apply this knowledge of the laws of the Universe for greater good in your daily life. Over time, using the principles will become a natural part of how you do life. This will give you greater confidence and serenity in any situation.

4/26/09

DEAR REV. MARY,

I was elated that my letter did not fall on deaf ears. I offer a constellation of thank you notes for the information you can furnish me. I offer a prayer of gratitude that you will be able to provide me with the necessary tools that will help me on my journey.

As of now, the limited amount of information I have had access to and that which has drawn me to Science of Mind is that there seems to be no separation, and what I mean by that is many of the religious beliefs I've studied imply that there is something to believe in and that is something apart from the believer. In other words, we have two things in a "partnership," the believer and his/her belief. A "partnership" can be dissolved. "Partners" can be divorced or separated, but what I've come to through the mist of Science of Mind is that the person and I make not two but a Single Thing, and since the believer and It are one, there is no way to separate one from It.

Another aspect that has attracted me to Science of Mind is that it seems to gently, compassionately rescue, reconnect, affirm, ignite, and celebrate the Spirit of the Divine in every child of God. It seems to respect differences in other belief systems, is unprejudiced, never superior.

It seems not to intimidate or frighten with threats of hell and eternal damnation. It has not claimed to have an inside track to God that's not available to everyone else or the world in general.

Your writings in the *Creative Thought* magazine and those of others have strongly compelled me to learn more about Science of Mind, for many of the writings parallel my philosophy concerning the way I live my life. So, this familiarity propelled me to reach out to you and I believe you, as my would-be advisor and teacher, can help me attain that which I need to know and come to understand. To quote what I read out of a *Creative Thought* magazine by Raymond Charles Barker, "You are a Spiritual Pioneer for those who have not yet found this path."

I thank you for taking the time to even acknowledge my missive, being in this other realm. I am intent in discovering the depths of Science of Mind teachings and all it will do to aid me in my evolution. Anything else you can share with me in my learning will be greatly and honestly appreciated.

Please enjoy the poem I've included with this letter.

I AM HE

I am not I, I am this one
Walking beside me, when I do not see
When at times I manage to visit
To his Realm of Darkness and at other times when I forget.
The one who forgives when I want revenge,
The one who loves when I hate,
The one who gives when I take,
The one who remembers with I forget,
The one who remains silent when I speak.
The one who is awake when I sleep.
I am not I; I am this one
I am not I; I am He.

6/3/09

DEAR MICHAEL,

Your letter of April 26 has been on my desk waiting for an answer. It is interesting that it waited until I felt I had something to offer your inquisitive mind. You are a quick study and I was deeply moved by your poem and hope you don't mind that I read it to the class I was teaching at the time. We were studying Ralph Waldo Emerson and his essays. Emerson's essays were groundbreaking works at the time, the mid 1800s, and still offer incredible insight to us today.

The difference between the first poem you sent and the second shows light years of knowledge have been absorbed. Congratulations! You are learning the truth of who you are at the soul level. You are correct that Science of Mind teaches oneness with Divine Intelligence, that we have been created from that Source, whatever we call it, to be here and learn about that connection. Our life experiences are happening *for* us, not *to* us. We can choose whether to use these experiences for personal growth or not. One of the primary tasks of adulthood is to access and reclaim the connection to the Infinite by learning how to use our unconscious mind.

I am preparing to teach a class that begins this week called "Writing as a Spiritual Practice." Perhaps you'd like to join us on the journey. I've enclosed the program agenda and my notes for class. The process is to write daily without stopping for a period of time, like ten minutes. No editing, no correcting spelling or punctuation, just write … let it out. I learned this technique from books by Natalie Goldberg, like *Wild Mind: Living the Writer's Life* and *Writing Down the Bones.* We ask a question and just begin writing. Within two or three minutes, our ego chatter fades away and we connect with a natural state of mind. Like Zen practice, the wilderness of our mind is where there are no perfectly lined rows of corn. The mind is raw, full of energy, alive, and hungry. The vital energy of our mind is in our first thoughts, the raw energy. In writing, you bring everything you know into it. In Zen, you bring everything you know into nothing, into the present moment where you can't hold onto anything. It is important not to read our writing for at least three days, to let it settle.

As Natalie says, writing is a great way to open up to the present moment when we feel disconnected and isolated as individuals. One way to reconnect is to begin with a connection to ourselves. The greatest lesson in writing as a spiritual practice is the lesson of impermanence. There is nothing to hold on to. It is a place to look at everything without judgment, no good or bad. I hope you find the enclosures of interest, and if you would like to join our class, send your writings and we can all share.

6/21/09

DEAR REV. MARY,

I have received your letter and assignments and, yes, I would really be honored to join you and your students on this writing journey. I am still in the process of learning how to write affirmations, yet with patience and practice I will master it.

The writings you are receiving are perhaps somewhat uncanny to say the least, because the world I dwell in is shrouded in propaganda and fictional television shows and things are not always what they seem to be to those on the outside looking in. I pray that my words, sentences, and paragraphs do not offend, shock, or disturb, but enlighten and provide insight.

Yes, I would be happy if you read what I have written with your class. In that way, I become a shadow member of your class. I will be behind in my writings, yet the second and third week of writings will be sent together at one time. I'm glad for the invitation and I thank you, Reverend. Perhaps you will notice my inevitable navigation toward the Science of Mind and how one can rise from the depths of the void of emptiness to the incandescence of truth and knowledge.

Many, many moons ago I desired wealth, fame, prestige, yet in order for me to attain these, I resorted to illegal means. I desired to be recognized as a big shot by my comrades. I desired to impress women with money, cars, and deeds. Yet these desires brought with them consequences that were negative. In order for me to make my desires tangible, I engaged in criminal activities, which inevitably led to my incarceration and a sentence of life without parole. Now, I desire truth, wisdom, knowledge, and students who are ready to learn what I know. I strive relentlessly for this, because in order for me to keep others from following in my footsteps, they must know that there is another way.

WRITING ASSIGNMENT: To expand the mind
Write down ten nouns and ten verbs, then use them in a paragraph.

Nouns:

man, strength, prison, courage, land, madness, labyrinth, omen, realm, death

Verbs:

awakening, hurt, driven, teaching, writing, elevate, listening, evolve, learning, pursue

There was a time when I *hurt* people to the point of *death,* but those ways I have purged through discipline and strength. "For when I was a child, I talked like a child, I thought like a child, I reasoned like a child. But when I became a *man,* I put childish ways behind me." When I entered into this *realm,* this terrestrial hell, this *land* of *madness,* it was essential that I adapt and sharpen my *listening* and *learning* the ways of this *prison labyrinth* to ensure my survival. *Courage* was my sword that allowed me to not fall victim of the foulness and crookedness that devour men. Being shown an *omen* was the beginning of my *awakening* and I have been *driven* to *elevate* myself beyond the mundane of this world and *pursue* the teachings that will allow me to evolve. I maintain my *strength* through physical and mental exercise, and *writing* brings me peace of mind.

6/28/09

DEAR MICHAEL,

As I read your beautiful letter and writings to the class, I was filled with emotion. The journey of the soul is mysterious, and it is so clear in my mind that you are in the right place for your enlightenment. As you open up that connection to Spirit, the mind fills with love and compassion. It is hard to watch the "walking dead" even in my life on the outside. I used to be disturbed by this and wanted to help others wake up, but then I finally realized that each soul is on its/their own journey and awakens when ready to.

The walls around all of us are as real as they seem in our minds. Some people I know are held back from even thinking about another way of seeing the universe. Their beliefs are often brought from childhood, never to grow up beyond God as a wrathful being, fearing the afterlife and eternity. It is an amazing thing to recognize on your unique path that this experience is bringing you to this awareness of your true nature.

Some thoughts as you read *The Science of Mind*: During your reading, take notice that you will naturally leave behind previous habits that didn't serve you well, such as false ideas about yourself and others, attachments, judgments, and compulsions. Living the Science of

Mind is to experience a sense of freedom in every moment, which results in inner peace and greater love. You will find yourself surrounded by more loving and compassionate friends; solutions to problems will come more easily; your inner support system will be stronger.

The journey called the spiritual path is a process of learning how to use our freedom of choice for our greater good by understanding and aligning with the laws of the Universe. Opportunities exist in every aspect of our life to enhance our good. There is no place we can go in order to get away from the fact that we are spiritual beings in a life experience as we find our way back to our true nature. This knowledge isn't something we can buy and wear like a jacket. It comes through practice where you prove to yourself, time and time again, principle works. One of my favorite spiritual teachers, Ram Dass, says, "It is a peculiar predicament that the knowledge can only be known by transforming ourselves into the knowledge itself." The essence of living the Science of Mind is a positive, life-transforming activity.

7/12/09

DEAR REV. MARY,

At the base of every metaphysical class, book, lesson, principle is peace of mind based on the fact that God is all there is. We live in a spiritual Universe with "God," the animating or vital Principle, which has given life to all. My favorite name for God is Infinite Intelligence, but most people are OK with just using the word God.

The laws that govern our lives are created by God and exist in everything. This creative power, therefore, is in, through, and around us. It is the person sitting next to us, the table, the flower, the bird, the tree. Do you see it in everyone? Can you look closely enough to see each person, place, or thing as Spirit in action? The essence of God is expressing Itself throughout all creation. God is for us. It could never be against us or It would self-destruct. Creation operates by law, a changeless principle based on love and God's desire for self-expression through creation.

Since the beginning of time, human beings have assumed there was an invisible power greater than they. From creating cave drawings to pyramids to the great cathedrals, people intuitively knew there was some greater power affecting their lives. They gave it names like Ra, the sun god, and created rituals and rites of passage to satisfy the gods in the hope of making life easier. Many of these practices seem kind of bizarre today, but at the time they were very logical for their level of understanding and whatever goal they were trying to attain.

Today we still feel an inherent desire for freedom from pain or fear, just like the soul's eons ago. We intuitively yearn for something that seems intangible. God created us with volition, the ability to make choices. We have volition at every moment. We can choose what we will do, how we will act, what path we will take. It is an awesome gift and, when we really understand it, an awesome responsibility. In my experience, God stands with open arms and says, "Here is your real self—and it is wonderful!"

To live with this knowledge is to recognize that behind all events, death, and destruction is harmony, the perfection of the Universe unfolding around us. We will delve deeper into this as we progress, but at the moment, just consider that all people are on their own paths, consciously or unconsciously. Some travel in pain and anguish, while others live in varying degrees of happiness and contentment. Try experimenting with the idea that each person is in their unique place for this play of life, where whatever their recognition of truth, it is right for them at the moment.

Each individual life experience reflects their play of divine consciousness. This brings out a sense of compassion in us, especially when it comes to recognizing the spiritual path in family members. It is one thing to recognize the truth in those we don't know well, but so often we think we can fix family members so they can avoid pain and see life more positively. But there is no difference—their life experience is their play of consciousness. Yet inner change often comes from having a direct experience with others. Each of us is a light and the clearer and brighter our light shines, as we live in the awareness of truth, we become a catalyst for change in others just by being who we are.

In walking this path to freedom from fear, be aware of the laws that operate in the Universe. The planet Earth, the stars, the sun, the moon, the seasons, the tides, the cycle of birth and death flow in perfect harmony. By studying life and the laws of nature, we get a better grasp of what a law is. We see gravity, for instance, works equally on all objects. It doesn't work more powerfully one moment and less the next; the laws of the Universe do not play favorites. Cause and effect is another principle that impacts every aspect of our life, working perfectly every time. These laws are not supernatural; they don't change over time; they just are. Why a principle exists we will never know. What we can know is how it works and live in alignment with these principles to find freedom, peace, and happiness.

7/24/09

DEAR MICHAEL,

Thank you for your letter and sharing your insightful writings. I shared them with my class and asked them to write about their impressions, which I have enclosed. You are living on the cusp of your greater awareness of the soul's journey and beginning to understand the gift you bring to those in your environment and to me and those in my class. Each one teach one—changing lives, one at a time.

I'm not sure if you have read any of Fyodor Dostoyevsky's books, but his biographical statement at the beginning of *The Brothers Karamazov* might be of interest.

> His life was dark and dramatic as the great novels he wrote. He was born in Moscow in 1821, the son of a former army surgeon whose drunken brutality led his own serfs to murder him by pouring vodka down his throat until he strangled. A short first novel, *Poor Folk* (1846), brought Dostoyevsky instant success, but his writing career was cut short by his arrest for alleged subversion against Tsar Nicholas I in 1848. In prison, he was given the silent treatment for eight months (guards even wore velvet-soled boots) before he was led in front of a firing squad. Dressed in a death shroud, he faced an open grave and awaited his execution, when, suddenly, an order arrived commuting his sentence. He then spent four years at hard labor in a Siberian prison, where he began to suffer from epilepsy, and he only returned to St. Petersburg a full ten years after he had left in chains.

> His prison experiences, coupled with his conversion to a conservative and profoundly religious philosophy, formed the basis for his great novels. But it was his fortuitous marriage to Anna Snikina, following a period of utter destitution brought about by his compulsive gambling, that gave Dostoevsky the emotional stability to complete *Crime and Punishment* (1866), *The Idiot* (1868), *The Possessed* (1871), and *The Brothers Karamazov* (1879). When he died in 1881, he left a legacy of masterworks that influenced the great thinkers and writers of the Western world and immortalized him as a giant among writers of world literature.

Somewhere I read a quote that was so beautifully put, that Dostoyevsky had to "see differently" to write his spiritual and philosophical novels. Rather than indulging in self-pity and withdrawing from life, he chose to explore his life circumstances and see them as carriers of relevant messages for spiritual growth. He wrote as a way to heal what happened to him and, in doing so, he investigated how he might see the events and people in life differently. If you do not have access to his books and are interested, let me know and I can have them sent to you. I looked on the prison website and you can receive books if they come directly from commercial booksellers.

Your writing about color was very interesting—grey, black, white. There are a couple of ways of seeing these things differently. One way is to take time to relax and look at one of the objects in your view, even if it is a wall, but look just to the side of it, or about six inches away. Keep looking. Keep looking. Soon you will notice a halo effect along the wall. It may only be white or it may have a color. It is the energy alive in the wall. Every cell of that wall is made up of atoms moving at a furious pace to retain its shape. They give off energy. The energy is always there, everywhere. When we actually see it, we may think we are crazy, but in actuality we are seeing the soul essence of what appears to be an object.

Try this with one of the guards. Look just a bit away from his body and feel in your body the presence of love, love for God's creation. Keep looking and you will see like a halo effect from his body. This is his soul essence. When we practice it enough on people, we can begin to see colors, which represent the type of energy the person is feeling inside. There are doctors who can see colors radiating from a person and are able to diagnose illness based on those colors.

7/28/09

DEAR REV. MARY,

Enclosed are my writings for three assignments.

ASSIGNMENT: Ten minutes of writing

Being engulfed by ignorance, stupidity, and ill-willed individuals, with the added burden of sensory deprivation and tactics of repression, has the effect of challenging one's mental stability and stagnates amelioration. By any logical and apparent reasons, I should be anything but what I am today, but sometimes the Spirit is stronger than the circumstances. Many people in the world of the free believe that "adversity creates character." However, adversity reveals character as well. Just as an inmate who suffers and remains just an inmate doing time, filled with rage, hate, despair, and no direction, there are those who are revealed and become forever filled with discipline, confidence, energetic, vigorous, humble with knowledge of self and inner peace. For these individuals, prison is a mere obstacle to overcome. They realize the seriousness of their situation and they apply themselves with the necessary vigilance, will power, discipline, and patience to ensure their success in prison and in life. Their days are filled with productive activity, such as reading, studying, exercising, and introspection of self and life.

The primary objective is to survive, which means one must redevelop his mind state to deal with and overcome any and all forms of oppression, degradation, and regression. One must challenge the mentality bred into us to be conditioned to respond in a certain way toward certain situations. Any brute can force his way through changes, either by being and feeding of anger, mental or physical violence, when it is physical. However, only through adequate thought will one be successful on a higher and more complete level. The brute only accomplishes short-term gain. The one who has meticulously thought things through and undertaken a correct form of action is assured of knowing the outcome will be in his best interest, whether it is actually favorable or not.

Experience gives one knowledge, wisdom, and understanding, which are key elements in fortitude. It gives one a sense of worth and purpose while dealing with the wilds of captivity. Those who do not remember their past are doomed to make the same mistakes. Those who do not understand their past will never know themselves or others.

ASSIGNMENT: Ten minutes of writing

Each one teach one. That is how we get down in these isolated death camps. We reach out to one another, teach each other, lift each other up, work together, strive together, collaborate, and conglomerate. When one sits in a cell and takes the time to think about his situation, his life, his struggles, he begins to see things for what they are. When you have good people around you to share real gems of knowledge and truth with you, then you begin to see things in a whole new light. You begin to transcend yourself above and beyond the madness. You start to walk a more truthful path in life.

It's hard to rise above this crazy lifestyle, but consciousness is a savior. One can use this time to better himself, to reconstruct his way of thinking and reevaluate his way of life. One uses this time as an opportunity to elevate himself. Each one teach one. That's how we learn, grow, and develop. It's how we share, unite, and reach levels of real understanding amongst ourselves. Each one teach one. We exchange knowledge, pass it on to those who are worthy. Plant seeds of growth and water them, nourish them, and let those seeds of realness grow through the concrete and through the walls. From tier to tier, wing to wing, and from unit to unit, we let it evolve. Each one teach one.

If I see a person who's a good dude struggling, I reach out and help him out. I lift him up, encourage him, whatever I can offer to help him get back on his feet again. Each one teach one. That's my motto.

ASSIGNMENT: Ten minutes of writing

Sitting in solitude, with my thoughts laid out on the hard, concrete floor and pasted to the walls, trying to make sense of them as I sit and stare, ponder and reflect. I don't know what the guy in the next cell thinks about as he sits there, but I often wonder...

Today someone told me that there are a lot of "dead" people around here, dead but still breathing. I've been thinking about that, thinking about how people can let themselves fade away and deteriorate. I've been thinking about how or why people in here can't take pride in themselves, take pride in their abilities. I've been thinking about what is this about, this place that has stripped them of their determination to win, succeed, or overcome?

I'm sitting here thinking, because I've since come to realize how beautiful it is to take the time to think, trying to make sense out of things, trying to see things underneath the surface for their external appearance. So as I sit here in the cell thinking, I'm trying to connect my mind to my soul so that I can understand the truth of things that I think about. Truth is a beautiful thing. Thinking is beautiful, too. If man thought his way to the moon, then I can think my way out of this cell. The sky's the limit when it comes to what one's mind can accomplish when put to good use. The mind is a dangerous thing when sharpened and refined. Dangerous! Some people might call it plotting. Others might call it contemplating, but I call it thinking. Thinking is a true act of self-empowerment.

As a prisoner, I am fascinated by the idea that anything made by man can also be destroyed by man. So, I sit here and ponder ways to destroy the construction that confines me. I think I have deserved, studied, and mastered my surroundings. All thinking is good, but there's a difference between idle thoughts and intellectual thinking. There's a difference between day-dreaming and logical thinking. There's a difference between wondering and contemplating—and there's a difference between fantasizing and creative thinking.

Creative people think. Intellectuals think. Be a thinker and learn to think for yourself. Think and breathe and allow your thoughts to inhale the breath of life. The mind is powerful, dangerous, unstoppable, deep, reflective, and very effective when it is put to its proper use. I cultivate my mind, exercise it, strengthen it, sharpen it. Train it and use it. There can be no limitations, restrictions, or confines put on the mind. Just a couple of thoughts from the graveyard.

8/12/09

DEAR MICHAEL,

Listening to what we are thinking is one of the greatest gifts we can give ourselves. It is listening to our inner voice in total honesty. In reading this lesson, the process for you has already begun. Holmes's criteria for the actions that come forth from deep listening should be based on: Does the thing I wish to do express more life, more happiness, more peace to myself, and at the same time harm no one? If it fits this description, it is right. If not, it is selfish. Whether it helps or hurts anyone, we will reap the consequences.

As we learn how to live life from a spiritual base, we see that life is a series of falling down and getting up as we learn to make better choices. Each step teaches us more about how this thing works and how to use it. This is the essence of metaphysics, the study of co-creation. Ernest Holmes explains it as, "The study of First Cause, Spirit, Mind, or that invisible Essence, that ultimate Stuff and Intelligence from which everything comes, the Power back of creation—the Thing Itself." Our efforts to understand the natural laws of life will result in positive change as we explore and begin to relate to life in alignment with the laws of its own nature. As Holmes described it, nothing moves but mind and by living from that center of knowledge, we taste the nectar of life. We dig deeper and open our minds and hearts to reveal our true selves, and it is sweet.

If all that moves is mind, let's relate this to the power of prayer. At some point in life when we have been in a tough spot, some type of prayer comes to mind requesting the intercession of God, an angel, or a saint to solve the problem. The word prayer comes from the Latin word precarious, meaning obtained by begging, to implore. If every prayer were answered, this world would be chaos since no one would ever get sick or die and God would get tired of making someone love one person, then another, and then another. Yet we have all had some prayers answered. If the Universe operates on principle or law, there must be a natural law behind the power of prayer that, when understood, enables us to have a higher percentage of success.

In the Bible, Jesus said that God "maketh His sun to rise on the evil and on the good, and sendeth rain on the just and on the unjust" (Matthew 5:45). Holmes says, "Since some people have been healed through prayer, while others have not, the answer is NOT that God has responded to some and not to others, but that some have responded to God more than others." The power of prayer rests with the one doing the praying. Again, we see that by going within we find the answer. The power rests in us.

9/15/09

Note: During this month, Michael took a class by mail with Rev. Mary, entitled "It's All God," from a book of the same title written by Walter Starke. It is an in-depth and challenging book for all serious students on the spiritual path and has become a classic in its own time. Homework questions were completed weekly by mail. Here are a few of Michael's answers.

1. **Take a moment to consider the costumes you wear and the concepts about your-self that create these outer forms. Which ones have you created intentionally?**

One that I did create intentionally was the costume of a mad, cold-hearted, ruthless killer. In an asylum world, the likes of the truly mad rise to the top. The crème de la crème of the demented. When I first entered this realm (prison), there existed a stringent, gruesome pecking order. I had taken a saying that I had read and turned it into my own personal concept to live by. The saying was this: "For what had Satan saw when God hurled him from heaven into the abyss; that it was better to reign in the pit than to serve in Heaven." For years, I believed this to be my hell, one of Satan's playgrounds as it is said. So, I created the strongest, the most cunning, most ruthless, the most dangerous character. I became and used violence to instill fear and intimidation within this world as my way to survive and stay on top of the bizarre pecking order that existed. Yet, as time passed in this hypnotic shell, I was able to wake up and go through a self-induced metamorphosis and begin to see myself in others and know that they, too, only wore masks as I did, because of the need to survive in this hostile environment.

There existed a prison called Missouri State Penitentiary (M.S.P.), which closed in 2003. It was also known as "The Walls," because it did not have any fencing around it, only high concrete walls. It was the first and oldest and deadliest prison in the state of Missouri. It rested in Jefferson City, the state capital. The whole economic system was spawned from this prison. The Walls was a place where, when many convicts made it there, they took a perverse kind of pride for doing time in The Walls since it takes on the aura of being decorated for bravery. A prison record that included time in the infamous Walls was like adding a purple heart to the uniform of a war hero. M.S.P. was the graduate school of the most brutal savage, and those who completed the course study were regarded as ferocious beasts. These are the ones with reputations, so they had to live up to them and they willingly accepted the glamorized toughness they had to demonstrate. Many of these men become leaders in other lands (prison facilities). Many will be soldiers to enforce the orders of other leaders.

Naturally, the competition to become a leader is stiff, so it is the mad who rise to become top nincompoops within a hippodrome of buffoons. They reap the benefits of respect, prestige, drugs, clout, and fear. Pleasure comes from trivial things in the system. I, myself, was infected with this madness, possessed by this costume.

2. Create a mission statement for your life and be sure to include compliments.

This would be a mission statement for my life: I have written many things. The truth of the things I have written has long been known by many, but not always believed outside of the "realm." The realm is the 9th Dominion. The 9th Dominion is what I refer to as the prison system, and the prisons of America are worlds within a world. What true life is in these manmade torture facilities has never before been truly revealed. I have taken it upon myself to reveal the truth like no other. The everyday struggle of a man trying to rise from the depths of degradation, oppression, inhumane conditions, hatred, racism, and humiliation is no easy task. It is constant and stupendous.

My writings are somewhat unusual for its honesty and tormenting truth, yet it unburdens one's mind on things thus far unspoken. It therefore strengthens and ennobles one. There is a web of lies that has existed about the prison system for centuries, not to mention the myths propagated to those on the outside and the inside.

I have been chosen by fate to experience a cruel and beautiful ordeal, both physically and mentally cursed and gifted. I have struggled to maintain my mind, soul, pride in a battle against mysterious forces that seem determined to destroy my sanity, dignity, and beliefs. I must admit that I am no saint nor angel, yet I am a father, a son, a brother, a healer, and a protector of those I love. I will sacrifice myself for that love. I have been denied the right to feel, to care. My only right has been survival, yet even that lasts only so long, for in time all men must die.

Living deep in the shadow of the unknown has made every mundane act of normality almost seem like a waste of time, an absurd attempt to paint a façade of typicality over an existence that is peculiar and uncanny. In an infinite Universe, the potential number of intelligent life forms is also infinite. Theoretically, anything that could be imagined must exist in an infinite realm. It is said that the perception of a child is an uncanny gift, for they have not yet learned to protect their perception by developing tunnel vision that keeps out 90 percent of the Universe. A child will see every sight their eyes happen upon, hear every sound in their ear's range. Men hear, but they do not listen. They do not listen because they do not believe—and there are none so blind as those who will not see.

Since my encounters with the anomalies of this world, I've been searching for the keys that open the portals to Truth, but in error I was searching outside of myself for answers that were already within. I have learned truths about myself and life in general. The 9th Dominion is where I dwell and Truth is my torch within this darkened realm. I have labeled myself many things: a convict in prison, a king in exile, a demon in hell, pretending to be other than what I truly am. In all things does God exist. The Greatest and most Formidable Mind that will ever exist, for without Universal Mind, man, beast, plant, and insect would not be aware of itself or its design or its purpose. I will teach others as I do learn all of what I have written is my mission statement, because to destroy the ill perceptions many have in this world, I must rely on a Truth which cannot be destroyed, which is the Love of God.

3. What absolutes have limited you in your progress?

Being taught that the Bible was the only absolute Truth and everything outside of it was falsehood. One of man's greatest concepts is to think they can know absolute Truth, possessing it the way a rich man possesses a rare and precious object. I believe what limited me in my progress was believing erroneous ideas and opinions that other versions of the truth are counterfeit and inferior and needed to be corrected.

10/19/09

DEAR MICHAEL:

Living in the darkness of prison, it would be easy to let the negative and hateful energy you encounter overcome you. One spiritual practice that is of utmost importance in this philosophy is prayer. Prayer is not confined to a specific place or time; it can be done anywhere at any time for success, to heal an event or the body, or to help someone in a different city or state. This powerful tool reaches out beyond the here and now and is what some call a "nonlocal" event. This means it works through the infinity of time and space. That's another challenging concept for our ego mind. We are a divinely inspired creation and infinity is inherently part of us. As Larry Dossey wrote in his book *Healing Words,* "In the West this infinite aspect of the psyche has been referred to as the soul. Empirical evidence for prayer's power, then, is indirect evidence for the soul."

How interesting that the success of prayer depends on the mind of the one praying, yet no one knows exactly what mind is. Mind cannot be located in our body, yet we have discovered how it works: through objective and subjective states of consciousness. Objective consciousness, our daily thinking mind, is aware of life around us and is where we find that committee (ego) that analyzes everything we do. Subjective consciousness is our unconscious state that acts upon our thoughts and is a place of limitless creativity. It operates through principle, by law, and always says "*yes*" to our deep desires or fears. It is the creative factor in us that has unlimited power to work out the desire of our conscious thoughts.

Subjective mind operates by Universal law, the one law, which connects each of us with all creation. Everything is consciousness, equally and simultaneously. Our conscious mind makes choices and the tendency our conscious beliefs hold sets subjective mind in motion to achieve these desires. As Holmes says, "This is the greatest discovery of all times." When our thought falls into subjective mind, it merges with Universal Subjective Mind, the Thing Itself." Holmes explains we are one with the whole on the subjective side of life. We are a wave of individuality on a subconscious ocean. Consciously understanding this process gives us a much greater ability to use the power of prayer for a successful conclusion. This is the key to freedom: the conscious/intelligent use of the law.

The Creative Process in the Spiritual World

Conscious Mind . . . . Subconscious Mind

Spirit. . . . . Law

Reasoning . . . . Mechanical Order

Decisions. . . . . Reaction

Volition. . . . . Effect

Individuality . . . . Creative

SEEDS of ideas/beliefs planted and watered in the

SOIL result in manifestations/experiences:
THE PLANT

Why is it this way? We may never know. At this point, it is enough to know that it is possible to learn how to think in alignment with the Law of Mind. This requires a new level of self-awareness, because we are unable to go beyond our own self-accepted image. Many people we meet are self-righteous, feeling their ideas, their work, their knowledge is better than ours. It is the delusion of the ego. The spiritual path is about awakening the dormant possibilities within and making decisions to let go of any tiny belief in lack and limitation or self-righteousness, so we can move forward in a clear understanding of the truth. "...the entire problem of limitation, evil, suffering and uncertainty is not God-ordained, but is the result of ignorance. The bondage of humanity must be the result of our ignorance of the true nature of Reality. The root of all suffering is spiritual amnesia" (*The Science of Mind*, p. 32-33).

I hope you enjoyed this as you awaken to the divinity within by recognizing all of life as the play of consciousness. As we become more aware of our individual power through studying and spiritual practices, we are able to walk more consciously on the spiritual path. It clearly is the road to freedom, our path back to God.

CHAPTER 2

2010

Searching for Truth
Through
Questions, Questions, Questions

God offers to every mind a choice between truth and repose —
In prison, kindness and compassion are outlawed — Man cannot imprison consciousness — The prison staff set one group
against another — Is violence the only answer? — How can one
combat injustice with those who only believe in hate and more
hate? — Liberation is gained from education — How can one
be of this world and not a part of it? — Shedding the skin of my
old ways — Anything accepted as Truth makes a subconscious
impression — I've been given a precious understanding so
unexpectedly that has changed me forever and for the better.

1/12/10

DEAR REV. MARY,

The world I dwell in, my social interactions, my experience, studies, and beliefs dictate my vision without obscurity. To emphasize it more clearly, I will quote from *The Essays of Ralph Waldo Emerson:* "He must worship truth; and forego all things for that, and choose defeat and pain, so that his treasure in thought is augmented. God offers to every mind its choice between truth and repose. Take which you please, you can never have both. . . . As long as I hear truth, I am bathed by a beautiful element, and am not conscious of any limits to my nature."

Rev. Mary, the gemstones of knowledge, wisdom, love, kindness, beauty, and truths you have shared with me have been priceless and have enhanced and elevated my life to Spirit three-thousand-fold.

1/20/10

DEAR MICHAEL,

How wonderful that as you learn these truths, you have enhanced your awareness of your divine nature, that you are in an individual expression of Spirit in action. There has never been anyone like you before. You are a divine inspiration of God. God reveals Itself to us through us. It seems extraordinary, doesn't it, that our life comes from a greater power and our daily experience comes from within! One of the primary functions of this letter is to consciously connect you with that Universal power.

Ernest Holmes, the founder of Religious Science, said, "There is a power for good in the Universe and you can use it." This Universal Mind, Intelligence, is limitless spiritual substance, not limited to any place in space. The unity of one power without limitation is where Religious Science differs from so many religions and life philosophies. God is universal, and as much of It as we are able to incorporate into our life is ours to use.

Most spiritual teachings say God is everywhere present, but often their core belief is that God isn't to be found just anywhere, but in a church or holy place. Could there really be a place where God/Spirit is not? If so, what would be there instead? Although there is much energy focused on the unhappiness and chaos in the world, without unity at the core of it all, our world could not exist for one moment. Attributing unity to good, if we look hard enough, we can see some core level of good in everything. So in times of doubt we must look behind appearances to find the answer.

We do not have the power of God to move the stars or create a planet, but we do have the ability to align ourselves with this power. Therefore, some things may seem like they have their own power, such as evil acts, but a belief in good and evil is a belief in duality. Evolving spiritually requires a conscious awareness of the truth that the only law is God's law and nothing opposes it. In *The Anatomy of Healing Prayer,* Holmes says, "Our whole work is based on the concept Perfect God, Perfect Man and Perfect Being. Our whole practice is based on the concept that God is where we are and what we are, and that there isn't anything else. Our whole concept is partially based on the theory that whatever appears to be wrong is not wrong in itself but is the wrong arrangement of what is right. There is no dualism in the Universe."

Since Spirit is limitless, we have an unlimited ability to expand our consciousness. This is the reciprocal relationship between Spirit and each individual. One of the great philosophers who Holmes studied was Dr. Thomas Troward, who explains that as we open up to universal truths, we will find our consciousness expanding. Our desire to fully express life, knowing we can express in greater ways than ever before, pulls us into a new dimension of understanding. As we open to a greater use of this natural power, the Universe pours into us a greater level of acceptance. Holmes explains in *Observations*, "There is an irresistible push and pull in the Universe which combines to maintain a perfect equilibrium." When we perform our daily tasks in this consciousness, we perform to the best of our ability, and principle sees to its accomplishment. "The Truth known demonstrates Itself."

2/9/10

DEAR MICHAEL,

I've been thinking about how much you hear about the news in the world. It is a difficult time for many countries and cultures. There are times when I feel overwhelmed by all of the bad news in the world. At those moments, I take my mind to the top of Mt. Shasta, a snow-capped mountain here in northern California surrounded by forest land, lakes, and rivers. I feel myself sitting there, looking out over the valley and the cities. I feel a sense of rhythm, a flow of divine harmony as I imagine people coming here from other planes of existence by being born, having a human experience with all of its intricacies, and then going onto another realm by leaving their bodies. It is a divine flow of coming and going, so how could any single experience in this process be less than perfect? As Walt Whitman wrote, "At the center of everything nestles the seed of perfection."

I have found that often the association we have with our body, our work, or our relationship strongly becomes the essence of who we think we are, our identity. But from the top of Mt. Shasta, I see that it is our consciousness that has chosen this form on purpose. The inner reality is Spirit in expression, and the outer reality is our individual way of expressing life in this form.

The infinite possibilities of how we live in this Universe show up as people involved in war, starvation, famine, parenthood, sickness, disease, as teachers, doctors, waiters, etc. The perfection behind this multitude of appearances is tough for our ego mind to grasp, because something that is infinite is beyond our limited mind. Our center of expression comes from our connection with Universal Mind and functions at our level of understanding of It. Unity is the one energy behind all things and cannot be multiplied or divided.

We live in one infinite whole, omnipresent in its entirety. Thomas Troward said it is logically correct that at every moment, all of Spirit is concentrated at any point in space and we may choose to fix our thought upon it and individualize it. He saw the relationship between Spirit and matter as that between idea and form. Spirit is conscious and therefore must be conscious of something. Through contemplation, It is creative. As individuals, we all share the reality of unity at the core level, yet are free to express diversity at our conscious level. When we were in the first grade of school, our ability to see all that we would learn by the time we graduated was very limited. Our acceptance of the nature of diversity is clearer when we are in an airport or shopping mall, observing the variety of shapes, sizes, and personalities, yet recognizing each one is perfect since each person is expressing life as only they know how.

3/13/10

DEAR REV. MARY,

Thank you for the gesture and willingness to send me stationary, but this is no longer permitted. Many years ago, family and friends were able to send these types of things, but the Department of Corrections does not allow gifts. Kindness and compassion are outlawed. It may seem strange that a rehabilitation system designed to turn inmates into law-abiding citizens would outlaw kindness, and if it was really a rehabilitation system, it would be strange, but it isn't. It is a debilitation system and the prohibition against kindness destroys the social bonds between the poor and the marginalized. Increasing distrust and encouraging a dysfunctional and pervasive sense of constant competition and danger and war, a world of all against all.

This element of the degenerating process creates brigades of paranoids hoarding worthless junk, incapable of transmitting anything beneficial to families, friends, or colleagues. By outlawing kindness, the act of giving, the prison system encourages selfish and narrow thinking and enforces callousness.

I have the tendency to sometimes vent when I write, so forgive me for troubling you with the idiocy which plagues this realm and for complaining about matters which I should be struggling to change.

What God has instilled in us is the way of leaning toward that which is beautiful, longing for that which is the source and thirsting for that which is eternal. In these days there is quite enough in the form of pain, confusion, difficulties, and obstacles. And in my opinion, an idea that can stand before the Absolute and the Eternal is immune to the effects of a dominion that gives its inhabitants snakes and stones instead of that which is needed, the proverbial loaf of bread and fish.

Always remember, you do have a friend in this part of the world who wishes you well and prays that no harm comes to you. It is said that a friend far away is sometimes much nearer than one who is at hand. Is not the mountain far more awe inspiring and more clearly visible to one passing through the valley than to those who inhabit the mountain?

3/22/10

DEAR MICHAEL,

It's tough, but it is reality: It is the nature of the creative process operating throughout the Universe to always say "yes" and give us what we believe. If we think we are not worthy of a high-paying job, one won't be offered to us. If we believe we are not attractive, we find ourselves with people who verify this. When we say something negative about someone else, the Universe hears "yes" and brings it back to us for our experience. Just as negative beliefs come back to us in negative way, so do positive beliefs.

By frequently checking in with our mind, we can determine whether our dominant thoughts, feelings, beliefs are helping or hurting us. Look at your thoughts today. If you were to place a black dot on paper for every negative thought you have had so far, how many dots would there be? Ironically "the power which appears to bind us is the only power in the Universe which can free us." Our thoughts of unworthiness bind us, yet when these thoughts are changed to worthiness, the Universe again responds *"Yes!"* How perfect!

Reflecting on your life today, can you identify your most deeply held beliefs? What do you think they are? Look closely and examine each thoroughly. Do you deserve greater good than this? Remember, "As much as we can believe will be done unto us." If you see several areas for improvement, choose one to focus on this month. As you work positively on this area, other aspects of life will automatically shift. In all activities of life, we find this Law of Perfection. If we plant tomato seeds and add water, the reaction of the seed with the water in the soil will soon result in tomato plants. If duality existed, we could not expect a particular outcome; tomato seeds might result in carrots or weeds. Since Law is mechanical, if we're too busy to water the tomato plants, they will naturally shrivel up. The Universe won't step in to save them just because we are doing something else.

We are dealing with an impersonal law which says, "No water, no tomato plants." Plants do not have volition, the ability to choose, like we do. Plants cannot decide they need water and crawl over to the hose and turn it on. Its life is a mechanical, natural event, which is impacted by many things in its growth cycle.

4/4/10

DEAR REV. MARY,

I recently came across a small book in the library titled, "The Magic of Believing." It had dust on it and had never been checked out. It was written by Claud Bristol. It was a first Pocket Book Printing dated October 1969. In the book, he mentioned Mary Baker Eddy of Christian Science and he quoted Emerson. He referred to Universal Laws of Cause & Effect, and how man has the ability to use it, as "Mind Stuff."

The book touched on many concepts I am already aware of, but all in all what he had to say was informative and interesting. He even attributed positive thought to the act of catching fish. He said that a fisherman he knew visualized the fish snapping at the hook and believed that it will work and the fisherman would pull trout after trout out of the water. He also mentioned Creative Force. Much of what he spoke on, I've been studying in the Science of Mind literature you have provided and other tomes I've come across. When I randomly happen to come across information that reflects my studies and thoughts, I take this as a sign that I am following the path truly destined for me and my way of perceiving the world.

There are times that incidents within this prison give me negative views, but I see them as no more than mundane distractions and I always replace them with a positive mental equivalent; therefore, it does not affect me, becoming something put in the past as insignificant and not important enough to dwell on.

Last week, I was coming out of the chow hall/kitchen. A guard, known to be a very belligerent individual, antagonizes nearly every inmate he comes in contact with. This guard wanted to pat search me, so I submitted to the pat search. After he searched me, he wanted me to take my shoestrings out of my shoes, because they were blue. Being true to my nature, instinctively I rebelled and inadvertently challenged his authority. This happened right in front of the kitchen, so close to a hundred inmates are watching through the windows, as well as other guards who came out of their assigned areas to watch what would unfold. Since I've been in prison, I have gained a notorious reputation for assaulting guards, and there was the expectancy from the inmates who dislike this guard, as well as other guards, for me to do what I've been doing for decades. But on this day, I gave the officer my shoestrings. Even though I did this, he was intimidated, causing him to pull out more of his posturing and bravado.

Because I did not follow the pattern of violence I was known for, many inmates and guards were disappointed. This guard gave me a conduct violation for creating a disturbance. When I was asked for a statement for them to put on the conduct violation, I simply stated "It was my fault."

Since I did not follow the pattern of violence I've been following for years, many inmates who wanted to see this guard get hurt were depending on me to do it for them. Some say I got soft. Some say I got punked. I knew this would come, but it did not affect me, yet in the past this was intolerable. I know that when I do not engage in the wicked games the administration usually sets up (making bets, etc.), it disrupts the system. In order for me to evolve, I must rise above the conformity of this realm and ascend the impetuous thought process that plagues this land with its noxious miasma.

You have given me valuable knowledge and when I apply what I've learned, it is profoundly rewarding to see the effects that it has on myself as well as my environment.

> Monsters hide here in human guise
> Than reside in the pits of hell
> But love, warmth and kindness arise
> In the heart of the beast as well

I must say that I am already living in another dimension as a reborn spiritual being. I am confined to a world of darkness within this realm. It is hard to envision or even imagine what life would be like outside of this necropolis. I refer to this world as the 9th Dominion. It has devastating effects on all who dwell here. I will not say that being here and going through this madness hasn't had any destructive or negative effects on me or hasn't done any damage. I could never say that. This suffering, this madness has done plenty of damage in so many ways and I may never recover from some of it, but the point is that nobody is immune to the constant isolation or constant prison madness. But as a reborn spiritual being, it is important to stay active, stay healthy, to keep resisting, keep striving, keep elevating, so that I may avoid deterioration.

Consciousness permeates through this infrastructure and fills the atmosphere of this kingdom. Man cannot imprison consciousness. Knowledge helps to liberate my mind from this constant oppression. It allows me access to increase my strength of consciousness so that I can take the initiative to rise up and above this constant death, destruction, and devastation.

As a reborn spiritual being in this land, I am an infinite voice of many souls lost in darkness. I am here to awaken the mind of the confined and unconfine the minds of the unawakened. I know truth, therefore I speak truth. Some truth hurts, some truths set us free. Truth can unleash one from their fetters. Truth can release one from pain. Within this dimension, I learn, I breathe, I live.

5/17/10

DEAR MICHAEL,

I have not read the book *The Mind of Believing* by Claude Bristol, but I looked him up on the internet and found a lot of beautiful quotes, which I have included with this letter.

If the reason we are here is the self-expression of God, then each person, place, and thing is important to the unity of the Whole. The greater harmony in the Whole, surely the greater expression of life in each of its parts. At the molecular level, each part is made up of particles with atoms, which, when combined with other atoms, takes on a multitude of forms. The smallest particle has an inherent perfection and is in pure harmony in its own way. As particles combine and build into the multitude of expressions we see in the universe, we could not remove part of these building blocks and expect a form to stay the same. Each individual expression of life, including our life, is significant to the whole. *The world would be diminished if we weren't here.* As we expand and grow in knowledge and our ability to use the Laws of the Universe for a greater good, it contributes to the further progression and expression of the Whole.

We develop the realization of the truth found in metaphysics as, time after time, we prove to ourselves affirmative prayer and living in principle works. "I think I can, I think I can," said the little engine to itself as it climbed the steep hill and made it to the top. "Whatever the mind can conceive, we can achieve," whether it be to do good or harm, to help or hurt, to give or take. At both ends of the scale, the Law works consistently. This is the seed of perfection. Holmes explained, "We experience good and evil because we perceive a presence of duality rather than unity." Our thoughts create the appearance of two sides battling for success, but spiritual practices work to bring our thoughts to peace and harmony. Reaching for a higher good is worthwhile. Take time today to reveal the inner goodness that is yours.

6/28/10

DEAR REV. MARY,

I have a few questions I would like to ask you, but first I need to explain and elaborate the situation. There are about 1,800 inmates here at this prison: 35 percent African, 60 percent European, 5 percent Hispanic. The prison staff (guards, wardens, caseworkers, parole officers, chaplains, secretarial, food service workers, investigators) are 99.4 percent European. There is one African male for each rank as guard—Major, Captain, Lieutenant, Sergeant and COI—so five African staff members hold what I call "token" positions. Many of the European staff members have never before been around Africans, so we are subjected to bigoted scrutiny.

In this prison, racism is so blatant that in the future it will end up in a bloodbath. The prison staff manipulate prison organizations in order to set one group against another. This helps them maintain divisions among prisoners and keeps the "illusion of power" and violence under the control of the prison staff. Violent resistance from specific inmates against staff have only arisen when it was necessitated by those who monopolize violence through their own power.

When prison staff repress every educational and legal outlet for prisoners to redress wrongdoings, then it is clear what kind of correctional services they are promoting. It is believed that violence is necessary to end injustice, because documented history has demonstrated that the oppressor never stops oppressing any other way. Yet is violence the only answer?

This is the 21st century, yet I've come across those who think this is the 8th century and treat inmates of hue as if they would have done in a rural Arkansas plantation. I've always told myself that if I ever ended up on death row, it would probably be here at this prison. I've been in many different prisons in Missouri, but none have had an epidemic of racist ideologies and maneuvers like here in Licking, Missouri.

I believe in the cause of justice and freedom, in the principles of love, truth, and peace. But how can one combat injustice with those who only believe in hate and more hate? There are a multitude of issues keeping inmates from inviting and presenting a concerted effort against these malevolent entities, who want only to see us destroy each other and self-destruct.

Without a doubt, the Department of Corrections of Missouri is the root cause of our polarization. After that, the different ideologies are a great hindrance to solidarity, especially the ones that teach ethnic superiority over others, and many of these people consider themselves Muslims, Christians, Odinist, Wiccans, Jehovah's Witnesses, Catholics, and Buddhists.

I've been working toward building better relationships with the different street tribes in hopes of bringing solidarity within these different units. I'd like to overcome the stereotypes and propaganda so we can, as an organization, publicly utilize our image to show that liberation is gained from education.

The search for Truth is often unsettling and if acquiring knowledge were easy, we would all have it. It's no easy task to bring stability from chaos, but inmates here need to break old habits that aren't productive and learn new habits. Doing nothing productive and deceiving ourselves that we rule or are almighty while under the boot of those who consider themselves "Grand Wizards," is the type of thinking that is absurd—and I'm not prone to embracing absurdity.

I have been met with obstacles ranging from prison officials to bosslings. One of the main obstacles that weighs heavy on my mind and heart is the barriers we have amongst us prisoners. I'm trying to penetrate the walls of ignorance that pervade the prison system. Every negative aspect of life is magnified and accelerated within this land.

Sometimes I feel that trying to teach and help others awaken is a waste of time, and even though I have a positive influence over many, I see the same ones I speak with fall back into negative mundane ways of thinking.

There are guards who have observed me with literature in my hand and a group of inmates around me conversing. Some guards might pull me over on the wall to search me. Then one will ask me, "Do you have any knives on you?" I'll answer, "No," and another guard will say, "Oh, Nichols has retired and he is now a private consultant." Because of past actions, guards assume I'm still on a destructive path and will crack jokes, for they are expecting me to be violent. So, I ask, how can one be of this world and not apart from it?

Is it prudent for me to become anti-social and just alienate myself from everyone? Is it prudent to complain and bring to the attention of governors and senators the corruption of this infrastructure? Is it prudent to see what is going on around me and ignore it and to never speak out against it?

Rev. Mary, I only ask for your insight, nothing more. I thank you for your support and information you have provided me with about Science of Mind. It has been a part of my inspiration.

7/29/10

DEAR MICHAEL,

Regarding the makeup of prison staff and prisoners, I have to go back to the soul's journey. Each of us is on this journey to go beyond what has held us back or stopped our growth previously. Guards were called to that career, just as those in prison for crimes were called and answered to that world. The two worlds don't get along, as one side judges the other harshly.

Alienating ourselves from others isn't an answer to creating change in the world. You are a light in your realm. Personally, when I get irritated at what I see as injustice, I write letters to legislators or companies in the hopes of opening their eyes to what can be done even better. In the prison system, there is much to be improved. God's love comes through us when we feel compassion for others.

Legislators, managers, and those who work under their direction are individuals with their own lives that may be frayed, and so they may also desire to alienate themselves, especially from the prison population. Our growth comes from loving what the ego perceives as the unlovable. If you were this unlovable person, how would you like to be treated? How would you like to be loved? Transplanting our feet into their shoes helps us let go of ego mind and replace it with compassion.

Compassion is the part of us that sees the rocky road someone has created and the pain that comes with it, and yet knows there is an answer, a way to get back to the smooth highway of life. Find a place of understanding in your heart for what that person at both the lowest and highest level in the system has experienced in their life. Feel it and let compassion swell in your heart. Understand, accept, and let go of negative feelings. We are all the same in the eyes of God, so be open to the grace of compassion by giving love.

What we long for the most is love from other people, yet there never seems to be enough. We take it so personally when someone doesn't love us *this much.* When our attention centers on us, we want everyone's attention—see me, hear me, love me. One teacher said we all want someone else to give us love, to make our life exciting and blissful every day, but seldom do we want to be the person who must give, give, and give, day in and day out to make that happen for someone else.

When someone finds it hard to show love, even in a simple form of friendship or respect for a stranger, they are deeply caught in their own feelings, pulled so far inward there is no awareness or capacity to do anything else. They live in an illusion that has nothing to do with us, it's just where they are in their personal growth. If we can be a light of love, we might be the catalyst for them to open up and take the risk of changing.

Just like all things, the Law of Cause and Effect rules love. When we give love, we receive a response—and we cannot receive love without having a response. It is the nature of love to be irresistible and transform everyone it touches in some way. In *The Science of Mind* we read, "Love is an essence, an atmosphere, which defies analysis, as does Life Itself. It is that which IS and cannot be explained; it is common to all people, to all animal life, and evident in the response of plants to those who love them. Love reigns supreme over all." Like the lamp that dissipates the darkness, love can overcome hate, fear, and sadness.

8/25/10

DEAR REV. MARY,

I must admit that when one ends up in prison, a sense of being in a free fall is forced upon you. The letting go of many different types of concepts, dependence on people, drugs, alcohol, and personal control of our lives is the free fall for many of the wretched of the Earth. It is positive in some ways, yet it can be harmful also.

When my only son and child was diagnosed with leukemia, I had written to his doctors, explaining to them that I was his father and I was in prison, yet I was willing to do a bone marrow transplant to save my son's life, because no match had yet been found for my son. I explained to the doctors that there may be some red tape that they would have to cut through to get this done. Yet these maladroit dragons never even tried.

When my son passed, my frustration, anger, and hatred for being helpless and not being able to receive justice blinded me for so long I didn't realize that my son was healed through his demise. To write about it even now brings back pangs of anger and pain.

9/12/10

DEAR MICHAEL,

Anger at those who make the rules can be debilitating. It's the impersonal nature of it all. What we really want is people in our life who love us for being natural and who support us with their love. By being open and honest, we experience the tenderness and the pain in the world. This is living. Our heart is touched and compassion blossoms. Holmes explains, "A life that has not loved has not lived, it is still dead." We cannot experience the gifts of the Universe if we have not developed our ability to love, because the Universe is based on love. Inner love is awakened by grace and its source is our own self. The source of all love is within and can be released through the expansion of grace resulting from doing spiritual practices.

When we maintain an atmosphere of love in any situation, the Law of Mental Equivalents brings us the experience of love as a reaction in our body. Anyone who is in an environment where they are the "helper" should watch out for the trap of being too formal and distant with the ones they are helping. The problem of being a helper is not the work, but our identification with it. The ego enjoys being in a helping situation by trying to organize it, saying, "I'm the helper, the one with knowledge and skill, and you are the one I am helping, so be quiet and listen to me." Instead of valuing the present moment and the gift each experience holds for us, we try to control the environment and the ways we might help. Our ego forms a picture of our self-image and the more we hold onto it, the more we alienate and diminish the people we try to help. By being an open vessel of love, the actions of being the helper are flavored with an energy that, as Ram Dass says, allows us to meet each other behind our roles, acknowledging our true identities as individual expressions of God, which adds richness to the experience.

Is God really just love? God must be love and only love or the duality would destroy us. The opposite of love is fear. Love overcomes all fear and cures all fear. Try it. Prove it to yourself. Love is more powerful than any bad feelings we can have for one another. Love softens our heart and reveals our inner beauty. We may try to attribute love and fear to God, but if both emotions were aspects of God, it would be chaos. God is only love. The Universe emanates love and support for all we do and all we want by saying "yes" to our desires and beliefs, so the more we embody the purity of this love, the more beautiful our life becomes.

11/4/10

DEAR MICHAEL,

The principles of co-creation may seem very intangible as you first study this philosophy. So how are you doing with all of this? The theory that we become what we believe according to Law is fascinating, but when we actually see it working in our life, it can be good news or bad news. We might look at our life and think, "Wow, I believe this?!?" Working through our thoughts and beliefs, the Law is always ready and willing to take form as our everyday experience.

The knowledge that life is a mirror of our beliefs has been around for centuries, but there is an undercurrent in society that greatly resists that fact. It is much easier to buy into a philosophy that makes others responsible for our problems. When we aren't happy with life, it may seem too overwhelming, practically impossible for us to change what we've believed for so long.

Many authors have presented these ideas in easier-to-swallow concepts. Years ago, Napoleon Hill wrote a very popular book, *How to Think and Grow Rich*. He believed in the power of autosuggestion, repeating prosperity affirmations to ourselves, which would, through the Law of Prosperity, show up in our experience. He described it like this: "Thoughts that are mixed with any of the feelings of emotions constitute a 'magnetic' force, which attracts other similar or related thoughts." In metaphysics we call this the Law of Attraction, which we know is not some sci-fi sounding invisible force, but an actual law, a principle. In attracting money, Hill described how our mind attracts vibrations, which harmonize with dominant thoughts, so by repeatedly holding thoughts of prosperity, we attract prosperity. Like metaphysics, he went on to state that when we know prosperity is ours, believe it, and trust in it, we attract it by Law.

CHAPTER 3

2011

This System of Hypocrisy, Cruelty, and Deception

A higher order structure emerges in my conscious, each more complex until there is only unity in all directions — My search for absolute Truth — Concrete walls, razor wire, electric fences can never hold down the thoughts of a prisoner — Malevolent influences imposed morbid teachings, manipulating the present by eliminating the past, rewriting history to accommodate its plans for the future — The world in which I existed ensured I would not succeed — In this world, darkness of the mind, corruption, wickedness, and hatred pay out with generous interest — A social disorder infused fear, doubt, confusion, and self-loathing into me — Learning my true history and searching for hidden truths — If I hold no goal higher than unraveling the secrets of the Universe, I must let the Truth into my soul.

2/6/11

DEAR REV. MARY,

You have encouraged me to write a book of my life experiences and spiritual growth. I did not realize that my writings would merit book status, so I regard your encouragement as a compliment, and, yes, I can provide you with writings of my life experiences and spiritual growth, but I must admonish you, for my life has not been that of the typical. I've been administered a high dose of morbid ideologies and philosophies from enslaved mis-education and genocide. Yet all of this has given me the strength to forge ahead and reach the level of wisdom and knowledge I have now attained. Those things which one would consider sinful are, for me, no more than an unequivocal reality.

The teaching lessons and information you have provided me with from *The Science of Mind* have been a momentous advancement in my studies. I have exceeded my own level quicker than expected. The Science of Mind teaching has given me the instrument to access the knowledge I had acquired only in the form of axioms, but did not know the methods of how to channel its dynamics. The abilities that can be obtained through a working knowledge of cause and effect can rectify one's thinking.

To know something, one must study not only the concept, but those things that relate to the concept. At each point in my psychological growth, I find that a higher order structure emerges in my conscious. The self identifies its being with that higher structure, so the higher order structure eventually emerges. The self dis-identifies with the lower structure and shifts its essential identity to the higher structure consciousness. Each successive higher order structure is more complex, more organized, and more unified—and evolution continues until there is only unity in all directions.

Every time a higher order deep structure emerges, the lower order structures are subsumed, enveloped, or comprehended by it. That is, at each point in evolution or development, what is the whole of one level becomes merely a part of the higher order whole of the next level. As the mind emerges and develops, however, the sense of identity shifts to the mind, and the body is merely one aspect, one part of the total self. In each point in evolution or development, a mode of self becomes merely a component of a higher order.

My search for absolute Truth has been of colossal transition. What is of worth to me is my path, regardless of the hardships it presents or the length of time it takes. The road in one's journey will not go to the individual. He will go to it if it proves of worth to him. If it doesn't, one cannot hold onto it. One cannot hold uselessness together successfully in this dimension of time, because it will fall apart from its uselessness. That is one of the reasons why many stagnated belief systems have become infected with hypocrisy.

The direction one should pursue is within each individual and only that individual can take that road. When one finds his path, he will constantly have an inner drive to keep on it, and when he is not on it, he will become restless and disturbed. When one finds his true path, he will find tranquility and purpose. The gifts will demand of him to know that he is distinctive, created by God the way he was intended to be.

One must change himself for the betterment. He must improve himself. One's complex personality is many faceted and bound to change by conditions. It is said that leopards do not change their spots, but leopards are not men and men can and do change. New circumstances, new commitments, and new experiences shape one into the realized and more beautiful being one is meant to become. One should commit himself to a cause that, in time, in scope, and in value, transcends one's thinking and purpose. One should involve himself in something that is of greater importance in the larger scheme of things.

> *If one advances with positive confidence in the direction of*
> *his dreams and lives a life he has imagined, he will meet with*
> *a success unexpected in common hours.*
>
> — HENRY DAVID THOREAU

Visions of cruelty of the past create false unrealistic illusions of reality. Under this grand wizardry, one will be a zombie in a dreamland of negative fantasy. Discovering Truth helps me develop a great character, which will be crowned and controlled by a consciousness that is constrained by God.

In your letter you mentioned how in California the prison system has an 80 percent recidivism rate. I would like to write on that somewhat, since I know this system well.

The 21st century subrosa *(in secret)* design of prisons in North America has been established on economics, warehousing of humans, experimentation, and strategically feasible games activated.

When a person studies mathematics, he learns that there are many mathematical laws which determine the approach he must take to solving the problem presented to him. In the study of geometry, one of the first laws one learns is that the whole is not greater than the sum of its parts. This means simply that one cannot have a geometrical figure such as a circle or a square which contains more than it does when broken down into smaller parts. Therefore, if all the smaller parts add up to a certain amount, the entire figure cannot add up to a larger amount.

A prisoner is not a geometrical figure, so an approach which is successful in mathematics is wholly unsuccessful when dealing with human beings. In the case of the human, one is not dealing only with the single individual, one is dealing with the ideas and beliefs which have motivated him and which sustain him, even when his body is imprisoned. In the case of humanity, the whole is much greater than its parts because the whole encompasses the body, which is measurable and confinable, and the ideologies and beliefs that cannot be measured or confined.

The concrete walls, razor wire, electric fences, the steel bars, the gas chambers, the death gurneys, the guns, and the guards can never encircle or hold down the thoughts of a prisoner. The North American prison system operates with the concept that since it has a person's body, it has his entire being, because the whole cannot be greater than the sum of its parts. But this cannot be true, because those who operate the prison system have failed to examine their own beliefs thoroughly and they fail to understand the types of people they attempt to control.

One must understand that the largest number of those in prison are those who accepted the legitimacy of the perceptions upon which the North American continent is based. Many prisoners have wished to acquire the same goals as everyone else: money, power, conspicuous consumption, and creature comforts. Yet in order to do so, they adopted techniques and methods of the xenophobes who established dominion and authority on this continent, that are now defined as illegitimate.

When these people are discovered of mimicry, they are put in prison. The prisoner recognizes his mistake of "getting caught," so he plays the game the prison system wants him to play if he wants to have his time reduced and get back out into the free world to continue his activities. Therefore, the prisoner is willing to go through the prison programs offered and speak lies that the prison authorities are accustomed to hearing. The prison system assumes the prisoner is rehabilitated, when in all actuality he is, since rehabilitation is another word for reinstate, which means to restore to a previous position. But to get funding for prison programs, "rehabilitate" is the label used and the rehabilitated prisoner is ready for society. The prisoner has really played the prison system's game so that he can be released and reinstated to resume pursuit of his previous goals, which equals recidivism.

It is said that great evil retains its greatness. Logic would say that anyone who wished to obliterate cruelty from the character of another must himself show no cruelty. The way one is treated in these American prisons by prison authorities tells one about those who devise such punishment. The story of exile and prison is the story of the lash, the iron chain and shackle, and every torture that the fiendish ingenuity of the supposedly "noncriminal" class can devise by way of teaching criminals to be good.

Reason rests upon truth. Wherever truth is disregarded, illusions appear. If we lose sight of the highest, the lower will appear to be the highest and an illusion will be created. The negative miasma that encircles this realm has an immense effect on many of the inhabitants of this land. Every person that comes into my scope, I patiently try to teach, if they have a desire to see the strength in positive thinking that will allow their true self to emerge. I know that no man can reveal to another but that which already lies half asleep in the dawning of their own knowledge.

The teacher who walks in the shadow of the temple among his followers gives not of his wisdom, but rather of his faith. If he indeed is wise, he does not bid you enter the house of his wisdom, but rather leads you to the threshold of your own mind. The astronomer may speak to one of his understanding of space, but he cannot give one his understanding. The musician may play to you the rhythm, but he cannot give you the ears that depict the rhythm. For the vision of one man lends not its wings to another man, and even as each man stands alone in God's knowledge, so must each man be alone in his understanding of God's knowledge and his understanding of the Earth.

Within this letter, I have included paperwork of an assessment of my "arrested development" from a prison program called ES/LS Employment Skills and Life Skills.

3/25/11

DEAR MICHAEL,

The ES/LS report is interesting, but recognize it does not represent the totality of who you are, just one aspect of life that can be improved upon. Opportunities abound. Life in the Universe is expanding, growing, flourishing. All around us we see the Law of Growth in action. Regardless of the exquisite beauty in a rose, as sweet as it smells, eventually it withers and then another takes its place as the bush expands and flourishes. Nature is always expanding and creating something new with greater complexity and splendor. We also expand and experience a greater life when we grow within ourselves.

Inner growth is the way we evolve. It requires letting go of behavior patterns or life-styles we've been clinging to out of safety and familiarity. Growth cannot occur when we hold on too tightly. By letting go, we release the old ways and create a vacuum into which the Universe brings a new and greater experience.

By letting go of what does not serve us, a vacuum is created into which we put our thoughts and desires. We make space for a greater relationship to show up in our life. Without focusing our thoughts and desires, without using affirmative prayer and the power of Universal Mind, a vacuum is always filled, filled with whatever happens to come along. Holmes explains it as a fluent force forever taking form and forever deserting the form it has taken. We can mold the direction of growth by using our personal power, so we don't just take whatever comes.

Living by understanding and applying metaphysical principles on a day-to-day basis gives us direct experiences of our innate power. This growth won't happen if we wait around for friends to approve of us. Are there any no-growth areas in your life? Our desires show the way we want to grow, and through spiritual practices, Spirit can show us how to make it happen. Working with metaphysical principles, we find our power center, knowing the Law is infinite and occupies all space. It fills every form with a differentiation of Itself. It will bring whatever is necessary into our experience so it unfolds perfectly. What has been brought into your life lately that may have been unexpected? Can you see the perfection?

6/16/11

DEAR REV. MARY,

What has been on my mind lately is the question of what is it that makes some people so angry and vengeful at the world and each other? And what part does self-loathing play? In my studies, I've learned much, and I cannot rule out the truths that I have experienced.

My personal odyssey and commitment to uncovering truth has been an uncanny, arduous, and unique journey. I could not be a conscious, moral person if I ignore truth. I cannot pretend to be ignorant to the realities of my world. They cannot be dismissed as psychological rhetoric. Prison forced me to wake up and regain consciousness. My survival depended on it. Otherwise, I would have perished of despair. Despair is born of hope-lessness. Hopelessness is the loss of appreciation for what it means to have faith, purpose, and life.

As a child, I believed what was told to me or what many others were taught to believe without examining whether they were truths or falsehoods. This began the contagion of morbid ideologies. I often ask those whom I teach this question: "If I told you a lie and you believed it, would it be truth? Then if I told you a truth and you did not believe it, would it be a lie?"

In North America, the majority are individually and collectively enculturated to hate life, hate foreign customs. People hate the natural world, hate the wild, hate wild animals, hate women, hate children, hate their own bodies, hate specific colors, and hate themselves. A web of culture binds man to a style of life and a definition of human nature. Man sees, understands, and makes judgments based on the codes, creeds, and values he grew up with. Knowledge of the diverse ways of mankind can give one a new perspective on man: who he is, what he can do, what he can hope to become.

Religious beliefs, folklore, art, science, history, social order—all reflect the way a peo-ple come to terms with life. Each culture stands as a monument to man's achievement and each testifies to the human capacity to find a formula for survival. The majority of humans see reality through veils of their culture, heritage, biochemistry, brain capacity, compre-hension, upbringing, socialization, group think, or race consciousness.

When a nation fails to learn the true history of its past, the people are doomed to reside within a fairy tale of delusions. Once that deception becomes ingrained into the popular culture, the task of the tyrant simplifies how the nation is transformed into a civic ordeal and betrayal of principles and heritage. The masses cling to the lies as fact. The new gospel for social order becomes transformed into a somber reality.

When truths fade from a people's memory, when their traditions lose importance, when old moral values no longer serve a need, when the enrichment of knowledge that enhances one, when the rituals of religious beliefs is not preserved, that world, that way of life and its ancient teachings, will come to an end and the history and culture will vanish as if it never existed.

Malevolent influences have imposed their own morbid teachings, crooked beliefs, and immoral customs and lifestyles on many nations, while in the process manipulating the present by eliminating the past, rewriting history to accommodate its plans for the future. This entity operates through a profound, deceptive, distorted illusion, propagating falsehoods as truths.

There are those who believe the literal meaning of what they read in the numerous versions of their religious texts. Many believe that the book is literally "God's Word" and cannot be questioned, even when it conflicts with common sense. There are people who have spiritually divided themselves because their feelings and faith are telling them one thing and their reason and the actions of people in their world are telling another. Then there is the spiritual and internal division that is created by the representation of a God in a particular ethnic image.

The child growing up under the influence of this image fails to see a natural relationship between himself and this God. The effect is a person who has a strong faith in the reality of a power of God but associates that God with an image completely different from himself. This creates a split in personality and causes one to believe in the power of people rather than themselves. This creates the need to see one's own self in contrast to the God image of power, purity, and greatness. So, one's own self becomes evil, dirty, powerless, and worthless, in contrast to the God image of power and goodness. This inevitably leads one into the ominous bog of low self-esteem, self-loathing, and pessimistic views.

I have asked many who I teach: "What is self-esteem?" Several have tried, but not one could confidently answer the question. One person answered and said that self-esteem is how a person feels about himself. So, I asked him, "If I feel disgusted about myself or hate myself, is that self-esteem?" Even though the definition varies somewhat depending on which dictionary is used, the core essence remains the same—that self-esteem is the belief that one is innately worthy of being valued by one's own self. That one is a human being worthy of acceptance, understanding, love, friendship, and respect.

Self-esteem tells one that he deserves to succeed in life by accomplishing goals and fulfilling the constructive desires that one may have. It tells one that their worth and value are an end within themselves and are in no way dependent upon the ideas of the greater or lesser value of others. Self-esteem is an attitude of acceptance, approval, and respect toward oneself. Self-esteem is this because its essence rests within the self and is not reliant upon anything one does or doesn't do.

Synonymous with self-esteem is self-enrichment, self-confidence, self-love, self-discovery, self-discipline, self-development, self-dedication, and self-awareness, all of which adds up to achieve responsible livelihood, both the end and the means of peace of mind. Self-confidence overcomes feelings of inadequacy and replaces it with confidence. Self-confidence is the belief of one's own ability to come to grips with problems and solve them; to know that we can and will succeed at worthy tasks, all of which equips one emotionally to meet life's challenges with equanimity and imperturbability. The one who is self-confident in turn dares to be an honest man. He accepts himself as a unique individual. He reflects a basic integrity of character.

Self-enrichment is a process of developing or augmenting one's mental faculties or spiritual resources. "Power lies within us. We do not find it in outer things." The object of the search exists within the search. The seeker who is searching is himself the object of the search.

The skunk is a very interesting creature. It has a very attractive and alluring looking appearance. A child who has not been educated about the quiddity of the skunk may very well wish to hold it and pet it. Once the veil of the creature's presentation has been pierced, the child finds it produces a stench of enormous disgust. So it is with the society in which I have lived.

The world upon which I have existed has always been that of a slave in service of a self-proclaimed master. The entire fabric of American society is riddled with racism and enforced via its institutions, which ensured I would not succeed or be given an opportunity to carve out a meaningful existence unless I was willing to part with my cultural identity and awareness.

In 1832, a member of the ruling elite in Virginia was documented as saying, "We have, as far as possible, closed every avenue by which light might enter the slave's minds. If we could extinguish their capacity to see the light, our work would be completed. They would continue to be on a level with the beast of the field and we should be safe. I am not certain that we would not do it, if we could find out the process, and that on pleas of necessity."

In the world where I've existed, there are many willing to see only the light that is visible, never the light invisible. Many have a daily darkness that is night, and many encounter another darkness from time to time that is death, the death of those we love, but the third and most constant darkness with many every day, at all hours of every day, is the darkness of the mind, the corruption, wickedness, and hatred, which many invite into themselves and pay out with generous interest.

To quote Voltairine de Cleyre (a late 1800s American anarchist who opposed state power and capitalism): "The reason men steal is because their rights are stolen from them before they are born. Some die because they cannot eat at all. Pray tell me what these last have to lose by becoming thieves and why shall they not become thieves? And is the action of a man who takes the necessities which have been denied him really a criminal? Is he morally worse than the man who crawls in the cellar and dies of starvation? I think not, and say truly to begin by taking loaves means to end by taking everything and murdering, too, very often. And in that you draw the indictment against your own system.

"If there is no alternative between starving and stealing (and for thousands there is none) then there is no alternative between society murdering its members or the members disintegrating society. Let society consider its own mistakes then let it answer itself for all these people it has robbed and killed. Let it cease its own crimes first."

If a people are systematically prevented from engaging in the constructive execution of their life processes and subjected to the dehumanizing experiences of being made servants of an alien culture, then one can predict that they might conceivably act in ways inconsistent with their own development and counter to their best self-interest. This inevitably leads into a self-fulfilling prophecy, which can be defined as a projective assumption or prediction which, as a result of having been authoritatively projected, causes the projected assumption or prediction to be realized, thereby confirming its own accuracy. The projected self-fulfilling prophecy becomes fulfilled because the act of prophesying itself prescribes actions on the part of the prophet or projecting party who creates and sustains the conditions necessary to bring into being the expected event.

Actions on the part of the projecting party create and sustain a conditioned reality, actually and in truth. This conditioned reality is channeled, created, formed, and bounded by a set of organized and regulated actions and interactions on the part of the projecting party. That is, the prophet first makes a prediction or expresses an expectation regarding his target person or group. If in a position of power, he then arranges the life conditions and experiences of his target in concordance with his predictions and expectations.

The target, in adapting to the conditions imposed on him by the prophet or projecting party and, in reacting emotionally to these conditions, is often conditioned how to think and behave in ways compatible with the power interests of the projecting party. The target's character and personality and emotional orientations and abilities reflect the conditioning imposed on him by the projective party or prophet. Hence, the target fulfills the initial predictions or prophecies of the projectionist.

Yet this can only be actualized with the unwitting collusive participation of the intended victim when the victim accepts falsified projections as truths. Only then can the projected expectations fulfill themselves. The acceptance of falsehood is made easy and efficient by the fact that information, whether true or untrue, is almost completely controlled and manipulated by "Frankensteins"—academic and propaganda establishments.

Information that misrepresents views of African history and culture are still accepted as truth in the psychological establishment. For example, the theory of eugenics. Eugenics was a term coined by Charles Darwin's cousin, Francis Galton, in 1883, which referred to the attempts to improve the human species by affording the more suitable races or strains of blood a better chance of prevailing speedily over the less suitable. This pseudo scientific theory postulated that there were genes within oppressed nations that were leading to the deterioration of the human race and that people in oppressed nations were predisposed to committing crimes.

The resolution to this contradiction was to isolate these people in institutions, mental asylums, prisons, reservations, ghettos, barrios, slums—or to sterilize them. The State of California was one of twenty-nine American states to pass laws allowing sterilization and conducted more forced sterilizations than anywhere in the U.S. These sterilizations were justified as efforts to prevent the passing on of mental illness and criminality. In the 1990s, eugenics became the Bell Curve Theory.

Pseudoscientific credence means providing credibility to an issue based on flawed science. Race superiority is based on a false contention derived from a pseudoscientific application of biology (also Christian concepts of manifest destiny). Race-based theories were also given credence by flawed science in the form of psychology.

A prominent Louisianan named Dr. Samuel A. Cartwright claimed that he discovered two mental diseases in 1851 that were peculiar to the "Negro" race: Drapetomania and Dysaesthesia Aethiopica. In brief, Drapetomania was a disease that caused Africans to have an uncontrolled urge to run away from their "masters." The treatment for this "illness" was whipping the devil out of them. It is well-known that a captured fugitive slave was often beaten as well as mutilated with a whip by his captor, a clear example of how this pseudoscience gave credence to the oppressor's brutality. Dysaesthesia Aethiopica supposedly affected the mind and body. The diagnosable signs included disobedience, answering disrespectfully, and refusing to work. The cure was to prescribe some kind of hard labor.

The American empire severely punishes through social ostracism, racism, discrimination, violence, and denial of fundamental civil rights, and many of my elders who survived to pass on the *Thanatos* (death instinct) to the generations to come impacted me and helped shape what I would become. I recognize that a social disorder infused fear, doubt, confusion, and self-loathing into myself and others, for this is all part of the pre-arranged program. So, in accepting this reality that I myself was shaped and formed by social disorder that preferred that I remain afraid, confused, self-loathing, and unhappy, because I am more predictable and controlled that way, I had to change. I had to learn my true history and search for hidden truths in the many different religions of the world.

I had adopted a culture, a pathological culture, which was rife with morbid and rotten ideologies. I accumulated these poisons and engaged in toxic behavior. My behavior reflected the poison I had ingested, so in order for me to become healthy, I had to purge the poison from my system.

There has been a time when many men have been broken down to ground level and then constructed themselves anew. I was driven toward the knowledge and wisdom of Truth. The realm I dwell in holds no social constrictions, and I decided that I would let nothing stand in my way. One must sate his thirst without regard to the encumbrances of this world and then he will be able to go far to amass the vast reservoir of knowledge that reveals Truth. So, if one is truly dedicated, if one holds no goal higher than unraveling the secrets of the Universe, one must let the Truth into his soul, for it is the only way to deal with the Demogorgons (demons) of falsehood.

The great-hearted man refuses to imprison his soul behind color, creed, or caste. In every other, he sees another human being fundamentally the same as himself. Despite all barriers, he enjoys meeting kindred souls. For him, dignity, grandeur, and nobility exist only in simplicity, sincerity, and sympathy. I've found Truth the only thing worth living for. But there is a hard struggle to obtain it. As a rule, we do not like to hear that which doesn't fit with our own ideas. One may find that when it comes to unpleasant truths, their mind shies like a horse at strange objects. Yet by constant use of the spur of reason, one will be able to accustom himself to strange truths to overcome prejudice, for this will allow one to find each new truth easier to accept no matter how unpleasant.

Rev. Mary, when one is in an abnormal situation, that person will have an abnormal reaction, yet he will believe it is normal. In this realm, there is an unavoidable influence of surrounding. This unique structure of prison life forces the prisoner to conform his conduct to a certain set pattern.

Is the theory true that many psychologists base their denouement that man is no more than a product of many conditional environmental factors? Is it true that the prisoners' reactions to the dominion of prison prove that man cannot escape the influence of his surroundings? Does one have no choice of action in the face of synecological *sub rosa* human experimentation?

Life tasks are very real and concrete. They tend to form a man's destiny, which is different and unique for each individual. Escapism embraced allows one to ignore his tortured prison existence and/or harbor false illusions and entertain artificial optimism. Each man determines if he will give in to a condition or stand against it, deciding what his existence will be in a dire situation, facing a fate he cannot ultimately change. He may rise above, grow beyond, and by so doing, change himself.

In the mindset of one who denies his reality lies a certain danger. It becomes easy to overlook the positive beneficial opportunities that do exist. For many men forget that their situation is no more than an external situation which can allow one to grow spiritually. Only a few are truly capable of reaching great spiritual heights, and these few are given the chance to attain human harmony and peace of mind, even though their apparent world is surrounded by failures, hypocrisy, defeat, and death, an accomplishment which in the ordinary free world they would not have achieved.

There are within the 9th Dominion (Missouri Department of Corrections) opportunities to become victorious in this experience, turning one's life into inner triumph. Or one could simply ignore life's tests and simply decay as the majority of captives within these lands.

Prison for many has been a laboratory, a learning institution, an asylum, a necropolis, a zoo, and much more. But it also allows for one to either make use or forge the opportunities that do exist to attain moral values that a difficult situation may afford him.

Those who are capable of reaching high moral standards keep their full inner strength to rise above his outward fate. When man is confronted with his destiny, he must choose the decision of meeting it with courage, honor, and pride or succumbing to the demons, stripped of morality, principles, and dignity, to become molded into the form of the typical inhabitant.

Many would argue that the social construct of one's environment does not play an important role at all in one's decisions to the path he takes in life, and that many have been raised in war zones, ghettos, poverty, etc., and have gone on to become great leaders, basketball and football stars, musicians, actors, politicians, or living very lucrative and successful lives. This is true, yet for the African male child under European rule, the world is an enigma and does not function to the equivalent norms.

At some point, we may begin to realize that there are contradictory differences in our world and the world of others. Sometimes this can be shocking and sometimes shaming. It becomes unequivocal that we are rejected or ridiculed by a larger world, whether it be that we are of a different color, religion, nationality, or have a disability. We feel profoundly different. Depending on the self-esteem we've integrated and our inner strength and resilience, we may react with violence, withdrawal, anger, hatred, or an increased courage to reach out to bridge these challenges and more confidently into the social groups that we want to be a part of.

If in our youth we have adults who can help us with these challenges and can affirm our developing sense of a positive self, we can grow stronger and expand our self-view in positive ways. At the same time, we learn to use our challenges to develop empathy and appreciation for the challenges of others. If no one helps us, then we must rely on our own views to make sense of challenges. We may find a path to ease our way along that is help-ful or not. Many youths turn to drug substances or alcohol or to anger and/or violence to finally obtain great achievement. Others disappear and live invisible lives, never devel-oping to their true capacity as beings.

It is a complex journey for one to learn to function successfully in a world based on more negative actions than positive, yet many liberate themselves from the suffering of a mundane existence and find that we are much, much more.

What people have been brainwashed to be can distort their perception. All of the pre-judices, beliefs, attitudes, ideals, and opinions filter out the truth. If one grows up to res-pect and revere authority and is never taught to question that authority figure, this belief will greatly inhibit one's ability to be objective about information that comes to him. In such a position, similarly if one believes that all police officers are corrupt and hired assassins, it becomes impossible to see beyond that projection of his own ideals, beliefs, and prejudices.

Rev. Mary, before I end this letter, I want to impart to you this tale: You have two young males. Both grew up in the same neighborhood, both are fatherless, both graduated from high school, both hung out in the streets, both had run into trouble with the police. At a certain point in their young lives, they both made decisions that would lead them each to different destinies in their hostile world. One chooses the lifestyle of a gangster, the other chooses the lifestyle of a football star. The gangster inevitably kills a corrupt ex-cop, now a gun dealer, and ends up with life without parole in prison. The college football star who returns from a party and is pulled over by Demogorgons, adherents of the David Duke belief system, in the guise of policy and is lynched by a barrage of hate-filled full-metal-jacketed bullets.

I came to prison in 1991 because I survived the murderous entities that would rather see me in a graveyard. That was my only crime. I was and still am a survivor.

There is much more I want to extend on, but I'll do this in another letter. I'm includ-ing pictures of me and the "Bearded Lady." SCCC has a program called Healing Paws; it allows inmates to train dogs that came from the shelter that would have otherwise been euthanized. Once they've become adjusted to being around people, they are put up for adoption. The program has a very successful adoption rate. The picture was taken on May 23, 2011, even though the date on the front is off by five years. Many of the dogs, including Roxy, the Bearded Lady, have been abused, so their fear of people is a process when coming into contact with so many inmates. They adjust pretty well, plus the fact that inmates always have beef jerky snacks for the dogs!

7/24/11

DEAR MICHAEL,

It's so wonderful to find a companion in a dog that is trusting and loving. I know she is bringing out the best in you and others.

For those around you who live in fear or a belief in limitation, sometimes an analogy helps us to understand this teaching. One is that by living in fear or any belief of limitation, we are standing on the hose of grace, which waters our life. God is the water tap, and the water is always turned on. We engage grace in our life by the use of spiritual practices, positive thoughts and beliefs, and affirmative prayer. Therefore, the water flows. But if we stand on the hose or kink it through negativity or limited belief, we slow down and can even stop the flow of grace, the flow of water on our garden of life. Spiritual practices give us courage and help us locate and unravel the kinks, so we become more aware of when we are stepping on the hose.

I hope you can take some time this month to take a personal inventory in the areas where you might have posted a "No Growth" sign, where you might be stuck in a rut. Are you ready to take the sign down and move on? If you're not sure, you will find out where change is needed by paying attention.

Do you notice that sometimes in meditation we just get our mind quiet and a thought comes floating by, trying to distract us? Ram Dass, a wise meditation teacher, says there is a place in our mind where we can watch our thoughts go by. Visualize a pure blue sky. A bird flies by. We can follow the bird, a thought, or stay with the sky. By staying with the sky, we allow intuition, our inner voice, to surface and bring solutions to problems into our consciousness without much effort.

Experience is the best teacher. Listening to the still, small voice within is surrender based on trust. We trust that in reality all is well and the answer to any of our questions will be given at the right time. In that place of spacious awareness, the immensity of any situation will stay in its proper perspective. Try it! I'm sure you will be surprised.

10/10/11

DEAR MICHAEL,

Since I haven't heard from you for a while, I thought I would invite you to see cause and effect in action all around you. Here are a couple of examples from my experience lately. Recently a friend of mine was out of a job and lamented how hard it would be to find another good-paying job. Of course, the Universe said *"yes"* to this belief, and the result was my friend ended up putting a tremendous amount of effort into finding new employment.

The other day I was driving to a meeting with a friend, and as we approached the location, she commented how impossible it is to find a parking space close to the building. Gently I used a phrase I learned long ago, "That's not my experience," knowing the perfect spot near the building was always easily available, and it was.

It takes effort to be aware of all the thoughts zooming through our minds each minute. How many of your thoughts are affirmative and positive? If the pattern is overloaded with negatives, consciously shift the balance to positive and build from there. One way is to catch those negative thoughts and immediately say to yourself, "No, that's not my experience."

Our thoughts create a more forceful result when we have positive thoughts that are powerful, that have a sense of completion in mind. One way to do this is to add words, such as, "This is a beautiful room that brings joy and happiness to all who enter." Take a positive thought and create a power thought. Through this process we develop a picture of the result and tag it onto the initial thought. It can become a natural process in our mind that can be used to turn an average thought into a power thought.

As a student of world religions, do you have any knowledge of Scientology? One of my students asked about it and I did not know what to say. Any clarity on this would be greatly appreciated. And here in California, the governor is getting ready to release a lot of prisoners to relieve the overcrowded jails and prisons. I know recidivism in this state is about 50 percent and has been that rate for over ten years.

CHAPTER 4

2012

Oscillating Between Two Realities

Every year, month, week, and day is the facsimile of the last year, month, week, and day — Humans encased in concrete cannot truly grow, development is arrested, the being regresses and becomes the living dead — The future is a non-reality, taken before it has been touched — Lifelessness, unnecessary victimization, the dark forest, coercive controls, self-loathing, manufactured criminality — Developing immunity, courage — Discovering the purpose of my existence — The hole — Denying myself freedom — The death of my son — Elimination of hope — The prison of my own mind — My ancestors — Coming to terms with who I am — The power of a committed mind erased negative emotions — Ancient African Science, esoteric studies — Grandmother and Mother, library card, trombone, marching band, ROTC, Uncle Jr. — The warrior's way of life — Prison, an opportunity to learn my rich African heritage and culture.

2/6/12

DEAR REV. MARY,

I write this letter to give you a broader insight on the recidivism problem, not just here in Missouri but across the North American continent.

But first, you said you do not know about Scientology. In Scientology, they teach about the type of people who are sociopaths. The Scientologists believe a sociopath is a person who has a suppressive personality, a cruel exploitative, brutal personality; and once one has come under that type of person, one becomes a potential trouble source. Scientologists also teach about reactive mind and what are considered as enemies within the reactive mind, called "egrams" or demons. And it is from the reactive mind of the enemy, who imposes upon one their sociopathic tendencies, that they are now potential trouble sources for themselves and others.

Regarding recidivism, every year, month, week, and day is the facsimile of the last year, month, week, and day. I'm alive, and yet I'm prohibited from participation in the cycle of life. Humans encased in concrete cannot truly grow; that is, their growth is not authentic. At best, their development is arrested. True growth implies an influx of variously consistent nutritious stimuli. Devoid of these necessities, the being regresses into itself and hence becomes the living dead. Prison encourages escapism. It is a fleeing from reality from the moment.

The being oscillates between two non-realities; namely, the past and the future. The present is where the being does not want to be, for the present holds anxiety and frustration. To be detached and not participate in the moment is to become an object of that moment. Objects differ from subjects. The former are thought about and acted on, while the latter think and act on or in accordance with its will; the being's will is simply to be free. In an act of dehumanization, the being is commanded to give that which it does not possess— its future, as the future is a non-reality.

The ultimate crime is perpetuated against this being: its future is taken before it has even touched it. The being is hurled into a vortex of virtual reality and dehumanized to the point that its name becomes interchangeable with a number. And that number is grouped with other numbers to form statistics. And so, the statistics sit and wait for the demigods, who have set themselves in authority, to grant it life.

The existence of unknown limits is a mindset that aspires with the end of uncertainty, and then comes the uncertainty of the end. It is impossible to foresee whether or when, if at all, this form of existence will end. The Latin word *finis* has two meanings: the end or the finish, and a goal to reach. One who cannot see the end of his existence is not able to aim at an ultimate goal in life. He ceases living for the future, in contrast to a man in the free world. This feeling of lifelessness is intensified by eclecticism, by looking at a diverse range of ideas, that one would favor another. Anything outside of this oblivion becomes removed, out of reach, and in many ways unreal. To one within this realm, the outside world appears almost as it might to a dead man who looked into this world from the realm of his existence.

Many of those seventy to eighty out of one hundred prisoners who get out commit another crime. That means another victim. So beyond simply employing failed programs, the DOC is contributing to future unnecessary crimes and future unnecessary victims.

Every successful program erased in favor of harsh authoritarian modes of control translates into more than just heightened recidivism and data. It creates unnecessary human casualties. This failed system of correctional science contributes to the robbery and murder of store clerks working their way through college; the rape and molestation of suburban and poor inner-city children left with a neighbor because their mother worked two jobs; the carjacking of elderly women and pregnant mothers; the drug addictions of high school kids who buy poisons pandered by ex-convicts who the system failed to correct. All of this by prisoners the DOC debilitated. Rather than employing modes known to lead to victimization of only fourteen to seventeen taxpayers for every one hundred prisoners released, the DOC opts to victimize as many as eighty citizens for every one hundred released prisoners. The system of corrections manufactures unnecessary victimization.

The DOC does not so much as release criminals hopelessly inclined toward crime, who are destined for failure 80 percent of the time, as they release bitter people who have been abused by this system.

While I have yet to adequately and fully describe the depth and breadth of the dark forest, I will move on to describe some of the trees that are part and parcel of it. I personally would say that there are a number of problems that contribute to this system's abysmal failure, except these are not really problems at all, and the system does not really fail to accomplish its goals. From the standpoint of someone whose empire is founded on perpetual human suffering and bondage; from the standpoint of someone who is a creator of atrocities designed to exist without purpose except for their own sake; from the standpoint of those who advocate blasphemy and hideous offenses against nature and mankind and other abominations from which the human mind recoiled in desperate defense against insanity, and from their standpoint this system of corrections succeeds quite nicely.

The dark forest produces the principle commodity of rotten fruit, and everything is thus geared toward the production of rotten fruit. I write this not from the standpoint of someone who has experienced the degrading and debilitating system (though I have), I say this as someone who has read many of the theories and data and the social and economic predictions.

No effort is made to persuade a prisoner to change his or her conception of the world to the way a law-abiding citizen sees it. The will of the prisoner is not won over by persuasion of example or through processes within an atmosphere conducive to real, lasting cognitive change or moral development. Instead, prisoners are coerced by threat of force, by force, and ultimately by direct violence to engage in outward behaviors that the gestapo desires.

Prisoners are temporarily physically controlled in a controlled environment. Outwardly, prisoners comply with the captors because they are being held hostage. They have little recourse. Outwardly, prisoners do things they do not want to do. Yet inwardly, very dangerous changes take place. Prisoners resent coercive controls, as any human being would, particularly when one knows deep down that the design of correctional science is diabolical. Resentment turns into hatred. Arbitrary controls that force prisoners to work against their own best interest plant seeds to always reject the law and the gestapo who push it on them. Prisoners become less likely to respect the law and instead loathe it for its hypocrisy. Prisoners conform to inane or silly demands forced on them by lawless and malicious authorities, and many prisoners dream of the day when the system no longer has them in its venomous jaws. The threat of violence, which is the basis of this control system, creates criminals in the system's own image.

Persuasion through experimental learning and reeducation creates adjusted citizens with the practical skills necessary for good and positive citizenship. It produces a recidivism rate of 15 to 17 percent at a fraction of the costs, and it can accomplish its work in a relatively short period of time. The vast majority of prisoners who get out of prison and become suitable for release would stay out and would not hurt anybody else.

Coercion requires years and years and billions of dollars to get its subjects properly hateful and maladjusted in order to guarantee recidivism. Coercion turns prisoners into cowards. They live in constant fear because they live in constant dishonesty. Prisoners convince themselves that it is morally acceptable to continually endure neglect and hardship and scorn and torture. Prisoners become like battered wives who come up with excuses for their abusive spouses, excuses for deserving the full extent of the humiliation, excuses for cowardice in not rising up, in not engaging in collective resistance to a system designed with harmful intent on prisoners and society alike. Prisoners live in constant self-loathing because they know they contribute to this system's vast lie. So along within the system, prisoners begin to hate themselves.

This hatred seeps out in strange ways as prisoners try to reassert control over their world, as they try to regain some semblance of being men and women capable of dignity and honor. Prisoners beat and shank each other over packs of cigarettes and boxes of Little Debbie snack cakes. For when one has nothing, that which he has becomes something of immense value. Prisoners unwittingly participate in a system designed to destroy them in essential ways.

Insightful hired thugs direct prisoners to obey lawful and unlawful orders because it is easier to maintain control, so prisoners are divested of any decision-making or moral reasoning. Submission to authority of this type allows prisoners' moral agency to be taken and stripped away. Is it any wonder then, upon release from this environment of constant control, that prisoners are incapable of decision-making skills?

I must admit that systems that do terrible things yet give the outward appearance, at least cosmetically, of doing the opposite are sure to cost a lot of money. And this leads to the next social ill created by this system and its bloated budget for the manufacture of criminality. The money that funds this abysmal failing system steals from social programs and the infrastructure of education. By deforming prisoners, the system guarantees job security for those in the business of human bondage, even long after prisoners are gone, simply because the long and expensive process of pressure-cooking hatred drains resources that would otherwise keep children from falling between the cracks. In fact, due in large part to the obscene spending on corrections, whole schools have fallen between the cracks. Those cracks are starting to look like sinkholes. The prisoners know that robbing them of their moral agency diminishes them, yet they continue to participate in this sickness—and this is one of the reasons why they hate themselves.

The prisoners know that this system purposely deprives them of loving contact with family and friends and deprives their family and friends, yet they pretend they do not know, for they are as dishonest as the system. Prisoners know there is no reason why they can only see their mothers three or four times a month; they know there is no harm in seeing them every day. Prisoners know that unlimited family contact could undo the covert work of the prison system's hate-inducing designs. Yet too many hugs and smiles might make a prisoner seem too human. Prisoners pretend the "rehabilitation" programs are not watered-down money scams, yet they participate out of perceived self-interest.

Prisoners know that this system debilitates, diminishes, destroys, and when these prisoners get out, they pass it on. There is a small gaggle of child molesters who have engaged in a decade long "Uno-fest" right in my housing unit. Does society think that all that experience cheating at cards will keep their kids safe when they let these aged puritanical furtive muddled-minded inmates out? I wouldn't count on it!

The DOC has at its disposal a number of promising and proven programs that would empower people who have made bad choices, that would engender a respect and appreciation for sensible laws, that would create a society that would build self-esteem and realistic belief in their own capacities, and that would send prisoners back into the free world equipped and prepared for becoming (perhaps for the first time) respected, productive members of their communities.

One could argue that after years of arbitrary brutality and senseless injustice, a released prisoner would think: "I never want to go back to prison again." Most people are in error of this though. The proof? The majority of released prisoners return. And the reason why is because humans adapt better than any other creatures on the planet. Put a human in the harshest environment and he'll find some way to survive, overcome, and adapt. I myself adapted, and so has everyone else who inhabits these dark lands.

In old vaudeville shows, they would put chickens on a hot plate and play the piano, creating the illusion that the chickens were dancing. But every so often, they had to replace the chickens because they would stop dancing. The chickens would realize that by lifting their feet, they had to put them back down and it would cause more pain; yet if they held still, the hot plate would burn their nerve endings and the pain would stop. In the U.S. prison system, there are 2 million chickens standing on a hot plate. They've adapted.

Contrary to what politicians in government say, the cruelty and barbarism of prison does not serve as a deterrent. It serves as a catalyst in the evolution of bitter, angry, vindictive, unemployable, mind-mangled criminals who have adapted to a bizarre world where everything poisonous and distorted becomes normal and one develops immunity.

Depending on the quality of a man, certain environments will enervate or toughen the cords of the mind and focused thought, allowing one the opportunity to make a decision, a decision which determines whether one would or would not submit to those powers that threaten to rob one of his very self, that self of inner freedom, which determines whether or not one would become a thing of circumstance renouncing freedom and dignity to become molded into the form of vermin. That which the prisoner becomes is the result of an inner decision and not the result of prison influences alone. Any man under these circumstances can decide what shall become of him mentally and spiritually.

When one has the consciousness of power to overcome obstacles one has put on his path, one can overcome these obstacles by having more courage than fear. (I have always been one with the courage to go outside of the box in my thinking and actions). Fear develops from negative thought. Courage is taking positive action in an atmosphere that appears negative. If there is no challenge in life, there is no opportunity for spiritual growth. The effects in one's life can be changed because of cause, for man achieves a great leap in understanding when he recognizes that everything within his personal life and environment is a mirrored reflection of his beliefs.

3/30/12

DEAR MICHAEL,

Our consciousness is creative and, in our organization, to get assistance in overcoming obstacles, one of the special gifts in this world of metaphysics is a licensed practitioner. These practitioners are advanced students who have taken the required courses over about a four-year period, then passed a written test and an oral panel. They are then licensed by Centers for Spiritual Living to offer their service to others in order to help uncover the cause of negative experiences or effects, working to carve a new path into consciousness in harmony with Law. We call this process spiritual mind healing. Affirmative prayer is the tool used for healing, and its level of demonstration is based on each individual's recognition of truth.

Three important qualities are necessary for spiritual mind healing: persistence, flexibility, and patience, which releases the Law to work at each individual's own level of acceptance. A guaranteed specific result is not expected with affirmative prayer, because affirmative prayer puts a new cause into motion, and by Law a new effect unfolds. Since cause is the sum total of the person's beliefs and attitudes, the way in which affirmative prayer will demonstrate is not predictable. We know truth is superior to the condition that is to be changed. This belief in ultimate goodness must be greater than any apparent manifestation of its opposite.

The result of affirmative prayer will always be a positive improvement, although it may not look like it initially. For months, a friend of mine lamented her desire for a new car and one day she was driving and her car caught on fire. She got out and watched it burn up. The result was a new car, but if she had loaded up her thoughts with a lot of negative feelings and beliefs, she might have missed out on the greater good awaiting her, and the end result would have been diminished.

Demonstrations following affirmative prayer are like pouring liquid Jell-O into a mold. We want the demonstration of solid Jell-O or a specific form in an area of our life, but the speed of our demonstration is based on the Law of Logical and Sequential Evolution, i.e., liquid Jell-O takes time to solidify. As Ernest Holmes described it, "There is no process *of* healing, but there is generally a process *in* healing. This process is the time and effort which we undergo in our realization of Truth." By trusting in the process without doubt, our demonstration unfolds perfectly. We know that conditions are not things. Conditions can be changed. The task is to reveal the truth and allow the Law to work harmoniously for our greater good.

4/26/12

DEAR REV. MARY,

Thank you very much for the books you sent me. I've recently just picked them up from the property room. I was in the high-tech dungeon, also known as solitary confinement, the hole, or administrative segregation (ad-seg), for a minor infraction with a guard who believed his clothes give him superhuman powers. I was locked down for six weeks.

I also received your letter and the typed version of the writing on recidivism. I would be honored if you would submit it as an article to the magazine you mentioned.

I've read the *Care of the Soul* by Thomas Moore and *Practicing His Presence* by Brother Lawrence. I have not yet read *A Return to Love* by Marianne Williamson, but it is on the agenda.

In the book *Practicing His Presence,* there was much I identified with. There were many things written that I've come to understand from other schools of thought.

I really appreciate the fact that you have given your time to abet me in my studies and have provided me with knowledge that is viable for my growth.

In the last two decades within this realm, I have learned much of the world in which I dwell and its inhabitants. I have been made ready for the part I must play in its shaping, discovering a purpose of my existence. I have accepted the casting, complete with my own ominous stage name.

In the 9th Dominion, in this realm wherein many men's logic can easily be discounted, where kings are exiled, there is the strength of forces being marshaled. I understand many things today that were hidden from me in the beginning of my journey.

Perhaps in every man's life there will be some cherished failure, some unfinished business that outweighed a man's many successes. Sometimes the future can be charted and plans made to meet it. But there are also times in human affairs when events that seem to have no possible connection, to be removed as if they occurred in different worlds, may react upon each other with shattering uncanny meaning. There are some tasks that cannot be achieved by simple means, and one must accept this fact without complaint, for much strangeness is too complex for one to unravel.

It is said that time could never destroy truth, it could only hide it among legends. What I am to discover at my final destination, I have no conception. That I will discover something profound, I do not doubt.

One must cling to this world while he is upon it, even though it may be another plantation in Lucifer's garden, on the road between the madness and deceptions that one has emerged from, and the goal that awaits one at journey's end, years from now. I have endured much and the endurance, the patience I have displayed have given me a different perception about many things and a strength and a discipline to refrain from the violence and the malevolent miasma that plagues this world.

I know that it takes faith, strength, and accumulated wisdom to go against my once-held deep warrior ethics. I pride myself for making the unprecedented, the unexpected choice. Because of my inaction, mystery has been added onto my prison reputation, rendering me even more frightful by virtue of my perceived unpredictability.

Coming to prison for me was like being sent to a hostile alien planet in which one encounters strange and unnatural ways of thinking and acting. I have always been enthralled by respect. I have risked my life for it, and I have suffered greatly for it. My mind had once upon a time been plagued with strategy, warlord ascendancy, and domination. My mentors were super alpha males who taught the art of war, in which the lessons included deception, lightning-fast death strikes, ulterior motives, and cunning. In this world, one learns to focus with superhuman intensity on whatever he sees fit. A man with strength and intelligence can form a "gangster image" to his advantage.

The very real threat of others is mitigated by knowledge of exactly what course of action to take. I still believe there exists an entity that wants me in pain, wants me in misery, wants me in despair, wants me to fail, wants me to succumb. I believe this because this entity, this enemy energy force, has the capabilities to will itself upon the puppets who inhabit these lands, manipulating them into performances of contrived odd behaviors. There have been times when these marionettes would approach me with malice in their hearts and minds, their will not their own, and then they would have the rare opportunity to bear witness to transformation, like that of a magical statue which mysteriously and magically came to life when the right words were spoken.

The 9th Dominion is a machination that produces intense change within its inhabitants—some positive but mostly negative. Those self-titled demigods behind this infrastructure play games with people in an elaborate laboratory to experiment on guinea pigs, rats, and monkeys to see how they react. And data is collected. I truly believe there will never be a benevolent form of imprisonment on the North American continent.

For many, the type of thinking I often express is complicated and it is because my opponents, my oppressors, are complicated and shift identities. I've come to the realization that one must be subjected to certain stimuli in order to tap into that which sleeps within my own soul.

Ephesians 4:22-24

> You were taught, with regard to your former way of life, to put off your old self, which is being corrupted by its deceitful desires; to be made new in the attitude of your minds; and to put on the new self, created to be like God in true righteousness and holiness.

Surah 3:118

> O you who have believed, do not take as intimates those other than yourselves, for they will not spare you [any] ruin. They wish you would have hardship. Hatred has already appeared from their mouths, and what their breasts conceal is greater. We have certainly made clear to you the signs, if you will use reason.

Dhammapada 10:144-145

> Let the dread of endless mediocrity spur you into great effort. Relinquish the burden of endless struggle with unapologetic confidence, with purity of action, effort, concentration, and by conscious and disciplined commitment to the path. Those who build canals channel the flow of water. An arrowsmith makes arrows. Woodworkers craft wood. The good tame themselves.

The Science of Mind, Chapter 14, page 191

> Man will be delivered from sin, sickness, and trouble in exact proportion to his discovery of himself and his relationship to the Whole. Law is law wherever we find it, and we shall discover that the Laws of Mind and Spirit must be understood if they are to be consciously used for definite purposes. The Spirit knows and the Law obeys. Hidden away in the inner nature of the real man is the Law of his Life.

It is asked, "Why remain in the darkness of ignorance when the light is clearly presented to you?" I often contemplate on what my ancestors went through when they were brought to the strange worlds of the Americas. I know my ancestors were exposed to stranger and worst malfeasances than I, yet my ancestors' captors' descendants have inherited through the bloodline of their forefathers that which is innate to their quiddity, their basic nature.

Everything has a history and the best way to understand something for me is to examine where it came from. When we have little sense of history, we have little sense of why things are the way they are.

As seen by those who are students of the occult, esoteric, or gnostic teachings, the medium, diviner, or seer has been known to use a crystal ball in an effect to foresee future events. For me, my crystal ball is historical truths that enable me to see into the future. For everything that has been written and documented in history books, I think about all the things that have not been written. If one builds his life on falsehood, on what our mind imagines things to be, rather than what they really are, then one becomes a slave to fantasy and illusion. True freedom comes when one sees past the veneer of illusion and responds to life as it truly is.

There is that which is called a mosaic, a surface decoration made by inlaying small pieces of variously colored material to form pictures or patterns. By kismet, I believe God chooses specific people for the benefit of the whole. Each person chosen by the Supreme Being I believe is furnished with requisite attributes that best know how to adorn the pattern that Universal Mind has been creating since antiquity.

Teleology is the explanation of phenomena in terms of their goals and purpose; the view that the Universe exists or events occur in order to achieve a particular end. Things grow and change in order to become what they were intended to be, according to their inherent natures. Teleological proof of God's existence concludes that such a complex and intricately designed universe must have a designer manifesting a Divine Purpose.

Man must further develop his own consciousness if he wants to know its full dimensions. An integral approach attempts to honor, acknowledge, and incorporate the enduring truths of our very own self. The enduring truths of the ancient wisdom include the ideas of levels or dimensions of reality and consciousness, reaching from matter to body to mind-soul to Spirit. With Spirit fully and equally present, all these levels are the ground of the entire display. Ancient sages taught that one must be adequate to the level of reality he wishes to understand.

It has taken courage, faith, and flexibility to grow in a labyrinth of steel and stone, but turmoil has driven me to discover and focus on my inner Spirit. I had to come to terms with who I am. I had to realize my weaknesses and identify and understand my strengths. I had to adapt and apply the characteristics of manhood to my persona, applying the knowledge I've gained to my everyday living. Then I had to become a loving byproduct of my intelligence. This allowed my actions to define my intentions.

The Law of Intent is defined that intention is the strongest element of every action of conduct. The activity one performs matters little, no matter how difficult or tedious, no matter how conscientious one's efforts, and no matter what one sacrifices to accomplish it. The purpose behind the activity, one's attitude toward the effect of one's actions or conduct determines the whole meaning of the activity and determines the result of action.

My growth has been a process of becoming more than a thing, more than a stereotype, more than an exhibit, giving me a determined pursuit of knowledge and a better way of living this life. My rewards have been the shedding of skin, progress, and pride—the pride being that I owe it to myself to develop my mind to the highest degree possible. The power of committed mind exceeds any other force I have come across in these lands. That which has been decreed for me has allowed me to retrospectively examine my travels through different stages in my life, which have prepared me for the next stage, until I finally reach my assigned destination.

My life was once a question mark and my purpose a mystery as I encountered different people, places, and things, faced challenges, overcame treacherous obstacles. I observed what was at that time hard for my mind to digest and experienced a world of oblivion. These things have determined the quality of my growth. I have erased all negative emotions, those called hate, anger, anxiety, etc. They have lost importance to me. I have not allowed negative emotions to supersede my ability to make rational and informed choices and decisions, yet my positive attributes do not define me in my totality. I am further defined in my expressions and recognition of my constant progression toward the elevated state of being, the pinnacle of God's creation.

My time in prison has allowed me to get rid of bad programming and conditioned thinking. This time has given me an understanding of this world: its beauties, its ugliness, its mysteries, its riddles. The more I understand, the more sense of peace I attain.

Long terms of suffering can develop in one the tendency to reflect on things, the realization one gains of the subtleties that underly everything. It obliges one to order his actions and speech according to his new knowledge and assist, in all possible ways, other people to open their own gates of awareness. When one thinks in a positive and powerful perspective, he can make his world rotate in exactly the direction in which he decrees it should.

For many people, prison is just a chapter in their lives. But for me, it is the whole book. Pertaining to the idea and concept of a book, if you decide that you truly believe I should embark on this task, I will, yet I want my world comprehended by my valor and my pain recognized, my misdeeds conceptualized. I want you to be able to understand my truths and my deceptions, the source of my generosities as well as my cruelties.

One would never know the magnitude and dynamics of mastery that has come from surviving prison. Most telling of all is that many young white, Asian, Hispanic boys and teenagers admire and try to mimic men like me and the street lifestyle, yet I have never had the desire to copy them.

6/2/12

DEAR MICHAEL,

Have you noticed that each segment of the lessons I've been sharing has its own relevance to your personal experience? This says a lot about where you are in your personal growth, the growth that is happening inside of you. Rejoice at this knowing. Much of the time, the spiritual path is simply the expansion and maturing of our own perspective.

Although Religious Science teaches us the benefits of surrendering to love and Law, only a small minority of students take the steps and practice the philosophy every day. Obstacles seem to come up and make it challenging to put aside the worries or activities of the day and focus on truth. This is why I have gone deeper into *The Science of Mind* text to bring the subject of race consciousness to you.

To understand race consciousness, we must understand the soul. Soul is the subjective part of mind, our subconscious. As Holmes explained, "The Subjective Mind, which we call Soul, is not a knower. It knows only to do without knowing why It does. It is a doer or executor of the will of the Spirit and has no choice of Its own." This is why Religious Science works with the mind, since it is directly connected to Universal Mind, that part of the Universe that existed before we did.

Our beliefs in subjective mind are the cause of our experience, as compared to objective mind, where we experience conscious individuality. *Changing the beliefs embedded in subjective mind changes the effect of those beliefs and the form it takes in our life.*

8/18/12

DEAR MICHAEL,

Something we haven't covered yet is something that resides in the depths of subjective mind: an array of beliefs I previously mentioned that are often called race consciousness, the consciousness of humanity. Ernest Holmes called it race suggestion and Thomas Troward called it race personality. Holmes felt we all have a tendency to recreate in our life the thread of beliefs that have accumulated over time. An example is the belief that we are not responsible for our experience and someone or something else is to blame (the government, our neighbor, our boss, etc.). Another race conscious belief is there is not enough to go around (money, fame, food, great men or great women, etc.); the world is a corrupt place; life is a struggle; it is rare to succeed in life; people will rip you off if you give them a chance.

In most cases, a race conscious belief is negative and deeply imbedded in our subconscious to the point where we don't realize its impact on our life. One way to change negative race conscious beliefs is to become aware of the beliefs we hold. This can be done through affirmative prayer, spiritual practices, contemplation, meditation, classes, reading spiritual texts, and discussions with practitioners of metaphysics. It is also the goal of affirmative prayer to neutralize the vibrations of our negative beliefs, replacing them with positive beliefs.

Thomas Troward felt our personality as a human being developed from race personality. He believed evolution proceeds "not by diluting the individual into the race, but by fostering greater individuality through choice and initiative." By visualizing Troward's concept of evolution as an infinite upward spiral, individually we move forward whether we want to or not. We can go along with this easily or it can be very, very difficult. By deciding to learn and grow, we move up the ladder of evolution more gracefully. If instead we live with a mind dominated by negative race conscious beliefs, our ability to move forward in an understanding of truth is very limited. Do you recognize the race conscious beliefs you hold?

The vibration of our individual atmosphere is what generates the power of attraction between us and other people, places, or things. When we meet someone who we instantly like, although we may not find their form attractive, this attraction comes from deep inside and bypasses our ego mind, which may prejudge a person as not worthy of our attention. Feelings and unspoken words are a very powerful guide in our relationship with others in the world.

12/3/12

DEAR REV. MARY,

You provided me with friendship, when friendship or companionship was never my intention. You decided to respond to my invitation to teach me, when others would shun me as soon as they saw "Dept. Of Corrections" on the envelope. Yet I do understand this pessimistic viewpoint, for there are many prisoners who only want pen pals to break up the monotony of idle time, and those who may receive prisoner's letters may realistically surmise that if a person isn't writing with ulterior motives, then they haven't reached the point where they would actually benefit by correspondence with those outside the 9th Dominion, beyond the superficial feeling of receiving a letter.

You have honestly shared ideas, life knowledge, and wisdom and you have made a profound positive difference in my life. You have given me an opportunity to expand my knowledge and application of that knowledge. The whole subject of race consciousness is fascinating.

In this realm, I've only come across two or three people among hundreds who were hungry for enlightenment. My one adept protégé is known as Mr. Ra Ra. He was able to understand the majority of the teachings I conveyed, expressed, and articulated pertaining to thought, logic, and war. I have yet to meet another in this realm interested enough to engage in esoteric studies, ancient African science, or religious thought outside of the more popular canon expressions.

On the surface there have been those who would timidly approach me in the guise or pretense of seeking knowledge, but beneath the veneer was only fear or awe. Even knowing this, I would give them something to read. Then two weeks later, the book still had not been read. I would never condemn them because I know that all men need to attain an essential peace and faith in understanding the Universal Mind. But I also know I have a diverse effect on the canaille (the "riffraff") within this realm through my words and deeds.

I learned the first couple of years in prison that the prudent man might seem cold, but not so. He has the perspective, the calm detachment, the ability to laugh that comes with vision, which gives everything he does a quality of lightness. He is simply more reasonable, more balanced, less vulnerable to his own emotions and moods. This prudence allows him to look deeply into both himself and others, to understand, to extend vision.

I have been able, in retrospect, to perceive the roots that brought about present events into the form in which they now exist. For each event, there was my thought and intention, which accreted over many moons, which inspired my words and then my intricate actions. Because of this, events unfolded, many positive and many negative. Different people have regarded me in different ways. Certain people have migrated to me as if winter were upon them, as I have been drawn to those under the Law of Attraction. There have been those who avoided me as if I were going to wreak havoc upon them. Some goals I've accomplished, some opportunities I have lost, yet and still I am grateful for the grace bestowed upon me. This understanding, I acknowledge, comes from the many gemstones of wisdom you have contributed to my studies. The life that is unfolding for me now will not be forgotten.

As a youngster, my great grandmother, grandmother, mother, aunts, and uncles were my teachers of life. They influenced me through their religious morals, precepts, and guidelines to become the man I am today. My grandmother grew up in rural towns in Louisiana, then migrated to Arkansas. My mother and her siblings were reared in the small town of Eudora, Arkansas, a town separated by rail tracks, with Africans on one side and Europeans on the other side. In my late teens, I had the opportunity to walk in the footsteps of my ancestors by going to a cotton field, which was the size of three football fields. That experience would have a direct effect on me like no other.

When I was born, my mother was twenty-two and a college graduate. As the first born and only child, I received the cosmopolitan side of my mother's years. I was introduced to many different worlds. I was curious and quick to catch on. I would watch my mother closely, the way she treated others, her interaction with family and non-family. I imitated her business savvy. I think very highly of my mother and her morals and principles. Following her example allowed me to be a good father to my son.

My mother would read me stories every night and made sure I said my prayers before I laid my head to rest. At a very young age, she introduced me to the Children's Library in downtown Kansas City. When I first got my library card, I was so proud. It made me feel like I had accomplished something. It felt important. During the summer months, my mother would drop me off at the library on her way to work, so the library became my babysitter. On her lunch break, she would come pick me up and take me out to eat. Then she would take me back to the library, then return when she was off work.

During these times, the library carried on an array of activities. They had computers, puppet shows, Mickey Mouse films, animal exhibits, arts and crafts, so there was always something to do. I was always occupied with things I enjoyed. I read so many books that I would set goals. I would pick a particular author and read all of his or her books, something I still do today.

One of the things that was very interesting is that if I wasn't the only child there, I would surely always be the only African male child there. The library made me want to learn, because it showed me the wonders of the world beyond, through books. I was given a reason to read.

In the sixth grade, I was inducted into the band. My choice of instruments was the trombone. My mother said that if I stuck with it she would buy me my own trombone. I had been through phases of wanting to do this or that, from the Cub Scouts to Little League baseball to judo. Some things grew on me, others things fizzled out. But I did love music, and I was a part of the band until I graduated high school. In my junior high school year, my mother eventually bought me a trombone from a pawn shop. I went to a few different high schools in different states. In the public schools, I was a part of the marching band and we would participate in parades and perform at football games with dance routines. At a different high school, our marching band would create difficult designs in synchronized marches and our music would be attached to our instruments because the music was too complex to memorize. In a Catholic school, named Bishop Hogan, I learned the beauty of orchestral music. In orchestra, we would perform in competitions on stages in front of audiences and judges. We did not have the typical band uniforms, so we would wear blue slacks and white collared shirts.

In high school, I experienced many different things because of the influence of my uncle. ROTC became a part of my experience—military warfare, the art of discipline, martial arts, and access to shooting. I found that learning had a strength of appeal that naturally sketched itself within my being. I believed at the time that one day I would get a band scholarship to go to Jackson State University. If not, I would enter into the Marine Corps, in which they would pay for me to attend college.

But there was a warrior's spirit within, plagued with darkness and shadows that manifested themselves with exuberance, which led me into that which I am meant to be. For what we are led to will be, and all will be well for my awareness to be expanded. I must include the reality and existence of the spiritual facts.

My mother exposed me to people, places, and things outside of my community. She taught me that life existed in many dimensions, not just what I saw but also the things I could not see. Her optimistic outlook on life allowed me to experience a variety of extracurricular activities that molded me, from swimming to skating to bike riding to running. She never limited my choices, but when it came to guns, these tools, rather fake or real, she abhorred. Enter my Uncle Jr.

My Uncle Jr. was my hero, the only strong male figure in my life, and I loved him deeply. He had been in the Vietnam War and the warrior's creed was etched into his flesh and psyche. A scholar once said, "What I fear is man's ability to adjust." By that he meant that humans inherit an evolutionary capacity to adjust and adapt downward to survive in alien, hostile, and destructive environments. Returning from a war zone, my Uncle Jr. in his own way in the Spirit of Ogu (the "Spirit of Iron"), was preparing me for the warrior's way of life. He introduced me to a world I knew nothing of. My Uncle Jr. loved to drink alcohol, and when he was intoxicated, he would do and say the funniest things that kept me in laughter and cheer. He was a hunter and showed me the way of the gun. He gave me the knowledge on how to live off the land. I was so fond of him and emulated his manners, gestures, way of speech, and outlook on life. Even today, Mom says I remind her of him.

I would sneak and drink his beer. It was an accustomed taste you got used to for the intoxication. My Uncle Jr. gave me my first dog, a female puppy German Shepard, whom I named Princess. This gave me a chance to show responsibility. Mom explained to me that the first time I didn't clean up after her, fecd, or water her, I wouldn't be able to keep her. I dedicated every day to Princess to make sure I didn't lose her, from shots to training, grooming, and playtime. I took on those responsibilities with enthusiastic liveliness. Me and Princess had many adventures growing up together. She was my play-mate and protector.

Perhaps when I was twelve or thirteen, on a New Year's Eve night, my Uncle Jr. got out his twelve-gauge shotgun and let me shoot it in celebration. Shooting it left a pretty big frog in my arm. In the future, the twelve-gauge shotgun became one of the weapons I wielded.

I didn't enter into the military services. Instead, I entered into the criminal underworld, which had the allure that one could truly attain the American dream. To my youthful eyes, this was the more attractive, iconic, and lucrative way.

Throughout my youth, I kept up jobs—mowing lawns, shoveling snow, selling candy, collecting aluminum cans, working at theme parks, at fast food restaurants, as a janitor, and also as a mucker. My mother had a lot of people whose taxes she would do to earn extra income and many of these same people, whether from her church or job, would become my lawn mowing customers on a regular basis.

There was an elderly woman whose grass I would always cut. Her name was Mrs. White. She was a widow in her late seventies or early eighties. After I cut her grass, she would give me twenty dollars, a cup of orange juice, and homemade cookies. She would show me black-and-white photos of her in her youth. She was a very attractive Person of Color. Her husband had been an airplane pilot. Years later, while in a prison library, I came across a *National Enquirer* newspaper from the early 1990s and there she was, Mrs. White, on the cover page, smiling. The caption read that she had shot an intruder who broke into her home with her twenty-two revolver. Being in her mid-nineties, she caught the attention of the media. I pondered how in one spectrum the gun can make you a hero, a veteran, a war tycoon, a celebrity, and in the other spectrum the gun can make you a murderer, a fierce tyrant, a prisoner of war, and a vestment for fear.

Sometimes the choices we make provide us with guidance and a way to grow from the experience. Growing up, the one thing I did not receive was the one thing I truly needed: the knowledge of my rich African heritage and culture. Prison has given me the opportunity to learn who I truly am, my true purpose, and my true history, which has reshaped my outlook of life and has given me a better direction in which to proceed forward.

My Great Elders, who I never knew, inspired me to write what you are about to read.

YIGUMU SEFUWI (Difficult Search)

At an early stage in life, I was affronted with the power of thought. In school every his-story book was typed in white ink. I could tell that most of the original books were in black ink, but the creation of a substance called With Out allowed the plagiarists to revise everything. While sitting in a tree in a tropical rain forest center planting, I started to reflect back to the day I was born.

I recalled immediately after I emerged from my mother's womb, the doctor made an incision on the top of my head and on the left side of my chest. He took something out of both places and handed them to two men who were standing nearby with shovels in their hands. The doctor handed them a golden box and some silk cloth and instructed the two men to wrap up whatever he took out and place it in the box and bury the box deep into the ground far, far away. He said, "It is very important that this African man-child never finds or retrieves this box."

For years, I wondered what it was that was stolen from me. Year in and year out, my growth and development were stagnated and blinded. I had no African-ness and I was incomplete. I did not have regards for anything or anyone. This mentally was destructive, and I had to find out exactly what it was that was taken out of me at birth, because I felt it was related to my decadence. So one day, I got a shovel and went all over the North American continent, digging up the ground in search of that golden box and its contents.

In every state of America, I left holes in the ground, but so far, my quest was futile. This disappointed me, but it did not discourage me. I ended up in the middle of the Sahara Desert and while digging, my shovel struck something, and I got down on my knees and pulled the object out of the sand and dirt. Upon seeing the gold box, I was jubilant and sad at the same time, because I wanted this to be the box and I didn't know if I could endure another disappointment. But I was compelled to open it.

As soon as I opened the lid, I was blinded by the radiance of light that came out of the box. I reached down and pulled out the contents, and as soon as I saw what it was, I began to weep, because in that box all those years was my African Pride, Dignity, Religion, and Soul. Once I re-implanted them, my consciousness spoke and said (which I later found in James Allen's book *As a Man Thinketh*), "Mind is the Master Power that molds and makes." Man is Mind and evermore we take the tool of thought and, shaping what we will, bring forth a thousand joys or a thousand ills. We think in secret and it comes to pass.

James Allen says: "The environment is but our looking glass." Matthew 7:8 reads, "He that seeketh shall findeth; and to him that knocketh, it shall be opened." James Allen adds: "For only by patience, practice, and ceaseless effort can one open the door to enter the temple of knowledge. ... Between these two extremes are all grades of character and we are their maker and master. For as one thinketh, for as one is. It is not a person's outward appearance that deems morality, but the content of their convictions and how they practice their transition, so remember that whatever appears to be wrong is not wrong in itself, but is the wrong arrangement of what is right."

Today, Monday, December 3, is important to me. It was the day I came upon the realization of a truth I had been denying myself for over twenty years. On this day I spoke with my mother. I also had a conversation with a comrade and a stranger. Now today, December 3, I received your letter and the books you sent. By this elaborate design, enlightenment was brought unto me. When speaking with my mom, she asked me what plans I had made for my return to the free world (albeit, I have life without parole, of which she is fully aware). My mother believes deeply that I will return home.

I had nothing to say because I have never envisioned myself in the free world. I have never even entertained the thought. So, I made up an excuse and said that my time was up and I couldn't speak any longer. Later that day, I was approached by a stranger who told me that he was trying to do the same thing I was doing. I asked him, "What would that be?" He said, "Trying to go home." I told him, "This is my home; here I am a ruler and king of this realm." Later on that night, a comrade asked me when I was getting out of prison. I asked him, "What is the end of eternity?" He said, "Never." I said, "Exactly."

That night, in reflection, it all came to me, everything I had experienced. I remembered that I had demonstrated before and bore witness to the manifestation. I understood that a miracle is what seems impossible but happens anyway. In 2008, I was assigned to administrative segregation (the hole) for an assault. I was put on Mandated Single Cell Confinement. This means that a prisoner represents a danger to staff and other inmates and should no longer be allowed around other inmates for many years. Under this rule, one can be in the hole five years or better. I know only a handful of prisoners who have been on this status over ten years and a few of them went insane.

The other prisoners who were on this status also would always say, "Man, we are going to be in here forever." In my mind I was always thinking, "I'm not," and the only input I had for the conversation was to tell them to stop putting their faith in men and their administration. When one is put on this status, the only person who can take you off is the Deputy Division Director in Jefferson City. The warden, case workers, and other staff who approved for you to be on Mandated Single Cell Confinement cannot take you off of it.

Many opportunities came my way that enabled me to be taken off this status and be released back onto the yard. My prayers were constant. My positive belief that I had already been taken off this status eventually manifested itself in May 2009. I came across a guard who worked in the hole when I was down there. When he saw me, he said, "Nichols, if I didn't see it with my own two eyes, I wouldn't believe it," for he knew the intentions and discussions they were having about me.

I realized I had been denying myself freedom, liberation, by creating a fallacy I used as an offensive weapon as well as a defensive weapon. Many prisoners with less time and parole dates have the tendency to mock and taunt prisoners with life-without-parole only to vex them. Yet when one embraces this world as his only world and claims to be its ruler as well, he then becomes the decision maker of who he will allow to leave it. My time factor becomes a weapon, which speaks loudly, and actions brought forth only strengthened my resolution. My actions of violence spoke volumes to the canaille of this realm. It told them that I lost everything already, so I therefore have nothing else to lose. My perception of reality grasped at a fact, a truth that obliterated the effect of mockery, it's voice, it's poisonous miasma.

Every man's effort to cause me pain was futile. Yet it also made me cold with indifference, numb. And then with the added demise of my son, my only child, my heir, something emerged that wanted all those who I saw as my enemies to feel my true pain. I had eliminated the word "hope" from my vocabulary, because to me that word only meant a false illusion, a fairy tale built from myriad imaginations.

Hope is a word I have seen break the hearts of men and their families, and to this day, I still do not use the word. But after contemplation and grand design, I know that, yes, I do have freedom, for in that moment of realization I had released myself from a prison I had erected with my own mind. My freedom has now been attained, no matter the form. I have always had it, yet I couldn't see the harm I was inflicting on myself when I began to believe that this world was my eternity.

My understanding of Truth allows me to be free by aligning me with that which has never been bound. That which limited me is the same which has freed me. Change lies in man. He must begin with himself, teaching himself not to close his mind.

Under the Law of Intent, intention is the strongest element of every action or conduct. The activity one performs matters little, no matter how difficult or tedious, no matter how conscientious one's efforts, and no matter what one sacrifices to accomplish it. The purpose behind the activity, one's attitude toward the effect of one's actions, determines the whole meaning of the activity and determines the result of the action. In back of everything manifested on Earth, and Earth itself, is one of many thoughts. The theme of every thought with its accompanying degree of emotion has dominion over atoms. This is the most valuable knowledge one can ever understand.

Rev. Mary, the knowledge you have shared with me has released me from the fetters I put on myself. I have expunged a wrong mental equivalent and replaced it with its opposite. For the right thought automatically deletes the wrong thought. For so many years, prisoners and guards who did not really know me have seen me as this unemotional convict with no heart, no love, a bringer of trepidation. I must admit that in this world, this type of mind-state ranks supreme, and in the course of gaining mastery over it, I became inhibited and was on the verge of losing my true self. I have changed my thinking.

Liberation is my thought, my mantra, for I know that a new pattern will emerge, for when the Truth is known it is demonstrated.

As the new year comes, I will have evolved shedding skin of no longer needed thoughts. You have been my ardent mentor, and I have taken heed of the lessons.

I had the opportunity to speak with Ike Crawford. I work in the gym and I have the pleasure of seeing everyone on the yard. Ike and I have been familiar with each other for over a decade. He let me know that he had the *Living the Science of Mind* book and a few more. I told him I have some enlightening books to read, if he ever needed them.

In the past months, I read numerous books. One is a seven-volume set entitled *Teaching of the Masters.* It is a DeVorss publication written by Baird. L. Spalding. Another book was *The Intention Experiment* by Lynne McTaggart. It had many similarities with the book you sent me, *Birth 2012 and Beyond* by Barbara Marx Hubbard.

Another book I read is one I would like for you to research on the internet for me. I found the book truthful in many aspects, but it also carried a bizarre oddness that reminded me of a grimoire. It is entitled *Ramtha: The White Book,* written by a Russian female author named J. Z. Knight. There is also an organization that exercises the teachings called Ramtha School of Enlightenment in Yelm, Washington. If there is any information you can locate on the internet pertaining to the Ramtha Organization and J. Z. Knight, please send it to me so I can share the information with the owner of the book.

I thank you for everything. Let this new year bring about new experiences!

12/16/12

DEAR MICHAEL,

The book on Ramtha has been ordered. It addresses questions on the Source of all existence, our forgotten divinity, life after death, evolution, love, the power of consciousness and the mind, lessons from nature. It has a wide following. Ramtha is sometimes looked at as a prophet, with the ability to look at the subjective tendencies in Universal Mind, which have been stimulated by cause, and see the outcome before it actually manifests.

Holmes explains that this talent is like watching two trains speeding down the same railroad tracks toward each other. If we stand on a hill observing the trains, we see the anticipated result—the prophecy would be a crash. The prophet taps into subjective mind and through logical deduction, sees the tendency toward completion. The tendency can be averted. Affirmative prayer removes a negative seed (the oncoming crash) and plants a positive one (a different track or a malfunction that makes the trains stop). There are an infinite number of ways to avoid the crash. Spiritual practices tap into Universal Mind, and by using affirmative prayer to change a core belief, the effect is changed and the outcome shifts.

One way to reveal race conscious beliefs and our dominant core beliefs is through meditation. Many of these beliefs were placed into subjective mind throughout time by our environment, experiences, and those who had authority over us. But we always have dominion over our life. We can take conscious control and tell subjective mind what we wish to experience.

In order to differentiate whether an idea comes from a deeply held race conscious belief, ask these questions: Does the belief express more life? Does it expand our good for the self and those around us? Does it express love? If it is in alignment with love, life, and unity, it must be in harmony with Universal Spirit. Those core beliefs will serve us, as well as everyone in our environment.

CHAPTER 5

2013

Doorways Begin to Open

The Law of Cause and Effect — New Thought research and religions — Teleology of the Universe — Science of Mind stepped into my true Spirit — In Potosi Prison, more reverence for man than their own God — The mind has a way of punishing itself for destroying life with no remorse — No story is a straight line — The madness that engulfed me — Curiosity, one of my strongest virtues — All along the answers were within me — Guided to my roots — There is grace, if one pays close attention — Only individual opinions are fixed and dogmatic; Truth is more dynamic — When a man changes his mind, he changes the world — See Truth only — I can endure and survive; this, for me, is a source of pride — How I value these lands in which I have evolved — I discover how truly necessary my life and another's life are to each other — Exploring new horizons.

1/19/13

DEAR REV. MARY,

Over the holidays, there are a few of us here at this prison who have been conversing about theological truths, as well as the transformation of the world in general. In particular, I brought up the subject of the massacre that happened in Newton, Connecticut. I asked my comrades to give me their honest opinions about that situation. Many of their viewpoints vary because of their different outlooks and beliefs.

Having lost my only child, I can empathize with those parents whose children were taken away from them. One thing I mentioned to my comrades was that the situation was the cosmic Law of Cause and Effect. I stated that how all during the year of 2012, all over the world, was the propagation of the end of the world, by tornadoes, floods, and earthquakes. All over the media, on television shows and in hundreds of books were messages of death, destruction, and chaos. It seemed like the majority of people were expecting and anticipating the worst to happen, and happen it did, perhaps not in the way many had imagined, not in earthquakes, but it did happen in a way that did shake up the world. The killing of innocent children has always been to me something cowardly and sickening because of my own morals and warrior ethics. I do know that many doomsday fanatics became very wealthy by selling destruction and havoc, to many people's dismay.

In your letter, you mentioned that you were finishing the last week of a ten-week class called New Foundations that reviews the rich history of the Science of Mind teaching and who Dr. Ernest Holmes studied with or took their writings to heart and included their ideas in his works. I have been researching many of the women and men of New Thought, from Ralph Waldo Emerson to Dr. Raymond Charles Barker, Minister Emeritus of the First Church of Religious Science in New York City. I've learned about Mary Baker Eddy and how she was healed by Phineas Parkhurst Quimby and became his student. And then she founded Christian Science in Boston. I've learned about Emma Curtis Hopkins, who was a student of Mary Baker Eddy and how she started her own school and how Dr. Ernest Holmes was one of her students. I've learned about H. Emilie Cady, who was a homeopathic practitioner and metaphysician who also studied with Emma Curtis Hopkins.

Rev. Mary, you have opened a doorway to a world for me that has heightened my awareness and given much needed guidance so that I may apply all truths learned and teach others a different approach other than the famous hellfire rhetoric so famous among ministers and preachers.

January 16 of this year, I celebrated my forty-first birthday. I've been in prison since I was nineteen, so I want you to understand that my life has almost entirely been spent confined, and my shedding off of skin in old behaviors of negative thoughts and habits has been arduous but not impossible. Many in this realm forsake the ability to make decisions that will improve their lives. I made a choice to come out of darkness and into the light.

3/1/13

DEAR MICHAEL,

The death of any child is so hard to imagine. I don't think a parent ever overcomes it but may come to terms with the seeming finality of it. Death is a deeply embedded race conscious belief, an accepted outcome of our life in this form. It is one of those beliefs that is so ingrained, it is often difficult to differentiate whether it is a universal law or a belief. History has shown that Jesus and others overcame this consciousness and resurrected.

Thomas Troward calls death "entering the Fifth Kingdom," a place where we are fully aware of our divinity. In the Fifth Kingdom, he says we recognize our body as simply substance, entirely responsive to our will. Troward concluded that eternal life in an immortal, physical body is the logical outcome of evolution. But few people throughout history have attained this level of realization. Therefore, the generally held belief is that we must pass through the transition called death.

Our ability to change race conscious beliefs can be improved by being aware of the pictures, images, and symbols brought into conscious mind by our intuitive, subjective mind. Intuition is that inner knowing, that gut feeling of right and wrong, which always tries to keep objective mind informed. Often, we are too busy to recognize the importance of intuitive thought because intuition is not always logical, but it is generally correct.

We can develop our intuition in a variety of ways, such as using affirmations, focusing techniques, imagery, inner peace through meditation, contemplation, journaling, and physical exercise. When an intuitive feeling arises and that gut feeling appears, take a moment and bring it into conscious mind. If the feeling persists, go with it. This was brought home to me recently when intuition led me to stop and get gas for my car at a station with a long waiting line. I found myself pulling in line before I consciously recognized that this is something I don't do. As I sat waiting, wondering what this was all about, I heard a frantic woman on a pay phone. Her car had broken down on the way to pick up her young son. Without thinking, I asked her if I could help. In a flash I was pulling my car out of line, taking the grateful woman to retrieve her son. All I could do was smile and give thanks to Spirit that I was awake enough to let intuition be my guide.

Plotinus tells us there are three ways by which we gather knowledge: through science, through opinion, and through intuition. Holmes complements this by saying, "Intuition is Spirit knowing Itself." Intuitive channels represent spiritual capacities; each is an avenue leading to self-knowingness. As we expand our awareness of intuitive thought, we can use it to identify race conscious beliefs. Over time intuition can help us clarify and strengthen our skill, until we reach a point where we just know the truth.

5/12/13

DEAR REV. MARY,

Spirit has found a great voice in you, in vibrant truths and joyful splendor. Spirit has found revelation through you, in resonant and reflective ways. Spirit has found celebration through you, in infinite expanses and endless reach. To all those awakened by the grace of your gifts, Spirit has found both wings and light.

My studies are going well, and I am improving in my application of the knowledge and wisdom. The application of the knowledge gained allows me to walk as an example of Universal Laws being exercised with understanding and humbleness. I have come across a few prisoners who have showed an eager interest in the Science of Mind. Yet there are those who cannot yet get past the complex synergetic patterns that exist within this realm.

I have witnessed at times where one person may have a dreadful thought that morning about a particular situation. He may discuss his anxieties and worries with two people, and before the day is over there will be at least thirty people all with the same dreadful thought.

I have been studying this pattern and analyzing its effect. Because it is easier for one to think negatively in this environment than to think positively. I bear witness to Universal Laws being used just as one thinks and believes. I will hear old clichés like, "Look for the best and expect the worst," or "If it weren't for bad luck, I wouldn't have no luck," and the list goes on.

Many of these prisoners practice a religious belief rooted in hatred, bigotry, and unity of race or ethnicity, and there are so many people who consider themselves to be followers of the same system of belief, yet it is in contrast to what others have been taught to believe. Within this world, I have come across Hebrew Israelites, the House of Yahweh, Sunni, Orthodox Muslims, Protestants, Roman Catholics, Wiccans, Buddhists, Asutra, Odinism, Nation of Islam, Five Percenters, Moorish Science Temple of America, New Christian Crusade, Native Americans, Satanists, etc. The majority of the members of these belief systems do not apply the knowledge in a way that gives them the faith to never doubt and experience an evolution in mind expansion. Many are skeptics of their own belief system, which hinders progression and gives the impression in mind of a religious belief that is useless.

I myself have come to the realization that the aim of knowledge is to increase clear thinking. For me, nothing is to be more esteemed than aptness in discerning the true from the false. To distinguish truth from falsehood can be a difficult task in the everyday affairs of man, as we engage and socialize. Man is confronted everywhere with alternative routes, some true, others false, and the eye of reason must choose between them. Those who choose well or in error will incur that which serves as a base of their beliefs.

There is a thing called Teleology, which is the explanation of phenomena in terms of their goals and purpose. The view is that the Universe exists or events occur in order to achieve a particular end. Things grow and change in order to become what they were intended to be in accordance with their inherent natures. Teleological proof of God's existence concludes that such a complex and intricately designed universe must have a designer manifesting a divine purpose. Therefore, man must further develop his own consciousness if he wants to know its full dimension. An integral approach attempts to honor, acknowledge, and incorporate the enduring truths of our very own self.

I recently had the opportunity to read two very interesting books. One is *Moses, The Man*, author unknown. The other is *Bloodline of the Holy Grail: the Hidden Lineage of*

Jesus, by Lawrence Gardner. It is a fact that history rewrites itself, that science and technology improve in some forms and rewrite themselves. Medicine in some form improves and rewrites itself. Within my studies, I've found that many religious belief systems do not evolve. They do not rewrite themselves or improve. Many systems of belief the world over are under the necessity of coming to terms with new conditions created by vastly increased knowledge and experience.

It is said that all truths are truths of a period and not truth for eternity, for that which is eternal cannot be abolished. Ernest Holmes said that facts are fluid. We never have the whole truth, even for our own lives. In fact, truth (like our lives) is a continuing growth in consciousness and in understanding. Truth is a brilliant jewel with many facets.

I would like to discuss a subject about the situation in Newtown, Connecticut, in December. The year 2013 was astrologically given the label of a time of destruction, devastation, riot, turmoil, and death. So far as the entity is concerned, it will depend on the attitude of the multitude taken. If it is dwelt on in the pessimistic manner and acting in that way and manner, those attitudes that endure fear something negative happening. And the universe acknowledges. The greater the fear, the greater the chance it will happen. The increased fear of the effect gives the negative seeds increased energy. This is implied in the Biblical commandment, "Thou shalt have no other gods before me" (Exodus 20:3).

One can make little gods of fear and unwittingly pray to them. Nothing happens by chance. The Universal Laws were at work. There was cause and effect and all was in order, yet man does not like to accept the embarrassment that comes from taking full responsibility for many things he would not rather face, including these things that appear to be the fault of others.

When I lost my son, I pointed a finger at the doctors, at the system, and at racism because they did not want to deal with the red tape of prison officials to save my son's life. I had written the doctors and told them to do a bone marrow test to see if my blood was in accordance with my son. They didn't even acknowledge the possibility existed. But after all these years, my understanding has given me peace of mind and respect and reverence for the Universal Laws that are unbreakable, unchangeable principles of life that operate inevitably in all phases of our life and existence, for all human beings everywhere, all the time.

6/19/13

DEAR MICHAEL,

It may be hard to recognize initially, but heaven and hell are states of consciousness. We choose the degree to which we experience heaven or hell, because suffering is a conscious choice. Ernest Holmes believed that someday we will have learned all we need to through suffering and will decide we've had enough. He believed we will reach this point through an evolutionary process and expressed it this way: "Evolution is the awakening of the soul to a recognition of its unity with the Whole." We will evolve into infinity.

Behind evolution is an irresistible pressure compelling us to be more, better, higher, greater. We shall make progress, expanding in a sequence from where we are to whatever we shall become, forever spiraling upward. Evolution is what both Troward and Holmes believed begins with involution, where Spirit becomes matter, where we go within to become a conscious co-creator with God, which then evolves into higher and higher degrees of consciousness. Evolution is the process of matter becoming Spirit—going back to our Oneness.

Mystics helped us know that we, too, could reveal the presence of God and have a deep spiritual perception. They didn't read our thoughts but sensed the atmosphere of God. In our escalating abilities, we can hear and read about God, but the best knowledge is direct experience. The best method is to learn it for ourselves, not secondhand. What we experience is all we can know. Mother Teresa had a great gift of experiencing Jesus in everyone. She would say, "Each one is Jesus in his distressing disguise." How blissful that vision must be.

Conscious evolution progresses with things as simple as letting go of a belief in duality and recognizing that right and left, up and down, are just two sides of the same coin. The speed of our upward movement depends on how fast we let go of the negative beliefs we have carried around for a long time, such as blame or judgment. As we choose to be in a witness consciousness, where we are the observer, we see beyond labels of good and bad, inside and out, and know the truth about any situation. The freedom of sensing unity with everything makes it easier to let go of habits and patterns that don't serve us. Then we can trust in Spirit, let go of negativity, knowing the Universe abhors a vacuum and will always fill it. The goal is to let go of the negative, be the observer, and know the Universe will fill us with love. Again, by letting go, our old habits die from lack of attention.

By letting go, does this mean we won't have any more temptations? No. Like Ram Dass says, our ingrained habits never totally go away, but instead come back to us periodically like little schmoozes that tickle us, saying, "Are you really done with this one?" It makes me laugh, because when that happens, I can really see how far I've progressed on letting go of that one! To me, it's the ultimate cosmic giggle.

7/7/13

DEAR REV. MARY,

A very interesting thing about Sri Aurobindo is in a book I've been reading, entitled *Dark Light Consciousness*. The author, Edward Bruce Bynum, quotes him in almost every chapter of his book. So, my curiosity about Sri Aurobindo was piqued and then you sent me his book! Another thing is that I have been discussing with other comrades serving life without parole, as well as contemplating writing to the governor as well as the president for clemency, and then you send me information that gives me a direction in which to proceed!

There is that which is known in the studies of E.S.P. called clairvoyance, precognition, clairsentience, intuition, and psychic. There is also another word, ipsissimus, the highest level for a psychic to reach where he or she becomes master of their own power. I know that in some degree all humans have these abilities, but they have the tendency to write it off as coincidence, déjà vu, or superstition. Yet your gift is very acute, as well as uncanny.

When my son was diagnosed with cancer, I believe this was the point that the dark nature of my being was inclined toward the forces of violence within this world where I now dwell. My need to vent pain led me into many violent confrontations with other prisoners and guards, so my institutional record is not that of a "model prisoner" and I know that this can play a factor in any decision presented before any board that would consider my freedom.

It is the society and culture in which I was born that shaped and molded my belief system that ultimately failed to lift me up. In erroneous ideology, I strayed from the nature in which I was originally created. There have been many religious disciplines and organized schools of thought rooted in the belief of God, in one form or another. I can now say that after the experience of studying many different religious systems, the knowledge I have attained from the Science of Mind teachings has helped me to step into my true Spirit of an ever-evolving consciousness—and break away from a society of customs designed to hamper the Divine Guidance that offers me a way into a much more positive world of thought.

The Spirit, which I have known only through the studying and reading of tomes, has now presented Itself to me, within me, and now I live and practice these truths. The grace and love I have received in the multitude of forms has given me the ability to rise from the ashes of doubt, anxiety, and negative and destructive thinking. I will always cherish and share with all of those who come within my sphere of influence.

Morality is often described as a set of standards that are generally accepted as right or proper, but what is left out of this definition is this question: Right or proper according to whom? If morality is defined by a group of people who rule over another group of people, then conformity to their interests makes these people, groups, organizations, or individuals accept what is proper and right in their enemy's view.

When I was in Potosi, another prison here in Missouri, this land was only for men with LWOP, life without parole, and death row inmates. I was there for about seven years, before the prisoncrats built and opened up eight more prisons within a three-year time span.

I knew and saw many men die there without reprieve. The only time men would not be executed was when the pope came to St. Louis for an exclusive Catholic gathering and a death row abolitionist would appeal to the pope, who would ask the governor not to execute whoever was next. This man's sentence would be commuted to life without parole, and the prisoner would live to see another day.

In the rare instances when this occurred, it dawned on me that men had more reverence for other men than they did for their own God. At these times when an inmate was taken off of death row, I would ask him if he prayed that he wouldn't be executed, and I would never get a straight or direct answer. More or less, the response was that it was "the luck of the draw," or "it just isn't my time this year," or "I got lucky," all a truth to him who believes it. Yet I always got the impression that these men did not sense a more profound or enlightened meaning.

I now recognize the quick and effective way to eliminate anything you don't want is to disregard it and turn your attention and interest to what is directly opposite, to what you do want.

7/28/13

DEAR MICHAEL,

A Buddhist monk, Thich Nhất Hạnh, writes, teaches, and practices nonviolence. Growing up in Vietnam, he personally walked the difficult path during the war, trying to shift both the Vietnamese and American governments away from their commitment to violent action. In reading his book, *Love In Action*, the numerous monks who followed this path in their quest for nonviolence can be great modern examples. Much like the crucifixion and suffering of Jesus, the monks were willing to accept great suffering in order to awaken others. Speaking out for nonviolence, they were condemned at the time as pro-communist neutralists.

Thich Nhất Hạnh believes "a government is only a reflection of society, which is a reflection of our own consciousness. To create fundamental change, we, the members of society, have to transform ourselves. If we want real peace, we have to demonstrate love and understanding personally so that those responsible for making decisions can learn from us."

Going to the essence of the problem, he sees blame, anger, and arguing as forms of violence. Should we just stand back and avoid violence? He explains the difference between nonviolence and non-action: "When we see social injustice, if we practice non-action, we may cause harm. When people need us to say or do something, if we don't, we can kill by our inaction or our silence."

Again, let's reflect on the soul. Subjective mind, the soul, knows only to do without knowing why. It is the doer. This is why metaphysics and affirmative prayer are so powerful. Affirmative prayer works with our mind, which is directly connected to Universal Mind. Our deeply held beliefs, positive and negative, are the cause of our experience.

Let the power of affirmative prayer, combined with your belief in love and goodness, replace any ingrained negative beliefs so that your life may more profoundly express those same qualities.

8/19/13

DEAR REV. MARY,

Well, the month of August has been a commemorative month known to conscious prisoners throughout the penal institutions as "Black August." For many, it is a month unifying revolutionary and militant philosophies and ideology. For me, it is a holy month.

It is a sacred month for me to pay homage to those who paved the way for my own existence, their sacrifice, their spirit of self-determination, their insurrections, rebellions, and resistance against tyranny, oppression, and enslavement.

Black August is not commonly known or talked about. It is by far the least recognized month of great historical and spiritual significance in the lives of African people in America. Since African people in Africa have not properly memorialized their loss and the Africans in America have not erected any edifice or monument to remind their children that some of them survived the greatest protracted crime in history, those of us who are aware are a constant reminder of African struggles for liberation against some of the most disturbing atrocities that are not taught or discussed in history classes in the public/private school and college curriculum. Certain historical truths cannot be taught because it could unwittingly uplift a child to become more.

There is a long list of great feats accomplished during the month of August. I will only mention some of them briefly:

- August 22, 1791 – The Haitian revolution begins.

- August 21, 1831 – Nat Turner leads a revolt of enslaved Africans in Virginia.

- August 1, 1834 – Slavery was abolished in British colonial territories.

- August 2, 1850 – William Still starts the Underground Railroad.

- August 3, 1800 – 550 Maroons leave Halifax, Canada, and go back to Africa.

- August 17, 1887 – Birth of Marcus "Mosiah" Garvey.
  (I've included an article on Marcus Garvey with this letter.)

- August 28, 1955 – Emmett Till, age 14, kidnapped, tortured, and lynched in Money, Mississippi, for allegedly whistling at a white woman.

- August 9, 1956 – 20,000 women march in Pretoria, South Africa, and defy the hated Pass Laws (a tool to facilitate the exploitation of labor and prevent Africans, Indians, and Coloreds from interacting and organizing against their oppressors).

- August 7, 1960 – The Ivory Coast becomes independent.

- August 11, 1965 – The Watts riots in California start.

There is much more that has happened during this month, but I will stop here. The reason I am bringing these things to your attention is because in history there are documented facts of the past. People without the knowledge of their past history, origin, and culture are like trees without roots. I believe that time present and time past exist here simultaneously, and the future is here, too, though we cannot see it. All time is eternally present and leads to an end that we believe is a result of our actions, but over which our control is perhaps only minimal.

The truth of the past gives me solace and inner peace. It gives me a better understanding of people when I interact with them today. I know that my history does not begin on the North American continent, as it is taught within the school system of thought, but on the continent of Abushakalan, Ginen, Kemet, Ife, Africa.

Without knowing the truth of who I am or my origins, I would not have been able to grow. I would not have been able to make my transformation out of ignorance and into wisdom. Many African people in America are in a sad situation, drowned through our fall into the abyss and reversed regression. Our true names have been lost, and the first step toward disorientation is the surrendering of one's true name.

Since my heritage and culture have been unknown to me and because of this lost knowledge, I adopted the ways of people unlike myself. I lost my natural weapon because I lost my natural way of being. So many Africans have greater appetites for the culture and heritage of other nations; many have lost their memory. Few Africans can tell the story of our people without beginning it with slavery. Many believe as if slavery was the only thing that happened in the history of Africans. This has a devastating effect on the mind state of an African child growing up. I know because growing up in ignorance to a greater truth affected me.

My spiritual transformation began in 1998 in a prison cell at MSP (Missouri State Prison) in Jefferson City, Missouri. There are some things impossible to discuss with or explain to someone who has not experienced them. I told myself I would never discuss my experiences with the supernatural with the average, because the horror was too personal, for it was for me alone to witness, to endure. This is a subject that I loathe to express because of the strangeness of it, plus to reminisce about one of the lowest and most vulnerable points in my life is somewhat embarrassing, but I will proceed.

During a nine-month stay in administrative segregation (the hole) for an assault on a guard, I was transferred from Crossroads Correctional Center to MSP. One day in my cell reading, I heard a scraping sound. There was an air vent that connected my cell with the cell below it, and the vent was next to the steel toilet/sink. When I heard the scraping, it sounded like someone was making a shank (homemade knife) so I went to the vent and put my ear to it, but the sound was not coming from the vent, it was coming from inside the metal tubing within my toilet.

When I looked inside the toilet, I saw something black. I did not know that I was looking at one of the wings of a bird. Looking intently at the blackness, the rest of the body of the bird manifested itself. What I had heard was the claws of this bird within the pipe, making its way to the surface. When it emerged out of the water, well its head anyway, it squawked. I admit it scared me, shocked me. I was amazed and intrigued all at the same time.

I grabbed the bird and removed it from the toilet. I tried drying it off somewhat with toilet paper. I contemplated keeping it as a prison pet but thought otherwise. I eventually put it in my laundry bag and told a guard what happened (which he did not believe, even though a wet bird was in the laundry bag) and gave it to him to release outside, which he did.

When this ordeal happened, every superstition I had heard about in my youth pertaining to birds resurfaced. So, I believed this anomaly to be an omen, a sign, a preceding for something else. But who would believe me? A man's belief in a statement relayed to him wouldn't make that statement true, and a man's doubt of a statement relayed to him wouldn't make that statement false.

I believed at that moment and time that it was an omen of the highest order. In many religious lore, birds have always been considered messengers of God. I have seen paintings and pictures drawn of Seraphs and other angels depicted with the wings of birds on their backs.

In an ancient African system of initiation, the truth seeker must pass through a second birth, and those who attained this exalted state were known as twice born. This new birth must be personally earned and involves a symbolic birth (similar to baptism rituals). This ancient initiation rite is known as *Bat Ge'* (Fighting the War). The Bat Ge' involves *N'wari* (the Bird God of the Shangaan tribe of Zimbabwe) and omens, which were very important.

The ancient ones believed that the Gods revealed things through the actions of certain creatures (for example, seasonal change through specific animal migrations) and the appearance of natural phenomena.

Signs and omens from the gods come also in the sudden appearance of a specific bird. Birds were particularly magical because of their ability to fly. Thus, they were associated with the gods who dwelled in the heavens. During the "Fighting the War" initiation rite of passage, one would encounter many spirits, some negative, some positive. Rather than resisting negative energies, one should sink into them, plumb their depths, and then come through stronger on the other side. Each spirit had a moral pull, but no one spirit prevailed in every situation.

Initiations into a new being are integral to one's spiritual strength and growth. One receives some of the highest forms of knowledge, learning to master self and forces of the visible and invisible work. One often submits to tests of endurance, courage, and intelligence.

Because the physical elements of existence reflect spiritual principles, one is assured that he does not exist in a universe that lacks reason or direction. Rather, all that is, whether it be seen or unseen, exists as part of a system in which valiant angels, lions, orishas protect all of God's creatures.

There are worse things than being frightened by the unexplainable. One could be frightened by almost having a car hit him, or by being shot at, or by almost drowning. A person could be frightened by all of these things and still function. But things that are not supposed to be can do more than frighten. They can offend a man's mind. They offend any sane person's mind, any sane person's sense of order. This offense one may be unable to deal with because it opens up a crack in one's thinking. One tries to justify it somehow, but you cannot justify it, because it goes against everything you have been taught to believe, against the norm one's mind has set.

How can one incorporate the paranormal, the unexplainable into his life? It doesn't digest. One's mind keeps trying to understand something that doesn't make sense to it because there is no rational explanation. Eventually the mind shuts down and one goes mad, insane, or into a mind state where it is impossible to function.

When the event happened of finding the bird, it was integrated into my memory, into my view of the anomalies within the world. Nonetheless, it haunted my mind's darker corner because the questions kept coming back to me. How could this bird survive through a complex outdated prison sewage system and end up coming out of my toilet? And if this is a sign of something to come, then what? These questions kept arising day in, day out. I got my answer about three days after the event. I began to hear loud disembodied voices. Whose voice I did not know, but there were many. These voices invaded my thoughts awake and in trying to sleep. I was at a point in which I could not think clearly, because I was so raptly listening to what the voices were saying.

When a person is spoken to, they have an automatic tendency to speak back, and when people see you talking to what they believe is yourself, they assume you are crazy. But rapt attention to the voices gives one an off look—and these voices have the ability to drive a man to the brink of absolute madness, which many can never return from.

I would ask myself, will this last forever, until I can no longer function? Will I be able to find the reason and answer to this paranormal event? Will I look for answers from God? (At this time in my life, I believed in nothing but gangsterism. I was an extreme atheist.) Defenseless against an unseen enemy, what weapon will I wield to fight off this unjustified intrusion?

At first, I believed I had tapped into the ability to read minds and, I must admit, the psychic nature within me was augmented during this process, but it had no discipline nor had I the training or knowledge to master or counter it. And even worse, a thought came to me, what if people could read my mind? The questions were endless.

Living deep in the shadow of this unknown made every mundane act of normality almost seem like a waste of time, an absurd attempt to paint a façade of typicality over an existence that was twisted and strange. In an infinite Universe, the potential number of intelligent beings is also infinite. Theoretically, anything that could be imagined must exist in an infinite realm.

When a man's spirit retreats, he can see visions from the past that he cannot bear. He can ask himself a question so terrible and so elemental that for a moment he feels in danger of coming completely unraveled and disconnected. To even think about the question makes him feel uneasy. Many criminal minds have no conscience, no feelings of guilt, but the mind has a way of punishing itself for destroying life with no remorse.

Through the descent, made up of despairs and without accomplishments, one can realize a new awakening, which is a reversal of despair. For what a man cannot accomplish, what is denied to love, what a man has lost in anticipation, a descent follows that is endless and destructible. If a man's mind is sick, he can think things that are not real, even the fears of madness.

I came to understand that no story is a straight line. The geometry of a man's life is too imperfect and complex, too distorted by the laughter of time and the bewildering intricacies of fate to admit straight lines into its system of laws. The madness that engulfed me carried the sensibilities primed and calibrated to register the slightest disturbances. Paranoia is a symptom of madness. I would listen to every word spoken by the other people with extreme concentration, but the language was being processed through a filter in my mind that was haphazardly imperfect, damaged, and cracked. The language I would hear became an instrument of bedlam, obfuscation, and irritation.

Words spoken in an innocent context could take an aggravated significance in my mind. Every conversation with me had the possibility of turning into a deadly dance with death. The slightest change of emphasis or shift in intonation could disorient my thinking rhythm and send me into an eerie paranoid zone, heavily booby trapped, bristling with observation points with variable passwords to gain access within my realm. Every friend eventually became foe; every foe became my enemy; every enemy became a threat to my survival; and every threat had to be vanquished. Something so dark would close in on me from the inside out—and violence was my only comforter.

> *A light shines in the darkness,*
> *but the darkness has not understood it.*
>
> — JOHN 1:5 NIV

I had to accept reality and realize there is nothing in this world that cannot be. The messenger brought with it something that was not of this world, something that belonged to another dimension, yet without it I would have never moved forward. Curiosity is one of my strongest virtues. I was determined to find out how this came to be and how I could heal myself. I began to study many different belief systems. I studied the occult, esoteric philosophies, and ideology. I took college correspondence courses in psychology. I took Biblical correspondence courses.

I was searching for answers outside of myself and all along the answers were already within me. In my search, I started to gain insight of who I was. I began to self-evaluate and, in the process, I learned truths of who I truly was. I was guided to my roots. I had to travel in time to get a better and clearer perspective on who I am and where I came from.

Destiny is made silently.

I have experienced several key moments in my life that helped shape my life. These things are known as evolutionary moments. Evolutionary moments bring the purpose of one's life into sharp focus. There are landmarks I have subconsciously filed away that I have used to plot my course. At various points, whether by apparent whim or Divine design, I made course corrections. Whether I received navigational aid from someone else, some event, or my own inner compass guiding me, I can look back and see vividly when these moments occurred. These evolutionary moments put me back on destiny's path.

Sometimes, when these moments occurred, I had a vague sense that something of great importance was happening, but I was too occupied to stop and make sense of it. I believe that, in some universal way, once I reached a certain destination point, I would inadvertently decide to take out a map and examine where I had been and where I needed to go. And by design, I would follow a deeper inexplicable impulse that would magnetize me toward Science of Mind.

In actuality, it is a series of seemingly unrelated events over the years that do not seem to connect until the purpose becomes unequivocal. In a sense, there are enough dots to connect to view a meaningful picture of our life's work. Every event in my life—the good, bad, hard, easy, rebellious, and compliant—shaped me into that which I will become and reinforced my goals and kept me on course in accordance to my inborn nature.

One's real life is often the life that one doesn't actually live. The dangers of denying one's quiddity to arise to the forefront of one's being can lead one into negative mortality because inauthenticity threatens one's quality of life at a profound level.

The path of Truth is one with a heart and is easy for me to travel. It has made me stronger in Spirit. Even though many truths are truths people would rather hide, they are truths nonetheless. Perhaps God has pre-written my path and my goal is to stay on this path. There have been many times I have headed in a different direction than intended, yet I've always returned to the path of Truth.

My experiences with the world of spirits was a necessary push into my metamorphosis. Many psychiatrists and psychologists call the type of behavior I exhibited psychotic or psychosis, but no matter the term used, the process has a lot to do with the violent destruction of the ego entity. My personal experience taught me that we are the most alive and the closest to the meaning of our existence when we are most vulnerable, when experience has humbled us and cured the arrogance which, like a form of deafness, prevents us from hearing the lessons the Universal Mind teaches.

Within textbook psychology, the psychotic hallucinates things that do not exist. My own understanding is that they perceive things that do exist, but they organize them psychically and emotionally in a way that is many degrees different from the ordinary. Or they perceive things the average person discards unconsciously, which results in the perception of a reality that for the psychotic is generally painful and many times self-destructive. The destruction of one's ego leads to a loss of certainty as to what is real. When ego has lost its sense of continuity due to the disassembling and dismantling of its reality, it will cause the psychotic to have serious doubts about their identity, since they are no longer certain about what the original characteristics of their ego were. Since it was ego that was the fundamental basis of conduct in its destruction phase, the psychotic appears to be erratic and incoherent.

Unless the insanity has to do with a tumor or genetic defect, an insane person is really one who has entered into an uncontrolled process of destruction of the ego, though not aware of it. The search for an alternative way of being is a rejection of anxiety, anguish, depression, pain, hurt, and fear. A psychotic is in a desperate search for freedom, a condition that can be accreted to an accelerated great personal spiritual upheaval or traumatic event. Yet the psychotic path does lead somewhere. It leads to freedom from an oppressive existence. The problem for the psychotic person is the lack of power to arrive at the destination of freedom.

I myself, during this process of transformation, finally accepted what was a simple truth: Life has many dimensions that cannot be explained by physicists, biologists, doctors, scientists, or mathematicians. I went temporarily insane, yes, but I did it without losing myself within the madness. I went through this process more harmoniously than I care to admit.

There is a grace in the natural order of things, if one pays close attention. The bird represented the mysterious. It was a foreboding of the unknown, and I had been taught to fear the mysterious as well as the unknown. These events led to my growth and evolution.

My true Divine Self has no fear of the unknown and can deal directly with the mysteries and interact with the unexplainable without interference from the non-comprehension of the rational mind. Thus, the awareness attained is a portal to the awareness of being.

> *The man who stands upon the crossroads of the paths and points*
> *the way, but does not go, is just a pointer, and a block of wood can*
> *do the same. The teacher treads the way on every span of ground.*
> *He leaves his footprints clearly cut, which all can see and be*
> *assured that the teacher went that way.*

— SOURCE UNKNOWN

There is what is known as temporal lobe epilepsy (TLE). In my studies on this subject, I learned that when a person has a seizure in the right or left temporal regions of the brain, there can be the direct perception of being removed from one's physical and psychological surroundings, while remaining completely conscious. These are often accompanied by the sensation of floating, elevation, rotation, or being autoscopic or viewing the body as distant and external to oneself.

The vestibular system of the brain stem is implicated along with the dynamics of the temporal parietal lobe sulcus. During these times, one may have the sensation of traveling through portals or tunnels of conversations with unseen others, or of hearing disembodied voices of one form or another, and other forms of psychic or spiritual experiences.

A psychological or neurological crisis in this context appears to parallel, mimic, or become entangled in a spiritual crisis or episode. When deep psychic or spiritual phenomena and neural structures emerge to give rise to TLE, a whole new reality of remote viewing, telepathic clairvoyance, and much more are experienced. All of these are latent capacities of normal human beings and can be developed under certain circumstances. It is the cultural prohibitions and fear of ridicule and present-day mechanistic scientific prejudice that preclude more from being known and taught about these universal abilities.

Without the knowledge of my ancestors, historical truths, and European historical truths, I would not have come to understand who I really and truly am. I wouldn't have come to understand that only individual opinions are fixed and dogmatic. Truth is more dynamic than that. History has shared a secret with me—that human culture and knowledge are constantly evolving. In my awareness, I have acknowledged the great mystery: In this life, I have been perfectly placed in exactly the right position to make all the difference in the world.

9/3/13

DEAR MICHAEL,

Are you comforted to know that enlightenment is an ongoing process? It is true, we never reach a place where our development stops; we evolve eternally. But since we also know that God is all there is, in what way do we relate this to all of life's ups and downs? I think Ken Wilber said it beautifully: "And so forms continue to arise, and you learn to surf."

Surfing is such a wild and exhilarating sport that requires intense concentration on the motion of the water and becoming one with it. Hard and fast, up and down, small and great, the waves of the ocean keep coming, just like life experiences. A surfer practices and develops strength and skills to work in harmony with the unpredictable nature of the ocean. Maintaining that sense of oneness takes focused effort and determination. With awareness and practice we, too, can hone our spiritual skills and surf harmoniously through life.

Inner peace and harmony come from living in the knowledge of our oneness with God and all things. But there are times when we become hypnotized by our earthly experiences. We might inflate our own importance a little too much, and it can be difficult to feel and see the unity around us. When we feel separate, our mind can be dominated by selfish urges, putting forth effort to have their own way to do only what we like, while we are unable to see at that moment how we might help those around us.

Jesus taught that we should not wait for a negative experience (a crash) to let go of our attachment to separateness, but should consciously turn away from those selfish needs and do something positive. By turning away from the darkness of separateness, we walk into the light.

Light accompanies an expansion of consciousness. When we connect with our soul in deep meditation, we can see white light. If it could be seen with open eyes, affirmative prayer would be seen as a pathway of light. Holmes said, "This light is not created. It is not a psychological explosion; it is something which preexists." And in this illumination, something is felt.

One way to see how perfectly both unity and individuality express in life is to observe rain. Eventually rainwater always returns to the ocean. Water may pause here or there in a lake or stream; it may evaporate into the clouds or be taken up by a thirsty plant; it may be the ice cubes that keep a glass of water cool. While water experiences its many forms, the ocean does not worry or fret—it just is. It waits patiently, knowing every drop of water is not lost, it is just on a journey of individual expression and will eventually find its way back into a stream, which eventually joins in perfect union with the ocean.

All spiritual teachers have said we also eventually find our way back to a true recognition of oneness, our true nature. It may take some people longer than others—pausing as long as water frozen in a glacier—but at some point, each one melts and finds their way back home.

10/28/13

DEAR MICHAEL,

My studies in metaphysics are my greatest passion in this life. To be able to share those studies with you and other prisoners is a gift to me and is the driving energy for every day to keep up with my studies, letters, and facilitating classes. This is not a philosophy we can just live by one day a week. It is a 24/7 commitment. I still have a way to go, but I cherish the joy it brings me.

It is also one reason I love Einstein's recognition of unity as energy and mass being equal, identical, and interchangeable. The basis for metaphysics is the concept that there is no difference between the thought and what it does; there is no difference between the thought and the form it takes. How could a thought change a form unless that form were actually thought as form?

That is the whole basis of affirmative prayer. Just as an acorn becomes a tree, a solid thought creates the thing. How? Nobody knows, and it doesn't matter. What matters is that it happens. Holmes explains, "Then our aim is not to speak the right word, necessarily, but a word that is so completely accepted that it can operate."

Do you remember a moment when you made a personal decision and it was so clear that nothing was going to stop you? Determination and clarity are powerful partners.

11/4/13

DEAR REV. MARY,

That which you have given me is priceless. I thank you for the time you have shared and the benefit of your thinking. One thing I have learned from you, that has been a supreme contribution to my education, is to see Truth only and avoid extreme views, to see people being human with human emotions being expressed, sometimes positive, sometimes negative, sometimes neutral.

Some say life swings on an ethical hinge and, if loosened, all of nature would feel its effects. Jesus had an ethic of inner perfection, and for me to walk this path will take patience, vigilance, and a genuine desire to escape a contaminated existence. In order for me to accomplish this, I must live it or make it so that all my learning of Science of Mind and my life are inseparable and indiscernible from one another. I strive every day to make this my way of life—and until the goal is reached, I shall view it as a way of life that I will encompass.

As I write to you, I am currently in ad-seg, also known as the hole. I was engaged in mortal combat with an administrative pawn. I tried every peaceful measure, but he was insistent in his provocation, which led to serious injuries on his part. When defining the word "violence," none of the definitions are negative when one looks at nature in its entirety. It has been almost five years since I had to engage in a battle of this magnitude, and in a world where violence keeps you at the top of the prison hierarchy, showing great physical force was the coin of the realm. *(Ecclesiastes 3:8: "A time to love and a time to hate, a time for war and a time for peace.")*

There is a limit beyond which no man can be expected to go and upon being in this realm twenty-three years and in my early forties, I still bear scars of earlier tortures and battles. This has assured me that I can endure and survive and still be in possession of my truths and my faculties of mind. This, for me, is a source of pride.

How I value these lands in which I have evolved and, increasingly, how I regard my status. Being an individual connected to other individuals is something I dwell on always. I don't glamorize this prison lifestyle or its ruthless ways, but I understand them. In ways I may never truly understand, my life is connected with many others, even though they seem separate. They both become meaningful as I discover how truly necessary my life and another's life are to each other.

What we think depends on what we perceive. What we perceive determines what we believe. What we believe determines what we take to be true. What we take to be true is our reality. So, we carry relative reality and absolute reality. Two truths. One points to what we believe, yet this may not be true reality of what really is. And absolute reality is what enlightens us to the real truth.

That which calls me to new horizons is honesty and integrity. This, along with poise, courage, and compassion, has allowed me to be attuned with my quiddity and embrace who I am as a whole. That longing for truth of the heart that penetrates the essence of things and phenomena leads me to great new vistas.

So, I always acknowledge change and know that nothing is set in stone. I will always look to you as someone great, someone of respect, someone to emulate. I thank you for everything.

11/16/13

DEAR MICHAEL,

In rereading your July letter, you mentioned receiving the book by Sri Arubindo and the information on clemency, just when you had been discussing it with comrades. Life is like that in so many ways. The more we observe the world without judgment, the more our intuitive nature connects with Infinite Mind and we experience more synchronicity. You, my friend, are in the flow.

I really appreciated your writing in August about Black August. I had not heard about it before. I agree with you that without knowing the truth of who we are in the sphere of humanity, it is difficult to grow. It must be very challenging for those who think their history begins with slavery. The richness of humanity that began in Africa dwells in us all. In most of my counseling work, I find unworthiness a common theme. And then the question arises, from where does one draw the knowledge of one's divine nature? Sometimes it takes a black bird.

Your experience with the black bird is mystical. And to look back and see that experience is what brought you back from the brink of madness into the realm of mystery says it all. It's the evolution of the soul.

In my classes, I often draw a big Superman S on paper and the bottom of the S curls around like a tail and on that tail, I draw a barrier. I share that every person is a soul created by Divine Intelligence to understand Itself. Just as the universe evolves, the soul is meant to evolve. Just as the universe continues to expand from the big bang, our soul has the opportunity to grow and expand when it takes human form (recognizing there are many dimensions or planes of existence of which being a human being on Earth is only one). When we leave or transition from this body to the next dimension, we will take along our beliefs, values, and understandings into the next state of existence. But to continue to evolve seems to require volition and the freedom to choose, at least here on Earth.

Using my Superman S diagram, my question to the class or client is whether they can identify the blockage in this lifetime that their soul wants to move beyond. We look at patterns in their life, habits that don't serve them, problems that keep resurfacing, and so on. It usually doesn't take too long for the person to begin to see that every time they hit this block and retreat or reverse course, life doesn't get any better. When we look at the block, which could be as simple as unworthiness, and go back to our spiritual baseline that we are all individual creations of the One, it becomes easier to see that it is almost like the soul is pushing us to get beyond that block.

The article about Marcus Garvey was very interesting. There is so much rich history that is not widely known. I found an article on his life that might be of interest that is also enclosed. The passion he had is amazing! The quote at the beginning was right on: "The ends you serve that are for all, in common, will take you into eternity." Every once in a while, I think I could get a new job doing this or that, but then I remember that it might serve my bank account, but my ministerial work is serving all. Every other week I submit a short column to our local newspaper for a page called Voices of Faith. The newspaper presents a question and invites various faith traditions to respond. It is always interesting to read the responses from the fundamentalist to the atheist.

Your continued enlightenment is in my prayers.

12/14/13

DEAR MICHAEL,

How you make me smile with your words on how you now value the lands in which you have evolved. "The great, the good, and the wise" have told us this "thing," this Divine essence is light, life, love, peace, power, beauty, and joy; divine attributes we can observe around us every day of the week. Troward describes these as attributes of Spirit and, as we contemplate each one, we become it. Spirit holds the possibility of everything and it resides in our individual consciousness.

You are evolving at such a rapid pace! This Divine Mind in which we live is the field in which we plant our seeds; it is the field of eternal action. In each thing, the presence of God must exist as the idea *and the potentiality* of that thing in which it is incarnated. The potentiality of a tomato plant resides in the seed. How the seed received this identity is the process of evolution. "Within us must be the potential of everything we shall ever evolve into," writes Holmes.

Just think of what has evolved over this past hundred years as a new century begins —computers, atomic war, airplanes, telephones, space stations. All of these things had the potential to exist many centuries ago. The potential was there, but it was the evolution of our thinking process, our knowledge and understanding, that put the pieces together to create a laptop computer.

Evolution is a *principle,* which manifests in all forms. It is the effect of Intelligence, not its cause. Evolution, the effect, only follows involution, the idea. When we embody the idea, the form appears, which is why we believe that behind everything is the movement of consciousness. Every idea we have is God expressing the Self. It is God's nature to know and crave expression. Every aspect of our life is Cause and Effect in action. Spirit involves and Law evolves mechanically. Evolution is an effect. Take a moment to look at your life and find the connection between: involution…evolution; thought…thing; word…law; purpose…execution.

Many sacred scriptures throughout the ages have taught unity and individuality. One text that focuses on spiritual self-mastery is the *Bhagavad Gita.* The epic stories found here are metaphors for the war between the forces of light and darkness in every person; the war between unity and individuality. In Chapter 2 of the text, spiritual teacher, Sri Krishna, reminds his student, Arjuna, of his immortal nature, the real Self that never dies, the eternal Self. The basic premise, as Arjuna begins his path of spiritual awareness, is that the immortal soul is more important than the passing world. But Arjuna is told he will not fully realize this until he can see beyond the dualities of life and identify with the immortal Self through direct mystical experience. Krishna calls for disciplining the mind and detachment from dualities like pain and pleasure. The goal of the story is to teach that by expanding our spiritual awareness, our reaction to events will not be based on habit but will be based on the freedom of non-attachment. Here again, we find the power of the witness consciousness.

Krishna goes on to talk to Arjuna about attachment: "When you keep thinking about sense objects, attachment comes. Attachment can breed desire, the lust of possession that turns to anger. Anger clouds the judgment; you can no longer learn from past mistakes. Lost is the power to choose between what is wise and what is unwise, and your life is utter waste. But when you move amidst the world of sense, free from attachment and aversion alike, there comes the peace in which all sorrows end, and you live in the wisdom of the Self."

When we enter this state of awareness, we feel bliss, then soon we again become aware of our body, our physical experience, and the sense of unity may fade like a dream. The moment we pierce the veil of illusion and touch infinity, our life changes. Consistent spiritual practices are the path to keep this channel of deep inner understanding open.

CHAPTER 6

2014

Refocusing on Growth and Evolution

Anything negative or false resonates weakness; anything positive and/or true resonates strength — This land, where ignorance is glorified and reading and writing frowned upon — The peculiar miasma that is a shadow over this land — Weary eyes filled with incessant rage, despair, insanity, and mental illness, the anguished eyes of sorrow — The Creative Process can allow one to focus his purpose and systematically create a positive change — Part of the whole, humans are the manifestation of God in the material plane — If I hadn't come into this realm, perhaps I wouldn't have learned all that I have — At each stage, a teacher appeared — Spiritual growth depends on taking a step in consciousness — Heart and soul expand to hold more love — My very soul is striving toward ascension and a transcendent understanding of creation — My life has been an intimate dance of light and darkness — I recognize the Divine design — My victory gained was that to love is a requirement of light.

2/16/14

DEAR REV. MARY,

I've been transferred to a different prison facility, and I was let out of the hole upon my arrival. Those in authority positions here deemed it unnecessary to continue my ad-seg assignment for such a minor infraction, but those authorities at the other facility seemed to believe I was a threat to the safety and security of the institution. In other words, I had been there for ten years and many of the guards, knowing me, would help me in certain ways to keep me from getting into a situation where I could end up in the hole. Under the science of corrections this is intolerable, but under the Science of Mind, friendships and associations (no matter one's job title) are inevitable.

The book you sent me, *Power vs. Force* by David Hawkins, was incredible in its knowledge. The physical concepts dealing with a person holding out their arm (muscle testing) has blown away the minds of every person who participated in the experiment. It brought amazing positive responses with many wanting to learn more about positive thought and the Science of Mind. I would explain how anything that was negative or false would resonate weakness and anything that was positive and/or true would resonate strength.

I had a conversation with an inmate who is a professed born-again Christian. The conversation revolved around positive and negative thought and the Law of Attraction. I was asked a question during our dialogue that I could not answer, so I ask you for enlightenment pertaining to the question. There were many negative calamities that came to Jesus in the form of slander by the Pharisees, torture, and physical death. Also, Ghandi and Martin Luther King Jr. suffered at the hands of those who did not agree with their methods of peace. Could it be that through the Law of Attraction they harbored negative thoughts that brought about the violence and hatred that occurred in their paths?

I know that thoughts can influence events in ways that can seem bizarre or even paranormal, yet there are other factors that are sometimes ignored but operate as well, such as the obscure but overwhelming forces that are called kismet, fate, destiny. Could these forces cancel out the Law of Attraction and bring to us that which we, perhaps, did not want to experience but needed to anyway?

4/1/14

DEAR MICHAEL,

Yes, you are on to something. Evolution as a constant. As Holmes said, "Creation is the passing of Spirit into form and is eternally going on…. The Spirit is conscious of Its own Thought, Its own Desire, Its own manifest Action; and It is conscious that Its Desire is satisfied. Consequently, It is conscious of that which It manifests; but It is not conscious of any effort or process in Its manifestation."

It just is. This is what is meant in metaphysics when we say Law is impersonal. Law does not know Itself; Law only knows to do. This is how Spirit operates; It creates by contemplation.

Fascinating, isn't it, to realize that by our thought we tap into Spirit, who only knows "to do," to react to our thought by creating every moment, which is why we call it Law. How was Law made? To our knowledge, Law has always been. Could there be a time when Law did not operate? It seems impossible because of the ongoing creative nature of the Universe. Continuing evolution is to coexist with God and therefore must be co-eternal with Spirit. All action must be Spirit operating as Law.

By looking at how all of this works together, we touch a deeper understanding of the concept of the Trinity. In many religions, we find the Trinity expressed as the Father, the Son, and the Holy Ghost. In metaphysics, we see the power of the Trinity expressed in several ways, such as:

The Triune Nature of the One God		
God and Law	Spirit and Creation	Substance into Form
Spirit	Soul	Body
Absolute Intelligence	Receptive Intelligence	Divine Ideas
Intelligence	Substance	Form
Cause	Medium	Effect

To apply the basic laws of metaphysics in our life, recognize there are two simple principles at its core, which cannot be physically grasped. One is the power of love. We have not physically touched love as it moves from one person to another, but we do see the results of love. Think for a moment about the last time someone wrapped their arms around you and said, "I love you." The warmth and joy of being loved is an inside job. The glow that emanates from being loved is how we see principle at work.

5/24/14

DEAR MICHAEL,

I am so glad to hear you enjoyed *Power vs. Force.* Yes, muscle testing is amazing. The soul knows what is good and not good for our body. The soul is so much larger than what we know of as our body, so that when we pay attention to it life improves. Whenever I feel ill but can't identify the cause, I go to a Chinese herbalist/acupuncturist and she uses muscle testing with all of her herbs to find out what makes me the strongest. It always, always works. My husband, Paul, being a retired pharmacist, doesn't believe in it because, in his training, pills are the way to go, but then he rarely gets sick.

The last class I facilitated was "Meditation Is More Than You Think," where we did a different type of meditation each week, which was really easy and fun. We enjoyed silent meditation, walking meditation, chanting, mantra (one to three powerful words said in repetition), and journaling. Since I will be gone for awhile on vacation, I will begin a writing class in summer, then we will go into the fall with more core Science of Mind classes.

One of the books I recently found is called *Prayer Can Change Your Life* by Dr. William Parker and Elaine St. Johns. It was published in 1957 by two of Dr. Ernest Holmes's friends. Elaine recorded every aspect of the three experiments Dr. Parker did with prayer in his laboratory at Redlands University. The experiments included people of all faiths, including ministers, doctors, and teachers.

The first of the three experiments was called Spiritual Psychological Counseling; the next was Ordinary Prayer, which is the type of prayer used in a lot of religions; and the last was called Prayer Therapy or affirmative prayer, which is what we use in Science of Mind. What they reported was that affirmative prayer had exceedingly good results—the best of all.

The next best was psychological counseling and the poorest results came from the ordinary method of prayer.

Their conclusion was the best results came from affirmative prayer because it is prayed with acceptance, a belief in consciousness, and embodiment in thought. The one praying accepted something for themselves or someone identified, such as, "This prayer is for John Smith." The prayer was made in the here and now, was affirmative, accepted, and identified, which showed the person praying was dealing with Intelligence. Holmes noted that later studies in prayer at Duke University came up with the same results.

Dr. Holmes stated that he was glad these results came out of a laboratory, so no one could attach it to a specific theology. He was so excited that we have within our reach the greatest good the world has ever known to definitely show the method and process that has been the hope and aspiration of all religious endeavors in the world.

7/11/14

DEAR REV. MARY,

As I told you in a previous letter, I've been relocated to a different prison. I've been here now close to seven months. I've been trying to locate two books you ordered for me, *Entering the Castle* by Carolyn Myss and *The Foundation of Mysticism* by Joel Goldsmith. I have filed grievances within this institution about the whereabouts of these books. The prison staff at my previous stay maintains that they never received the books, which of course is an excuse for their negligence, so my plight to regain that which you sent so far has been unfruitful and the books may have been lost in the chaos of my transfer.

I did receive both books by Thomas Troward—*The Edinburgh and Dore Lectures* and *The Creative Process in the Individual.* Letters, books, pictures, and literature from the free world are blessings for one like myself. So much has aided me in my struggle for ascension. The knowledge I've gained has cured me of the many maladies I suffered from in the past.

This new land I now reside in is somewhat outdated. What I mean by this is it feels like I've somehow stepped through a portal that has taken me into a time where ignorance is glorified and reading and writing is frowned upon. The mentality of the majority of the inhabitants of this realm remains stagnated. Many of the belief systems in the 9th Dominion of prison that inmates follow and adhere to do not help them in quite the same way Science of Mind has helped me. Their systems of belief do not allow them the ability to overcome the peculiar miasma that is a shadow over this land. Many here do not realize there is an alternative way of being, a way to allay the excruciating pain of merely surviving within this environment.

I have often wondered if my own eyes would come to reflect those I see all around me —eyes filled with an incessant rage, weary despair, insanity, and mental illness; eyes filled with despondency of an old man who can no longer fight injustice; the anguished eyes of sorrow. I used to sometimes wonder if someday my own eyes would show all these symptoms of oppression and self-loathing.

The Spirit of Liberation compels my being to resist all types of oppression. I will continue to work on completing my book and seeking all the avenues that will lead to physical freedom. The person I've become has been forged by enormous odds, unexpected blessings, and magnificent friends. During my stay within this new realm, I will explore all the possibilities that exist here for my enrichment.

Have you heard about the book called *The Kybalion* written by the Three Initiates? It was first published by the Yogi Publication Society of Chicago in 1908. I've read that this was a book that likely had an influence on Dr. Ernest Holmes. I would like your most honest insight on this. Many of the Science of Mind teachings speak about how many types of illnesses are derived from a certain type of mindset one can carry, and in many instances, I agree. I know that anger and hatred can cause blindness, strokes, and migraines. I know that anxiety, worry, and apprehension can cause high blood pressure, skin ailments, and can even affect the nervous system. My question to you pertains to children who become afflicted with illness such as leukemia. Even though they have no ideas of the disease, how would this affliction be determined as a mental state?

My son, who passed away of leukemia at age 12, had an uncle, his mother's brother, who also had leukemia and passed away, but he was much older when he passed. My son's mother named our son in memory of his deceased uncle, so he was given the same name. Do you think it is possible for the mother to somehow transmit her concerns, worries of her son having the disease to a point where it actually did happen, or would this be more in the realm of dealing with genetics?

7/30/14

DEAR MICHAEL,

As you describe those around you with eyes filled with rage, weary despair, despondency, perhaps you can think back to when you were first incarcerated. Does any of that resonate with your early memories? The good news is no one or no thing or experience now can take you back there. You have evolved into a wise man with so much to offer others. You have a calling.

You asked about illnesses being created by certain types of mindsets. Not long ago, I received a call from a woman in southern California who was in a panic because she had been diagnosed with hepatitis C. She had been in this teaching for a long time and was scared about how this happened. Since she had been a student, I asked her if she had ever read Louise Hay's books about the mind/body connection. She was familiar with Louise, so I asked if she would mind if I pulled out her book, *You Can Heal Your Life,* while we talked. She was fine with that, so I looked up hepatitis and it read: Resistance to change. She gasped and I asked how that resonated with her. She said six months earlier she retired from a job she loved and she has had regrets every day since then. Every day she thought about that job and cried. I said, well, it's time to find a hobby because this regret, this resistance to change, is going to kill you. It's time to be in the present moment and embrace the future.

8/12/14

DEAR MICHAEL,

Regarding your question of whether it's possible that your son's mother, whose brother died of leukemia, transmitted her worries to the point where your son ended up with leukemia: It is very hard to figure out, because, number one, it is the soul's journey. At the same time, we believe that the health or poor health of our bodies are the effects of what is in subconscious mind or what we consciously tell ourselves that sits in the subconscious until it manifests.

It is possible that your son felt his mother's pain at the loss of her brother. I have an example of a friend of mine I'll call Kelly. Kelly grew up in a home where her older sister, Marilyn, had Type 1 Diabetes. Marilyn received the bulk of their mother's attention. Feeling somewhat abandoned, when Kelly was about eight years old, she shared with me that she decided she not only wanted diabetes, but wanted it to be worse than her sister's. All of this was so that her mother would pay more attention to her. Kelly ended up with severe diabetes, and although she eventually got married at age nineteen, after she had her first beautiful baby girl, Kelly died from the disease. For me, I can see the thread of the Law of Cause and Effect, along with other related issues, but the other important thing to remember is that when the soul is done on this plane, it leaves.

A simple example of conscious thoughts creating undesirable experiences is my friend, a practitioner, who had a job she hated. For months, she told everyone that she needed a break from her job. It wasn't long before she tripped on a cement thing in a parking lot, fell, and broke her shoulder. She got her break. But a few months later, she fell again and broke her wrist. She came to our practitioner meeting laughing, since she realized that after the first break and before the second break, she had not changed her story about wanting a break from her job.

Another practitioner had been saying she needed to replace her car because it was unreliable and she didn't feel safe driving it. It wasn't long before she was driving and the car caught on fire. She got out and watched it burn up. Thanks to her insurance company, she got a new car.

Since Law is creative and impersonal and responds to us perfectly every time, we cannot demonstrate anything that is love if our thoughts are based on its opposite, fear. How can we demonstrate freedom if our thoughts are based on bondage? Another way of looking at this is through the Law of Mental Equivalents. We experience the equivalent of our (mental) beliefs. As it says in the Bible in Galatians 6:7, "Whatsoever a man soweth, that shall he also reap." This is another indicator that when we do anything negative, physically or in mind, it comes back to us because it is the Law. And yet it can take years or even decades to reach a clear enough understanding of this principle before we choose to shift away from negativity in our thoughts, words, or deeds.

This does not mean we should bury negative thoughts, but should instead open up to a different way of thinking through contemplation and meditation and use affirmative prayer to shift that understanding. Jesus understood this power. He had a great sense of Oneness and alignment with the Divine Presence and understood the Universal Law of Mind. He gave thanks and commanded the Law to work, and it did. Holmes explains, "Practice is a definite statement in mind, a positive affirmation. It is an active, conscious, aggressive mental movement and in such degree as it embodies an idea—and there is no longer anything in our minds which denies the idea—it will take form, because it now becomes a part of the law and order of the Universe in which we live." Our problems are primarily mental, and the answers are found in spiritual realization.

8/24/14

DEAR REV. MARY,

Thank you so much for your insight about the questions I asked in my previous letter. I am still making progress in reading *The Life Divine* by Sri Aurobindo. I ordered the glossary of Sanskrit terms from the Siddha Yoga Meditation Prison Project out of Emeryville, California. It helps with pronunciation of the words and gives a correct way of understanding the vowels and consonants and the variations that differ from English. It is very helpful when reading this book, plus I don't have to constantly turn to the end of the book when I come across an unfamiliar word.

Since I've been incapacitated from the freedoms of human sanctity and cursed to gaze upon nirvana within a penal colony, I've witnessed the de-evolution of men and also the evolution of men. I believe the inhabitants of an environment have a deep influence on someone who has for the first time entered into these lands, and which land the person ends up in can determine which path he will follow.

The majority of the inhabitants within this land in which I now dwell fall short of living their fullest potential. They struggle to consciously manifest what they desire. It is hard for them to attain because of being out of balance internally. Because of this imbalance, satisfaction, pleasure, and participation in their own destiny is missing. The creative process is a way that can allow one to focus his purpose and systematically create a positive change in all aspects of life.

Troward expresses throughout his book about evolution the recognition that he is a part of the whole. A whole atom is a part of a whole molecule; a whole molecule is part of a whole cell; a whole cell is part of a whole organism. As God is macrocosm, so is man the microcosm. Man is the manifestation of God in the material plane. Thus, the gods of nature, as aspects of God, are also in many. So God is in man through the qualities inherited from the Creator.

Each man within this realm has the potential to be a master of balanced change. We have the means to transform from struggle and survival to enlightenment and clear purpose. One must grow and evolve in his capacity to perceive the deeper layers of himself, which disclose higher levels of reality. One's true self does not speak in words or banal phrases. Its voice comes from deep within, from the substrate of one's psyche, from something embedded within one. It emanates from one's uniqueness and it communicates through sensations and powerful desires that seem to transcend one.

I cannot understand why I am drawn to certain activities or forms of knowledge. This I cannot truly verbalize or explain. It is simply a fact of my nature. In following this innate voice, I realize my own potential and my deepest longing to create and express my uniqueness. I know it exists for a purpose, and it is my task to bring it into fruition.

One's habitual old thoughts can create a solid structure that one will come to believe is one's true self. This can become a belief system that can trap one in the past. This way of thought can cause one to react to present-day experiences from a limited scope of choice. The far-reaching ramifications from one's experiences of his youth can greatly weaken one's foundation and affect many, if not all, of his future experiences.

Changing the workings of the mind from a personal viewpoint is no easy task. I myself spent numerous years in negative thinking. I considered myself an atheist and believed in no man's God. I had no respect for religion. I had to learn my true nature, what it is that I am. For me this was a vital point to concentrate on, because not knowing my true nature, I would not be able to live in right action with the world around me. I needed to understand what I am through the understanding of what I've been and move toward that which I will become. Clearer vision and a conscious shift in attitude, both spurred by an anomalous event, allowed my mind to come back into balance with all aspects of my being.

When one witnesses his own perceptions, he can harness a great force of change. For me, it was very painful to see the fullness of my mind's chaos. For example, as a youngster I took on the persona of a gangster. The images of gangsterism flooded my vision. It was glorified in media, Hollywood, music, and throughout the neighborhoods in which I dwelled and grew. So, I entered into this great mythical world of beast and became a hybrid, part man and part monster, to create this great apathetic gangster.

I have three uncles with whom I'm very close, and all have taken a small part in raising me. All three of my uncles are Vietnam veterans, yet my Uncle Jr. and Uncle Carl were the two whom I tried to emulate the most. Both of them were womanizers and alcoholics. They both carried guns and had run-ins with law enforcement personnel. They both lived off the land by hunting and fishing. In my young mind, they lived many of the ways of a gangster, so I favored them. My Uncle Ray, also a Vietnam veteran, didn't carry guns. He didn't drink alcohol. He had a wife and worked a steady job. In my delusional mind state, I believed my Uncle Ray to be weak and soft and not a gangster. I would dismiss any wisdom he would offer me, and from a gangster's perception, I decided I didn't like my Uncle Ray as much.

The power of negative thought was even able to dictate my emotions. I didn't love or care for him as I did those whom my myopic eyes saw as gangsters. So, throughout the years of my young life, this was something in my mind that had taken root as a belief, but I didn't recognize it as a falsehood. During the long periods of immaturity, one often transfers these idealizations and distortions onto people, projecting onto them what one wants and needs to see. One's view of people becomes saturated with various emotions, worship, admiration, love, need, and anger. Viewing people through a distorted lens, one's view becomes warped.

After decades of study and attaining knowledge, this was a profound realization for me, the recognition of so many flawed thoughts that led me to literally wipe away my old ways of thinking and start with a clean slate and give my mind new guidelines to follow. My mind had been stuck in a quagmire of muddled negative thoughts. I was perceiving the world through a kaleidoscope of negativity and tangled up falsehoods. I was at the point that I was unable to distinguish falsehoods from truth.

The thoughts of gangsterism became a joke. I could not believe that a thought based on a non-truth could take root so deeply, yet now being able to reflect on and laugh at this foolishness, the negative has lost its ferocious power it once held over me. A new way of being for me emerged after the chrysalis of tradition and habit had been cracked open and burst asunder, allowing escape into the light of freedom.

Such a transition necessitates destruction of old forms both of thought and action. Many people of antiquity, in their rebellion against outdated ideology and worn-out ways, created and produced works that disrupted habitual mental ruts and attitudes. They introduced the unexpected, the unnatural. Instinctively they prepared the way for something that has to come, something utterly new and different, although they themselves may not have known what it could have ultimately been.

The new awakening and the creation of something new, unique with a new thought, is one of the reasons I study so diligently. It is why I contemplate my incarceration, because if I hadn't come into this realm, perhaps I wouldn't have learned all that I have. I believe my dark experiences began my path, and at each stage in the journey, a teacher appeared. The Most High will often use the dark to provide a tool that leads to the light of wisdom. He uses the forces of evil against itself to accomplish something positive. Sometimes the loss of something will strengthen a person's soul to the point where he can endure without it. A man's soul knows when it needs to go to the next level.

Trusting in a Higher Power makes the seemingly impossible possible, knowing that there is an Authority so great and so powerful that there is no doubt that Spirit is Truth. When one can bear witness to his mind through Spirit, one's awareness shifts in a way that allows clear perception. One can cultivate his mind and use all his experiences to benefit growth rather than to inhibit it.

I have seen the tremendous pull that keeps one fettered by his habits, negative ideology, and falsehoods. I've uncovered and brought into use many of the laws, and I've been able to maintain a steady march of ever-changing living conditions. For it is said, one does not alter his beliefs to conform to reality, one alters reality to conform to his beliefs.

The gangster persona that I chose to become my public face with which I would meet the world included an array of qualities and personality traits that I presented to others as being my true self. I wanted people to see me as a warrior—cold, calculating, dangerous, intimidating, powerful, alluring, in control—versus an honest, real, and intelligent person.

I selected, organized, and created an entity that I had set up over decades, allowing it time to settle in to camouflage, to become like an insect, a part of its environment. I had mastered the skillful use of artifice, not knowingly but instinctively, to create something more powerful and more lasting than an illusion. And I was able to create moods and feelings that were real.

In discovering my true essence and learning how to respond to life in a manner that was productive, I found myself faced with a great challenge: my ego and the false identity

I had adopted. The goal was to learn to discern what was authentic and to separate it from the many false identities I had acquired in my struggle to find my way in life.

One of the hard pills of truth I had to swallow is that life is characterized by continual change. It is the nature of our existence. It is movement of energy without hindrance. It moves through man and his habits, resistance, and denial. Change is the truth of life that one can observe directly. There is nothing man can find that stays the same. Each thought occurs and then decays. Change is the end of attachment, the end of fear, for there is nothing that binds man and there never has been.

The ever-flowing river of life delivers small and large misfortunes, all of which are sometimes beyond one's control, from small, mundane daily disappointments to major, life-altering disappointments. A person's reaction to difficulty, disappointment, and uncertainty can create degrees of thoughts and feelings and make it hard for one to come to understand his true self. The power that appears to bind one is the only power that frees one, so when one looks closely, he sees that suffering is created by ignorance of the Law. One's spiritual growth depends on taking a step in consciousness from a tangible and limited mind to an intangible unlimited mind. As man moves into a larger conscious state, his heart and soul expand to hold more love and energy. A person moves from limitations to unbounded possibilities.

In *The Creative Process,* Troward makes one aware of the fourth and fifth kingdoms. In my studies, these kingdoms are akin to the fourth and fifth dimensions. Each mystery, as it becomes discovered, understood, and applied, gives one the use of greater forces, yet these forces must be applied not for destruction but for positive advancement.

The unknowing man would consider that an iron ax had more strength than one of gaseous substance. Yet let him see the way in which an acetylene blowpipe cuts through metals even under water, whereas an ax would be quite unwieldy. When fourth dimension forces are used, they are able to master anything in the third dimensional world. The fifth dimension forces are more powerful than any of the others. These mysteries belong to different laws and conditions. The designs are immutable, immovable, and held there by the primal force of creation.

The forces that traverse physical space are powerful indeed. They can burn, melt, mold, and change matter from lower dimensions than their own. But the forces that dwell within the greater higher dimensions still must wield the ultimate power over it. The higher dimensions must always rule and overpower the lower ones, and this is a Universal Law one must always bear in mind. This allows one to realize that mind can always rule matter and that Spirit can rule them all.

Once we can harness Spirit, it is one's duty to develop, and by means of which, learn to know and control the hidden powers and entities and individualities of the invisible dimensions. The gifts that those who develop themselves through living in accordance with cosmic or Divine Laws may help to advance them.

9/21/14

DEAR MICHAEL,

Life is never without some shadow. How would we appreciate beauty or joy if we could not compare a good experience with a not-so-good experience? In our busy day-to-day world, it is easy to ignore spiritual practices, connect with our soul, in favor of joining in the rush of life or personal or materialistic pleasures.

In my experience, the shadows of our mind surface to refocus our attention. At first there comes a feather, a soft touch that may tickle us into awareness. But if we ignore the feather, then subconscious mind tosses a pebble, which makes us a little uncomfortable, but it may not be enough to awaken us to reconnect with our soul, our path, our purpose in life. If the pebble doesn't work, next a rock hurtles toward us, which hurts and challenges us to stop, look, and listen. But with such a busy life, it is easy to dismiss the bruise and assume the rock wasn't really meant for us. Then comes a boulder, a major negative experience jarring us to the foundation of our being. This experience could be serious health problems or personal trauma.

How many warnings have we ignored? Is there an area in your life where you are ignoring a feather or a pebble?

Every moment is a choice, and we can choose to soar like an eagle, using one wing of grace, our personal connection with Spirit, and one wing of personal effort. Connect with the harmony, joy, peace, and love of God expressing as you, expressing both unity and individuality.

10/5/14

DEAR REV. MARY,

Like my ancestors before me, who integrally evolved throughout history, I too at this present time evolve. I have sought out the mysteries and found the explanations of this development in the underlying cause of scientific and metaphysical progress and in uncovering the laws of nature.

I have seen how these laws of nature, as they were uncovered and brought into use, produced a steady march of ever-changing living conditions. I've been able to decipher the message of these changes and understand in what manner many people have failed to acknowledge them and to ascend in their evolution. I have experienced the tremendous pull that keeps one tethered by his habits, traditions, negative falsehoods, and ideology.

For me, the knowledge I have attained has given me the fortitude for mental and spiritual growth. I've learned to wield these magnificent energies with my mind in ways, sometimes in that moment, I could not even fathom, yet it brought me into a better existence, so I deliberately cooperate with the Divine plan of being.

Throughout history, there have always existed individuals who identify with what exists beyond the physical. They have exercised their mind's thinking abilities far beyond the norm. They have embraced and lived their systems of belief that enabled them to overcome harsh obstacles and detractors. Their experiences of positive accomplishment enabled their faith to include every molecule and breath of life.

These people have dedicated their lives to understanding wisdom and to answering the universe's most profound questions. They were not too proud to embrace the thinking and experience of others who might accelerate their own quest toward enlightenment. They are the ones documented in history as insurrectionists, abolitionists, heretics, and the wretched of the Earth. They are the heroes and heroines, some well-known and many seldom even heard of. They are the philosophers who mastered the Law of Relativity. They are the scientists who mastered the Law of Cause and Effect. They are the inventors, musicians, and artists who mastered the Laws of Creation. They are the kings and queens who mastered the Laws of Divine Birthright. They are the spiritual leaders who mastered the Laws of Existence. These ancestors possessed the same universal structure of mind and functioned within the same Universal Laws as I do today.

Each of these individuals displayed enlightenment of an advanced soul. In this lifetime, I have dedicated myself to the Universal Mind and use the gifts I have been endowed with to build greater wisdom, learning and understanding to progress to a higher level of existence. For my very soul is striving toward ascension and a transcendent understanding of creation.

In *The Creative Process,* Troward says, "It is very important to realize that evolution is not the same as creation. It is the unfolding of potentialities involved in things already created, but not the calling into existence of what does not yet exist. That is creation."

I've studied this concept through the process of dialectics, which is the art of investigating the truth of opinions, testing the truth by discussion. Dialectics was first introduced into society in ancient Greece. It was made popular by Socrates through a process by which he examined a question, proposition, or statement from every conceivable angle in order to arrive at the truth of it. In this manner, truth was perceived as being many faceted, like a gemstone.

In a discussion with a prisoner on this very subject taught by Troward, he would argue that a chair, for example, existed in someone's mind as an idea and was put on a drawing board before it became reality. To this argument I pointed out that it is actual concrete conditions that give rise to many ideas. I cannot in fact say all, but I can say many. I would explain that in antiquity, before there were chairs, the idea of making something to sit on sprang from the actual practice of sitting, first perhaps on a large stone or a fallen tree. Sitting on a stone, once it becomes practice, eventually gives rise to the idea of improving upon it by making it softer, by adding skins of animals or something else, and then seeking something lighter or more portable. Hence, first here is reality, then the idea arises which improves upon reality in a step-by-step process until the Chippendale is arrived at thousands of years later.

The priority of objective conditions is displayed in a two-fold manner in this example. First, that the objective practice of sitting gives rise to the idea of chairs. Second, how it was impossible for man to think of a chair as complex as a recliner until the production process made it so. The tools and technology eventually existed that would make a recliner and a Chippendale feasible. Everything man has created, from tools to stories, began with a thought, an inspiration.

I recently applied for a tutor position to help guys get their GEDs, so this is something I'm looking forward to. I've worked as a tutor before, so I'm familiar with most of the work.

11/15/14

DEAR MICHAEL,

In the rules of the game of life, to be more, see more, experience more success and happiness, we have to look inside, be honest, and take action. In metaphysics it is often said, "Treat and move your feet." Do an affirmative prayer (spiritually treat the mind) and then take action. The following points are powerful action steps to put Law in motion. They can be used together or individually. Our co-creative nature and the Universe will support you—it's the Law.

Let's begin:

1. Decide to be happy. Know you have the right to be happy and Spirit, God, the Universe supports you.

2. Stop telling anyone, including yourself, that you are not happy. This only reinforces the pattern.

3. See the good in life. Even the smallest positive act of children, coworkers, spouses, or friends should be praised. Loving words allow you, as well as others, to see the beautiful part of you.

4. Catch any negative mind chatter and stop it midstream, replacing it with positive verbal statements. Verbal expressions carry more forceful energy.

5. Do something new or different. Get out of any rut and expand your horizons, whether in creative endeavors, new friends, new food, or new books. Enlarge your life.

Taking action in any of these areas expands your circle of experience. Each time we expand our circle, our life experience expands and things that may have seemed challenging in the past are now not so difficult. We start each day in a new place where we are greater than the day before.

It has been trendy these past twenty years or so to be blatantly honest and let out our feelings, not repressing thoughts about what we feel. But throughout history, sages taught the power of quieting the mind, disciplining the mind, strengthening the mind, and therefore freeing the self. The more we reinforce negative thoughts by acting them out, the more challenging it is to find inner peace. Desires and emotions come in an endless stream, and by using spiritual techniques we can sort them out.

One of the things Ernest Holmes made clear is that we are not here for the purpose of making an impression on our environment. Instead, we are here to express ourselves in and through our environment. At first this may seem to be in conflict with the tradition of establishing goals and dreams, but what he is saying is that it is not necessary when we die that our obituary makes the headlines or is even two sentences long in the newspaper. He says, "All that means anything is that while we live, WE LIVE, and wherever we go from here we keep on living." Think about this…and a burden is removed.

Holmes says, "We don't have to move the world—it is going to move anyway." The Universe, Spirit, God supports us, because in doing so It expresses even more fully. This is why you are the precious one in whom God is well pleased. Express yourself today in joy, love, happiness, and success. This is your purpose.

12/4/14

Note: This is a letter that Michael sent to Rev. Mary's husband, Paul.

DEAR MR. PAUL,

It has been over five years since I first contacted my mentor, Rev. Mary, and I truly believe the time has come that I engage in proper introductions, considerate formalities, and acquaintance with you, Mr. Paul.

First and foremost, you are a man and any man would have concerns about his woman. The words convict, prisoner, inmate, slave, offender all come with a stigma in the minds of the mainstream public. Perhaps one would assume that a prisoner who corresponds with a loved one to be an interloper or unctuous meddler, for it is only a natural state of mind for one to think this way.

Mr. Paul, out of heartfelt respect, I have no malignant designs or intentions of solecism toward my mentor. Her dauntlessness to reach back to me, when others didn't, spoke volumes and also gained my utmost regard, as have you, for the support you have given her endeavors to help and teach one considered the wretched of the Earth.

Since my arrival into this realm of captives, misery, and turmoil, it would dawn on me that the continued trade in flesh has many guises. Within this world, I chose to do something the majority of prisoners do not. I chose to learn and improve. No easy task amongst madness, deception, negative intentions, and corrupt disciplines.

My studies have included psychology, sociology, medicine, physics, quantum physics, metaphysics, philosophy, art of war, theocracy, theology, esoteric philosophies, occult knowledge, Santeria, Hinduism, Buddhism, Nordic and Celtic Wicca, Greek mythology, atheist concepts, Satanism, Luciferian faith, Coptic, House of Yahweh, Jehovah Witness, Sumerian, Mesopotamia, Babylonian beliefs, Hebrew Israelites, Lutheran, Catholic, Baptist, Seventh Day Adventist, Methodist, Sunni and Sufi Islam, Nation of Islam, Moorish Science, Temple of America (MS.7.A – an Islamic branch), Asatru, Odinist, Christian crusaders, Christian identity, Kingdom Identity Ministries—and much more.

In my studies in the different schools of thought that exist, I am able to see how others perceive their truths and how they walk the paths they adhere to. Many of these systems of beliefs are very popular in the 9th Dominion (prison) and are coveted for their ideology that is supposedly exclusive. Many are based in bigotry, hatred, separation, superiority, and chaos. I believe any appeal to what is morally good must be an appeal to what is good for anyone, not just what is good for oneself or for one's kinship group or ethnicity. Any religious concept that does not do so is counterfeit. It is the form of the will to power masquerading as virtue and a perverting moral sense.

Each man is the result of what he believes. The chaotic, unbalanced, and distorted doctrines and holy texts I have had the opportunity to study are written in a format to superimpose personal hatreds and dislikes and have been arranged in a preferred way of living. Of the many religious texts and tomes that exist, the majority have been written by man and come from a culture of thought and the experiences of man. I always take this into account when studying different systems of belief.

Morality is often described as a set of standards that are generally accepted as right or proper, but what is left out of this definition is the question: Right or proper according to whom? If morality is defended by an aristocratic group of people, the conformity to their interest makes non-aristocratic individuals acceptable and tolerable to what is right and proper in their oppressor's view. However, in the struggle to define self, while pursuing a destiny independent of aristocratic boundaries and limitations, the aforementioned will be labeled immoral according to their efforts of resisting oppression. A perfect example would be the earthquake that struck Haiti in 2010. Pat Robertson, from the Christian Broadcasting Network, stated that the Haitian Africans' disaster and misery came from a pact they made with the devil over 200 years ago.

This "pact with the devil" in truth was a slave revolt against the European French slave owners and Napoleon's armies. Boukman Dutty, an African priest, held a religious ceremony in preparation for their dangerous undertaking. On the eve of the revolt, they invoked their gods to ensure victory. When the insurgent African slaves went into battle against the French troops, they hurled themselves against the French battalions with Divine courage.

This war lasted twelve years. It was Toussaint Louverture, who had risen to military commander of the slave revolt, who defeated Napoleon Bonaparte, the French general who had conquered the known world. Haiti declared its independence in 1804. The U.S. refused to recognize it until 1862 because of the Haitians's resistance to oppression in the eyes of some of those who had great influence, who considered them minions of a devil and immoral.

There is such a thing as collective insanity, a type of dementia that overtakes an entire population, leading to massacres and atrocities, ending the lives of millions of people. History is a witness to this type of madness. History is filled with many truths, but one must diligently search for them. Like the honey bee gathering nectar from different flowers, the wise man assimilates the essence of different schools of thought, seeking truth in all its diverse forms.

The way to attain personal knowledge of the Higher Self may easily be told, though it may not so easily be practiced. Knowing this, I research the backgrounds of those men and women who founded or contributed their knowledge and experiences to a system of belief. In certain epochs of civilization, when these persons contributed their knowledge, there also was a dominant thought among the masses, and piousness was exhibited through xenophobia.

Any information, knowledge, encouragement, or instructions given to the subconscious mind must be in compliance with the compartments already there, otherwise the thoughts will be expelled. Suggestions that are in compliance with one's personality will take immediately, and others will be mulled over and mixed with the compartments already in the subconscious mind.

Synergy cooperation theory has been described as the unpredictability of behavior or a system of a whole because of the separate behaviors of any of the parts is real co-operation. Blending and cooperation between two energies is necessary for physical phenomena, such as that seen in group thought. It can account for the most monstrous and magnificent moments in human history. Also, a negative collective consciousness, like a germ, can inflect people and take hold.

Germany, for example, may have been affected on a quantum level, making it easier for Hitler, an intoxicating speaker, to create a collective consciousness that fed on itself and condoned the devastation that laid waste to so many. This type of group thought can be seen in nineteenth and twentieth centuries and in Puritan and colonial America. The archetypal ideal injected into a group mind by being realized and lived with destroy ideas antagonistic to it and coalescing with ideas that are sympathetic, thereby changing the whole tone of the group mind. This is something that, as a student of Truth, I cannot ignore.

Dr. Ernest Holmes states, "Race suggestion is a very real thing and each individual carries around with him many impressions which he never consciously thought of or experienced. Each individual's subjectivity is his use of the One Subjective Mind and when subjective unity is maintained between all people, their mentalities are sympathetic with each other. This is the meaning of mental influence." Race suggestion is a prolific source of disease, and many have not been able to avoid it.

Phineas Quimby said, "Disease is what follows the disturbance of mind or spiritual matter.... Disease is what follows an opinion. It is made up of mind, directed by error, and truth is the destruction of this opinion."

Slave codes in America, Barbados, and Jamaica in 1661 and 1664 named punish-ments for African slaves "who shall offer any violence to any Christian." It was understood that "Christian" signified European. Because of the relationships between Christianity and slave owners, many African slaves came to the conclusion that they could win their freedom simply by getting baptized. Destabilizing the racial-religious hierarchy, these African Christians caused a belief crisis for America's developing "slaveocracy." Lawmakers responded by explicitly rejecting any connection between religion and free/slave status. Becoming Christian would not remove the chains.

The Christian/heathen distinction was phased out of European laws in favor of explicit references to skin pigmentation. For religion to have no effect on the legal status of African people was actually favored by many Christian missionaries, who feared that if slaves could free themselves by accepting Jesus, they might use the religion to their advantage to try and improve their conditions. This fear was manifested in a Baptist preacher and leader of a slave revolt named Nat Turner.

Hundreds of laws placed restrictions on the spiritual lives of African slaves, and many wrong beliefs and teachings have been passed on from antiquity until today. Time catches up with empires and kingdoms and crushes them. It gets its teeth into doctrines and bends them. Time reveals the foundations on which any kingdom rests, and it destroys them by proving them to be false. To accept the past and learn one's history is also learning how to use it, to apply it. A fabricated imaginary past can never be used. It cracks and crumbles under the pressures of life.

I had to study history in the correct way. I had to bring to my attention the worldview of a historical period, the ideologies, feelings, thoughts, likes, dislikes, and beliefs. History is not just the evolution of technology; it is the evolution of thought. I have grasped how my everyday view of the world developed and how it was molded by the reality of those who lived before me. I now understand how the reality of this age is being defined by those who hold great influence over the minds of millions.

I believe each person who walks this planet is a translator. The infinite wisdom of the words of God yields different meanings when read in different states of being— and every single one of them is intended. Perhaps, in time, the world will right itself, but until that time of evolution has arrived, one must trust in that wisdom that is greater than his own.

Mr. Paul, I have expounded on certain aspects of history in order for you to comprehend my perceptions somewhat. I know things grow and change in order to become what it is they are truly intended to be according to their inherent natures. I myself had to grow and evolve in order to perceive the deeper layers of self, which disclosed higher levels of reality. The human heart chooses truth or lies, light or darkness. It was darkness and dark experiences that started me on my path, yet at each state in my journey, God appeared. The Most High will often use the dark to provide a tool that leads to wisdom, using negative forces to accomplish something positive.

My life has been an intimate dance of light and darkness. Light has attracted dark and dark has attracted light. I've recognized the Divine design of this, the loss of my only child whom I love dearly, while I was within this realm was something that vigorously forced me into a very dark place of madness, violence, rage, and pain. Yet sometimes the loss of something or someone can strengthen a man's soul to the point where he can endure without it. The Soul knows when it is time for one to go to the next level of spiritual discipline, training, and learning.

Within the 9th Dominion, I have been seriously challenged by the dark on a physical level as well as on a spiritual plane, in my battle against it. My victory gained was that to love is a requirement of light.

Isaiah 45:7 reads, *"I form the light and create the darkness: I make the peace and create evil: I the Lord do all these things."*

Science of Mind was a system of belief I was unaware of, had never heard of. But the name alone emitted an awareness to that which lay dormant. By inquiring about it, I knew the knowledge gained would give me guidance and direction to knowledge I had already attained.

Rev. Mary wrote something in a *Creative Thought* magazine that compelled me to write to her. To have my humanity acknowledged by such a beautiful person was, in my eye, a Divine gift. The inner alchemist has taken control of the forefront of my being and has transmuted, refined, and enhanced that which I deemed imperfect. One speck of God's created substance adheres to another of God's creation, for no parts of God's substance can be misplaced or placed where it is not wanted. Dr. Ernest Holmes stated, "Creation means giving of form to substance of Spirit. Spirit being All and Only, there is nothing for it to change into but Itself."

Since my incarceration for my foolish transgressions, I have often contemplated my life, knowing I am the culmination of a series of events that have allowed me to arrive at this moment. I have been sent on a path and as part of my destiny and kismet. I was taught how to defend myself and focus in on a discipline and survive. I considered all of my religious studies and how they prepared me to pray and increase my faith while under siege. I considered the different landscapes of this realm that I have inhabited and the information that came to me, whether in the form of a book, a teacher, or an observation.

The path I follow has been filled with experiences, temptations, tragedies, losses, gains, ambitions, disappointments, blessings, unexplained phenomenon, negativity, positivity, and a constantly changing series of decisions and choices. All these have been strewn along my path, and I consider them all signposts pointing in the same direction to a new and Higher Truth. Truth in itself is ever the same, unalterable and unchanging. Yet while I could see it as changing, the reality was that I was changing, because my perception of Truth changed as I traveled through this life.

There is still much I have to learn, and I will put all the knowledge I have acquired to paper in a tome that will assist others on their quest to reach what Science of Mind calls the Christ Consciousness.

12/18/14

DEAR MICHAEL,

Your words to Paul meant a lot to him. We both took ministerial training together, so we have a special life relationship. At a spiritual level we are all one, yet life looks so different to all of us on the outside. As an example, think of a colorful balloon bouquet. The air in each balloon is the same, yet on the outside each one is different in color, shape, and size. If we break a balloon, all of the air merges with "the air," the Oneness, yet for a while, each one appeared different to us.

Looking at this spiritually, if we were a balloon, we might judge other balloons by their color or stature, yet we would have the ability to find out that on the inside, we were alike. We would not have to wait until our outer shell burst and we again became one with the air to discover our unity, but it would be our choice. Like a balloon, when our outer shell bursts, we die and again become one with the Universe. If we learn and understand our true nature while we are still here, life can be a blissful experience. As we grow in our understanding, we take the new knowledge with us as we make our transition. Our outer shell bursts and we move on.

12/22/14

DEAR REV. MARY,

The power of prayer is something I have borne witness to. There was a time that I would negate my prayers by allowing doubts to creep into my thoughts based on appearances and others' pessimistic opinions. I've learned to pray aright and now hardly ever let confusion, uncertainty, and doubt enter into the Law of Cause. This has been the apex of my studies of Science of Mind, for my faith strengthens day by day as I cultivate and nurture my faith with patience and forgiveness.

Early in my prison sentence, my mother and sisters came to visit me. My mother told me that she and my little sister had gotten into a physical altercation. I was so upset at my sister because this to me was the most disrespectful, unforgivable act, for a child to lay hands on their parent. Only last year, I decided to write my sister and let her know that I had forgiven her and I did not hold it against her. I knew there was something deeper that eventually led up to it, that I never had her side of the story. But holding indignation toward her was hurting me in ways I didn't even realize. After deep reflection, I wrote to her, which released my negative resentment. I felt so much better.

The mind can contain so many small, noxious peeves that can hinder one, so I search my mind and heart daily, trying to purge all negative seeds that have taken root over the years of my life. There is a book I came across a few years back called *The Celestine Prophecy,* and if my memory serves me correctly, two books that are related called the *9th Insight* and the *10th Insight.* Have you read these? They were stories of spiritual discovery that led me to a higher awareness and way of being.

CHAPTER 7

2015

Signs and Guideposts
Light the Way

Rediscovering my humanity — Tired of prison life — I can teach. I can lead. I can play more. I can make people laugh — Understanding the nature of Spirit — Shedding habits, behaviors, and things that no longer contribute to my life — The great work of influencing our environment is accomplished by mental power — If the Universe is mental, the mind must be the highest power affecting its phenomena — Completing the "Impact of Crime on Victims" program, including apologizing, making amends, and serving our community — Coming into this environment, I created a persona that would enable me to navigate this labyrinth of madness — The ideology that somehow misery and suffering are ordained conditions haunts the prison system — I've created a mantra that brings me peace: "God doesn't think frustration, so I shall not." — In the hole for another five or six months.

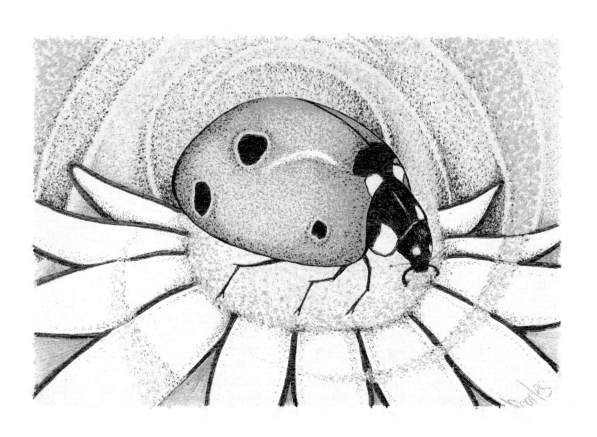

1/25/15

DEAR REV. MARY,

I have been moved from 4-house to 6-house to 3-house within the past couple of months. The administration is unsure where they want to place me, but it has given me a chance to get the lay of the land, as they say. Right now, I was put on mandated single-cell confinement. Under this sanction, an inmate will spend at least ten years in the hole or more. This is usually applied to prisoners who have caused death by violence or other means, or prisoners who have taken staff as hostages. I fit into none of those categories. I had an assault against another prisoner at the time, but I refused to believe that would remain under this sanction. After reading the literature you sent me, I knew I would not remain on this status.

During the time I was down there, I took an anger management class, a program called "Taking a Chance on Change." I got a poem published, and I also got my ordained minister credentials. To make a long story short, I was involving myself in an idea in order to then evolve the idea into a tangible form. I was contributing to my prayers. I was in a predicament that 99 percent of prisoners would remain when on it, yet at the right time I came across the right information and contacted the right person who was able to teach me about right thought. Then and only then was I released from the hole in 2009. Pure demonstration through the creative power of prayer. It is because of this situation that I will never doubt this, and my faith has increased.

In his introduction to the book, *The Essential Ernest Holmes,* Holmes wrote, "What's really important here is your study of yourself." What Ernest or anybody else has had to say is secondary to the immediate, personal experience of your Source that you are having at all times. There are no special revelations, because everybody is receiving spiritual insight and revealing the spiritual quality of nature with every thought and act. "You, then, are your own healer, guru and guide," he wrote. "Everything you seek is where you are now. A sense of oneness is right where you left it."

I have completed several journal pages that I thought might interest you:

Journal Page:

I believe that when doing healing work, many methods should be applied. I personally believe the human body is programmed for health, not illness, and can, with the use of different methods, overcome many diseases. I say this because there is one certain cure known in every medical school in the world as the one single method that will produce a guaranteed healing effect. It is known disparagingly as the placebo, and many medical professionals are taught to dismiss or ignore it. Every new drug on the market, in fact, will have been tested against it in order to rule out the placebo effect and ensure that the drug itself is doing the work. How is it that the one thing we know will guarantee healing, the mobilization of the body's natural resources, activated through the power of faith and belief, is not taken more seriously?

I believe right action is complete by using whatever means necessary to engage the client so that she or he is party to her or his own healing. The client's power of faith and belief are activated by our own treatment of right action and the energy of the illness. It is cause rather than effect. The how and the what is defused, allowing the physical symptoms to disappear. The placebo effect, as I am using it, is a way of empowerment, so that the patient's faith in his or her own abilities and strength is changed. In this aspect, if one has a specific outcome aimed toward healing, recuperation, and strong thinking, I don't believe it will have a lesser outcome or execute itself. For even the patient will have a specific outcome within his or her mind that may be more powerful and play a more important part than those doing the healing work.

I do not believe the role of feeling has been stressed enough. I say this because if one were to engage in a prayer treatment, perhaps he has just lost a loved one, this person's feelings might not be negative in effect, but he is going through emotional variables and this could affect the outcome of a treatment that he has partaken of.

Journal Page:

This morning I awoke with an incessant thought in my head—that I have to rediscover my humanity. Being in prison for so long has had a deep effect on my psyche. Even in my dreams, whether I dream about family, friends, or anything beyond, it is the prison landscape that dominates. Being incarcerated for a long time allows one to be conditioned by prison life, and it takes a lot of mental toughness to break that conditioning. Getting transferred to this new facility made me realize that I'm tired of prison life. I've outgrown this prison mentality and this prison lifestyle. I've outgrown my punishment. Rediscovering my humanity is one of my activities for this month.

Journal Page:

This week I started in a program called Impact of Crime on Victims Class or ICVC. We do weekly writing exercises with the whole group. We craft detailed descriptions of our crimes and our role in them. In vivid detail, we try to describe the harm we think was done to victims and their family and friends. Finally, we write a letter of apology to the victim and to the family of the victim and devise a plan for making amends and serving our community. Guest visitors who have been victims of crime also come and speak to us.

Journal Page:

This week in ICVC, I was elected as the person to begin and end the classes with positive quotes. I was given a small notebook to write my quotes in, and I have many. "The ability to forgive and the ability to love are the weapons God has given us to enable to live fully, bravely, and meaningfully in a less perfect world," by Rabbi Harold Kushner.

Journal Page:

This month I prepare myself for inevitable changes that I must make to elevate my being and to reach my highest aspirations. Benjamin Franklin once said, "Your net worth to the world is usually determined by what remains after your bad habits are subtracted from your good ones."

Journal Page:

Today I've realized that fantasies are aspirations without a plan and without the work. And when that cloud turns into rain, the fantasies will come crashing to the ground with it, because there's nothing real to hold it up. I know that a foundation is something I must build and all my aspirations must be built on a foundation in order for me to succeed.

The world is a far more mysterious place than most people realize. Every moment of life is woven through with meaning. The world is filled with mysteries. Every mystery will either explain itself or it won't. One cannot force nature to draw back her curtains and reveal the hidden machinery that constitutes the true workings of the world.

Last night, I was considering the immensity of the universe. I conceived of something so beautiful that it brought tears of happiness every time I brought it into my consciousness. A thought occurred to me that this life I am living now in the present is actually a past to a life I had already lived in a parallel future. And that my future parallel self has left behind symbols, signs, and guideposts that would help me for the time ahead, foretelling an encounter or an indication that I was at the right place at the right time and moment. Symbols that revealed the progression to the next stage of my spiritual development include signs and experiences that would aid me and affect me profoundly, spiritually, emotionally, and personally.

I've learned that the great work of influencing one's environment is accomplished by mental power. In back of and under the various teachings I have studied remains ever the constant principle of the Mental Substance of the Universe. If the Universe be mental in its substantial nature, then it follows that mental transmutation must change conditions and phenomena in the Universe. If the Universe is mental, the mind must be the highest power affecting its phenomena. If this be understood, then all the so-called miracles and wonder workings are seen plainly for what they are.

My understanding is that there are many people who have progressed greatly in their learning, yet they have not taken their understanding beyond the borders of limitation. There is truth in everything and there is also refinement in all things, for each moment refines truth. God is in a state of ever becoming. Each man and woman can continually progress in his or her understanding to encompass more unlimited truth. Any teachings that teach limitation are coming from those who simply have accepted that to be their truth and, as Emerson wrote, "The finite alone have wrought and suffered," but a greater and more refined truth is that those who have taught that life is unlimited will experience ongoing-ness. In this way, "The Infinite lies stretched in smiling repose."

Journal Page:

The philosopher Lao Tzu said, "When you let go of what you are, you become what you might be." I now know that I had to let go of who I thought I was in order for me to create a completely different life. Coming into this prison environment, I created a persona that would enable me to navigate this labyrinth of madness. It wasn't until I let go of what I thought I was and embraced what I know I really am that things began to change in my life.

4/11/15

DEAR MICHAEL,

Can you recognize that even one thing that happened to you these past weeks is the result of seeds sown earlier, last month or a year ago? If so, what a beautiful expression of evolution for you! We learn by trial and error or more gracefully by the assistance of spiritual teachers, like Ernest Holmes, who wrote, "We are not punished for our sins but by them." This may be good news or bad news, but it is true. As individuals, it is up to us to mentally lift ourselves above the Law of Averages and reach a higher understanding of Spirit and Law. In the Law of Averages, if we choose not to work for a greater understanding and a more positive life experience, we get potluck and the result is an average existence. By studying spiritual laws and using this knowledge, we will not have a potluck life.

If all it takes is a little effort, why wouldn't everyone live a heavenly life? We let ego and willpower tip the scales so we think brightly colored balloons are goals in and of themselves. In life experiences there are three actors: the changeless Self, which doesn't shine as brightly as it could due to negative aspects of our personality; the individual ego, which is how we identify ourselves; and this sense of separateness, the illusion that adds confusion and holds us back from self-realization. Part of the power of self-will comes from our five senses. Outer experiences have a great hold on our quest for knowledge and beliefs.

To make sense out of this, it helps to begin by developing a greater understanding of why we are here. The sacred text *Upanishad* says that as a spider weaves a web out of itself, God weaves the web of the Universe from Itself. When Holmes wrote, "The nature of God is reenacted through us," he meant we are part of this web of life, that our nature is identical with God's nature because we are God's divine creation. The Universe is nothing but the play of God's energy.

God as the Universe in full expression is vividly described by astronaut Edgar Mitchell in his book *The Way of the Explorer.* He writes, "We've discovered that matter is interconnected and 'resonates' in some mysterious manner throughout the entire universe, and patterns repeat themselves as though a template were being used over and over again on different scale sizes." Through the "butterfly effect," he describes the impact our individual decisions have on everything, large or small, just as minute changes in the atmosphere can dramatically change a weather pattern.

Patterns in our life repeat themselves, but it is our personal choice and belief that influences their direction. Like Holmes and Troward, Mitchell writes that life itself is the only vehicle for learning. He believes this is true not only for us but also for the Universe as a whole. He believes each life expresses one of nature's emergent potentials that may prove significant for the whole of creation.

4/21/15

DEAR REV. MARY,

I just graduated from the ICVC class last week. There was a victims' panel from the free world who attended our graduation to share their stories about some very negative experiences in their lives. Everyone in our class was given an opportunity to give a brief description of their crime and what they got from the class. I also presented the victims with the book of quotes I had been reading in our classes daily, as a token of the whole class's appreciation for them taking time to come into this environment and speak with us. I intend on participating in other programs that will benefit me in my revival with my own humanity. You will be receiving the worksheets a couple of days after you receive this.

Also, since I do not have any resources here that impart on Hinduism, if you can send me Sri Aurobindo's book *The Life Divine,* I will make a workbook from it. At first it will just be an outline sample, and I would like your critique on how to improve it. The library has typewriters, but we have to purchase our own ribbons and typing paper.

Today, religion properly understood is the science of evolving from the state of spiritual infancy to a more perfected state. The word science comes from the Latin *scire* (to know, denote, to mark out plainly, indicate, to make known, a system of knowing). A scientist is one who is involved in the study and practice of a subject following a set of rules that confirm and certify the fact that knowledge has taken place. Science gives you the ability to know that you know, a requirement that most people in their scholarly pursuits are oblivious to. A major key in science is the factor of experience and experimentation. In studying Science of Mind (it was the name that drew me to inquire about it in the first place), I find it is based on certain knowledge—a combination of faith, metaphysics, quantum physics, mysticism, sociology, and Universal Laws. The adherents of Science of Mind are not guided by a specific doctrine or dogma but by scientific understanding of the human mind, actions, and man's relationship to God. This is to me what makes Science of Mind a science.

Dr. Holmes taught that the relationship of Science of Mind with other religious concepts is the thing of unity. Like the honeybee that collects its nectar from various flowers, so it is with New Thought. It has accumulated knowledge from many different "flowers" of thought. The entity historically identified as the Egyptian God Tehuti, also known as Thoth, is known to ancient Greeks as Hermes Trismegistus. The written work of Tehuti has come to be known as the Hermetic Philosophy. I call it the Hermetic Principles of Tehitu. This philosophy and the concepts were also studied by Dr. Ernest Holmes and is discussed throughout his written work. By accepting the lessons, experiences, and ideology of the past and taking the best from everything, we should press boldly forward, looking ever for truth and ever ascending higher and higher into the heavens of reality.

4/28/15

DEAR MICHAEL,

In *The Science of Mind,* Holmes says, "Nothing could give form to a formless stuff, which has no mind of its own, but some Intelligence operating through it." The lowest level is atomic intelligence, physical things such as rocks, trees, dirt. Next is the simple consciousness we find in the animal kingdom, followed by personal consciousness, which we also experience in degrees, and eventually cosmic consciousness. From one end to the other, all is perfect— all will eventually move up the scale, no matter how erratically or slowly each one progresses. It has been said that a cloud cannot obscure the sun forever. We cannot obscure our true nature forever. Eventually, all forms of life will see the sun and reach cosmic consciousness. The degree to which we develop our personal consciousness in this lifetime is how we influence this process.

The conclusion of experiments studied by Dr. Edgar Mitchell suggests that all of nature is in a sense wavelike, field-like, and mind-like and that nature's energy moves forward through irreversible processes on a macro level. At this level, the processes of decay and creation operate continually, moving forward (i.e., Troward's upward spiral), all without a loss of energy on the micro scale. We know that in every moment we are either the creators or destroyers of our heavenly experience, which is why I find Mitchell's theory, which he terms the Dyadic Model of Reality, helpful. It is a more technical understanding, which gives greater definition to meta-physics and co-creation, yet no model is big enough to include the Truth.

We know by experience that as we correct errors and shift to a more positive way of creating joy in each moment, our life experience improves. In this model, the Universe does the same thing at a fundamental level; the Universe learns through a feedback loop process. If the Earth is eventually blown apart by nuclear weapons, the Universe learns and shifts and will continue evolving on a new and more successful path.

5/2/15

DEAR REV. MARY,

I'm responding to what you wrote about the prisoners in Florida studying with you and how different their ability is to be allowed to study Science of Mind. Within the State of Missouri, there are at least eight level-five prisons. I have been in five of them. Within my twenty-four years of incarceration in these prisons, the religion preference has always been the same. It is different sects of Islam, Wicca, Asatru Odinism, Catholic, Christian, and Native American. Many of these religious groups are gang structured, and their beliefs keep the inhabitants within these realms divided. All are in conflict with each other. The Department of Corrections encourages this type of behavior, and I believe it may be the same in prisons across the United States. Religions that are under New Thought, Buddhism, Vodun, Hinduism, or Santeria are not on the chaplain's list of religious preferences.

Prisoners who have come into contact with me are now aware of Science of Mind. Before, that was practically unheard of within these realms, but I believe that is going to change. Science of Mind is a system of knowledge that would elevate the average prisoner into a new mind state of positivity.

I have learned so much from Science of Mind, it has rearranged my whole way of being. There was a time when I constantly had to tell myself, day in and day out, "No negative thinking; think positive." It became my daily mantra. Now it is as natural as blinking and breathing. Because of Science of Mind, I've been able to heal myself when negative thoughts plague my mind. It would arouse anger, resentment, dislike, hatred, hostility, which would give me migraines. I haven't had a headache in a few years.

One of the things about you, Rev. Mary, is that you, unlike many, will actually respond to those in prison who have reached out to learn about Science of Mind. I truly admire you for this. You are hands-on if one is truly willing to learn. I truly believe that the more prisoners who embrace the teachings and apply them will upset the dynamic of prisons' religious attitudes.

5/10/15

DEAR MICHAEL,

Although the scientific study of this process is still young in the history of the world (and in prisons!), we can clearly see how humanity has misused thought and spiritual laws to create many sad and ugly conditions in the world. The negative consciousness in every society casts a shadow that is always equal to its height and width. This is why the phrase, "Change your thinking, change your life," is so powerful, because it is that simple. Jesus presented this same message when he taught the Law of Life, "It is done unto you as you believe," and not any other way.

It takes effort to corral our thoughts without bargaining or trying to coerce the Universe. It requires us to embody the attributes of what we want and then consciously let go and allow the Universal Power of Mind to operate through us. Intent is the key. The challenge is to live each moment being aware of what we are thinking and doing; to check in with ourselves and look at our intent, our motivation, to determine if it is based on fear or love.

5/15/15

DEAR REV. MARY,

Journal Page:

I have personally seen Unconscious Invitation, as described by Dr. Ernest Holmes in classes of the same name, in many different scenarios. I've seen this happen when the mind is too rigid or settled into a static position. I've seen it in the environment in which I dwell as intimidation and paranoia. When circumstances have frightened one, the imagination tends to take over, filling one's mind with endless anxieties, the imagination vexed with insecurities. They will sometimes envision dangers where none exist. They will try to interpret what others say or do as somehow implicitly involving them, and this will cause them to turn their thoughts inward.

I've seen Unconscious Invitation in the syntax used frequently termed "bad luck" and "good luck." Many people believe that events of life are determined by factors beyond their control because the events may be physically removed from them. Thus, one hears on many occasions people speaking of their bad luck or good luck as though it were something happening independent of themselves. They may feel that events, especially those that are unpleasant, are against them.

I've seen Unconscious Invitation arrive through descriptions, the descriptions of things, places, or people that compel one to behave always according to the terms it indicates. Therefore, many actions emanate from a description that subsequently tends to revalidate it. Descriptions can keep one chained to a form of being and behavior, that while it may appear absolute and definitive, it can be interrupted, opening unlimited possibilities in what man can be or do. When one allows suggestions and/or thoughts to enter his mind as an erroneous condition, circumstance, or influence, he lays out a welcome mat and in comes Unconscious Invitation.

When I read what Holmes wrote—"The person who can throw himself with a complete abandon into the Limitless Sea of Receptivity, having cut loose from all apparent moorings, is the one who will always receive the greatest reward."—it sounded so freeing. There is something greater than me at work and it takes incredible faith to see the spiritual perspective of a challenge. God is creating something and it is enormous. Many times, that which seemed to me a great challenge will appear in my life and it is simply a herald of prosperity, if I choose to see beyond the outer appearances. These are the times when I am urged to see the bigger picture, that God is in everything and everyone, and that something bigger is trying to be birthed through the challenge. Throwing myself with complete abandon into the Limitless Sea of Receptivity, I am no longer subject to doubts or negative schemes. By paying attention to that Divine Voice and Force within, I am able to become what I have been fated to become.

True faith is untouchable. By definition, anything that attacks it is not only false but, also doomed to be exposed as such, which is why I believe there are martyrs. The ultimate that can be offered against any true faith holder (Holmes's description of identification) to force him to change his beliefs is a threat to destroy him utterly, to cancel out his Universe, leaving only nothingness. But for the true faith holder, even this threat fails, since he and that in which he has faith are one, and by definition that which he has faith in is indestructible.

One may ask, why can't someone who merely believes be just as immune to having his personal universe destroyed? The answer is this: because merely believing, if one defines the word separately, implies something to believe that is something apart from the believer. In other words, we have two different things in a partnership: the believer and his belief. A partnership can be dissolved, partners can be divorced or separated, but the faith holder is his faith. He and It make not two, but a single thing. Since he and It are the one, there's no way to take it from him. (Sorry for my crude explanation!)

Journal Page:

For the last couple of months, I have had six different cellies (roommates). All have had different beliefs and mind states. One of my cellies, who did not consider himself any denomination but studied and quoted from the Bible, told me that he always asks God that he be given a celli who is spiritual. He said that he knew that I was a spiritual person before he even came to the cell. To me this was prayer manifesting itself on this plane.

I began to think this is the perfect prayer to release into the universe, because it can eliminate those negative thoughts that can pop up in one's head. Like I hope my celli is like this or that or I hope he is this way or that way. Asking for a person who may come into my cell to be a spiritual person is a mental equivalent that banishes all other thoughts.

Journal Page:

One thing I have learned and understood from studying Troward and Holmes is that we have the ability to see increased realms of possibility, alternatives unseen by others. Understanding the concepts that center on things that were or could be and on illusions that spoke of reality, there is no reason why something couldn't be because then it could be. And if you wanted it to be, then you only had to find where it was, for the possible is always there. One must first believe firmly in his mind that what he sets about he will accomplish and only then can one succeed in translating his powers from that which can be to that which is.

A stated reality cannot be dispelled in its entirety. Alternatives are possible within all circumstances. The knowledge I've attained lies in knowing these circumstances and when to apply the knowledge and harness the energy required for success in all endeavors. The Universe is undisturbed by human stupidity and ignorance of what one can really be. The Universe waits for one to come to his senses and know himself aright. Once one knows himself as Mind, he forevermore controls his experience through ideas, and not through the manipulation of material events alone.

You previously shared a case where a medical diagnosis for a friend of yours was not helpful until looked at from a metaphysical viewpoint. My understanding is that diagnosis is defined as the identification of a disease; to distinguish, to know; the art or act of identifying a disease from its signs and symptoms; to distinguish characteristics. A concise technical description of a taxonomic entity is giving its distinguishing characters; investigation or analysis of the cause or nature of a condition, situation, or problem.

From a medical viewpoint, a diagnosis is identifying a malady by its symptoms, such as a fever could indicate to the physician that one has a cold. Also, a medical diagnosis identifies an illness as either organic or neurotic in origin. It also aims at eliminating the disease or disorder. Successful treatment may be measured objectively. A patient is more likely left with uncertainty and doubts when the doctor cannot locate the ailment in the body or decide its origin. When the explanation of sickness is given in biomedical terms, the patient usually does not understand—and curing the disease does not change the person's social lifestyle and relationships. Many physicians and doctors do not rely on their own experiences of sickness.

From the medical viewpoint of prognosis, the metaphysician also considers that the body is not separate from the essence and perfection of reality. Metaphysicians state and know the nature of spiritual reality. A prognosis from a metaphysical viewpoint does not put any limitations or boundaries on curing and recovery. The metaphysician knows that the intelligence within the human body is a lower form of intelligence that responds to the higher form of intelligence and that within *ad infinitum* there is no disease.

The metaphysician is any doctor, practitioner, spiritual healer, or psychic who is interested in a person's correct health or their desire for good health. He or she suggests healing remedies and practices that lead to better and more positive lifestyle preferences for the patient, whether they are orthodox or unorthodox therapies and medicines. The metaphysician knows the human body is naturally programmed for health, not illness, and will naturally overcome such disease. It is the metaphysician's job to listen to the message of an illness and inform the patient of holistic changes that may be necessary to the life force and environment in which one lives, so that the disease does not return once it is removed.

Diagnosis from a metaphysical viewpoint explains that there is no distinction between mind and body. There is no clear distinction between the oneself and others, for illness can be socially created as well as self-created. Metaphysical diagnosis aims at transforming the experience of illness, as well as the self. Healers rely on Divine Power and Universal Laws and authority when diagnosing the cause of an ailment. Sickness may be interpreted as a positive experience that can save a person from a negative life situation. Healing includes changing a person's social life, dissolving false beliefs, and reconciling with God. Healers often draw on their own sickness experience. It is more than a way of treating external symptoms. It is a process through which a patient will experience the world in a sacred and more profoundly meaningful way.

The patient will also relate to humans in more novel ways and develop a new understanding of what provoked their illness in the first place. The patient can begin a meaningful, enriching, ontological journey, a palingenesis, rebirthing voyage, in which their whole being is renewed. Healing of an illness is turned into a constructive and positive experience.

As a malady becomes more solid and physical, one will become increasingly aware of their emotions and may sense that something is definitely wrong. At this point, the malady is entering the mental self, and it is here that mind goes to work on the problem. One may become consciously aware of some event in the past that still haunts them and seems to have a connection to their feelings and illness. Or perhaps one's mind also becomes affected by the spiritual fallout from an event of which one may still be unconscious. In these cases, mental illness can result. Finally, the effect on the spiritual side will create a physical problem.

The cause of disease will manifest along these lines: from the spiritual (the unseen world) to the emotional to the mental to the physical (the seen world). Stress is a perfect example of this process in action. There is no such thing as a "stress." We cannot examine it or experience it in the way one could a broken bone or a bodily wound. It exists as a phantom in the world of the unseen, yet many are affected by this, emotionally and mentally. It leads to relationship problems, mental anguish, anger, panic attacks, depression, and so forth.

I know that everything in support of wellness is in essence a spiritual remedy. The shamans of antiquity would use specific plants and molds to heal, and they were always thankful to the plant used, because it contained *ashe,* a West African philosophical concept of power, the breath of life within. They knew these plants came from the Creator and could aid in the well-being of the patient. Nowadays plants' healing potency has been modified into pill form, ointments and lotions and teas, but they still contain the essence and aspects of the One who created it.

Journal Page:

This week I was able to grasp a new understanding of the word "religion." The word religion is composed of the prefix re, which means to tie, unite, yoke, as well as the Greek legend, which corresponds to logic and law. I believe that those who composed this word had in mind something that, on the basis of logic and law, reunited that which had been illegitimately separated. Many of my religious studies have shown me that religion is a system designed to help people reunite themselves with God, through the essential qualities they share. So now, understanding this word anew, I truly grasp what the word says.

Journal Page:

I have the tendency to read at least three books at one time. This is something I've always done. I will spend a couple hours reading one book, taking notes, and then I will spend a couple hours reading something else, taking notes. There have been times I will take in information so fast that I simply overlook something. Then I will go back and read the book again and realize I have a different understanding of it than when I previously read it. Rereading *The Essential Ernest Holmes* has given me a brighter clarity from the first time I read it. I also believe that actually using the student workbook gives one an opportunity to actually contemplate what is being taught.

Journal Page:

Today I experienced something I'd like to share that supports mindfulness as a practice. I was sitting on my bunk, eating a couple of cinnamon rolls with peanut butter, when suddenly, out of nowhere, I recalled an incident of my past when a workout partner of mine explained to me how he only ate seven vanilla wafers when he got really hungry. I pondered this discipline awhile as I sipped coffee and ate a cinnamon roll. Immediately, I vowed to eat less. I was present in the moment, chewing slowly, and enjoying the taste and the smell and said a prayer of thanks for the food, which is a blessing.

During those moments of mindfulness, I realized how easy it is to eat less but still enjoy the wholeness of the experience. In the past, I often ate based on cravings and to get full, however that eating habit caused me to gain weight. Eating habitually can go against a reasonable discipline. Mindful eating is as simple as eating less and drinking more water, since that also makes you feel full. Sometimes one has to fool the mind. The wise one knows that the right effect means to try to do one's best diligently toward the right direction. So now I eat for nutrition and begin a way that will lead to less weight and to a healthier life.

Journal Page:

If one wants to succeed in their endeavors for peace—that is, to achieve the anticipated results—one must bring their ideas into correspondence with the laws of the objective external world. If they do not correspond, one will not be successful. After this, one must contemplate the lessons and correct ideas to make them correspond to the laws of the external world. It is a profound truth that external causes become operative through internal causes.

Things can be complicated and are decided by many factors. Many peace activists are within a specific social class and are not living under the yoke of oppression, genocide, or xenophobia. It is not enough to set tasks. One must also solve the problem of the methods employed for carrying them out. If one wants to cross a river, he cannot cross it without a bridge or a boat. It is idle to speak of crossing the river unless the problem of finding a method is solved. The myths and illusions that support the institutions of war have to be challenged. Those who encourage peace must be able to give people better alternatives, offering real hope and real solutions. The mind of those who perpetuate war must be changed, for this is the root: War derives from how people think, so this is where peace must begin, in thought, in mind.

Journal Page:

I have many thoughts about justice, which, from my point of view, is an elusive thing within North America and the world abroad. Violence against women and children, oppression of people of different ethnic origins, discrimination against those of different religious beliefs, and much more are still being played out on a major scale. If memory serves me right, in Great Britain the death penalty was abolished after one person was found innocent who was on death row. In America, the death penalty is still in operation after hundreds have been found innocent who were on death row. If a justice system is flawed, where is the justice to be found in continuing a practice that malfunctions?

I do sense a difference between human justice and Divine justice. "Do all of us get what's coming to us, regardless?" I believe in kismet and destiny. Sometimes people will encounter and experience something or even go through something that will spark a revolution, a change in laws, or begin a movement against or for something. Yet without certain types of people going through a specific thing, it could not or would not change or happen.

I think of the lives of Jesus, Gandhi, and Rev. Dr. Martin Luther King Jr. Gandhi challenged the "Great British laws." Jesus challenged the Pharisees. Dr. King challenged the pre-civil rights laws, the Jim Crow laws, the systemically racist laws, all of which perpetrated injustice. All of them became martyrs, killed presumably because they were a threat to the existing order.

I believe the world was not then and is not now ready for the full power of love as an approach to resolving conflicts, yet students of the philosophy of Science of Mind are practitioners of the Law of Mind. Those who follow this philosophy understand that there is a direct relationship between thought and environment. And they also understand that humankind's primary difficulty lays in the fact that most people's thoughts are largely negative. It is thought that all should look to the mind for the answer to all problems, and then begin to think rightly.

Synergism is the simultaneous action of separate agencies, which together have greater total effect than the sum of their individual effects. Now replace the word "agencies" with "people" and the word "effects" with "power" and it reads: Synergy is the simultaneous action of separate people, which together have a greater total effect than the sum of their individual power. For example, 100 people gather in a room for some common purpose and on a scale from one to ten, each person has a belief in that purpose at the level of ten. Simple math would indicate that the total belief in that room equals 1,000. But the force of synergy, the power of all that combined belief and energy, the total is actually 100,000 or 1 million. Synergy feeds upon itself with results. A concept like this is mentioned in Dr. David Hawkins's book, *Power vs. Force,* where he says that the power of the few individuals at the top counter-balances the weakness of the masses.

For example, according to Hawkins's map of consciousness, one individual at level 300 counterbalances 90,000 individuals. Below Level 200, one individual at level 400 counterbalances 400,000 individuals below 200 and so on. What this tells me, as a student of Science of Mind, is that as human consciousness rises, it creates an exponentially larger capacity to affect others, like in expanding energy waves. Science of Mind students and practitioners have the ability to come together as a single unit of a combined belief, and this organized center of gravity acts like a magnet on individual development. If one is below the average level, synergism has the tendency to pull that person up to the average acceptable level of consciousness development.

Dr. Holmes recognized that it is difficult to control thoughts. He stated, "It is not easy in the midst of pain to think peace, in the midst of poverty to think abundance, in the midst of unhappiness to think joy." Some adherents of Science of Mind ask if there are places for moral indignation and social activism in the Science of Mind philosophy. I say yes, there are. For me, moral indignation is defined as a person being aroused by something unjust. One's conscience is instantly telling them that they are witnessing something that is wrong, and social activism then becomes productive action.

7/10/15

DEAR MICHAEL,

With the increasing acceptance of metaphysics in the world, more people are realizing, as Holmes taught, that we have learned all we need to through suffering and pain. God could not wish us to suffer, but this level of awareness gives us the ability to create our individual life experiences. We move forward at our level of understanding, learning from our mistakes as we make the great discovery of our true perfection for ourselves. Jesus said, "Fear not, little flock, for it is your Father's good pleasure to give you the Kingdom" (Luke 12:32). A powerful way to connect with this kingdom is through spiritual practices. Mitchell writes, "Whenever successful meditative disciplines are employed in the pursuit of insight, they result in reduced stress, an elevated sense of calm, buoyed spirits, a greater awareness of synchronous events, and a heightened receptivity to nonlocal information."

An example of spiritual realization is found in the book, *To Love Is to Know Me,* by Eknath Easwaran. He shares his personal cosmic experience: "Light pervaded everywhere in the form of the Universe. I saw the Earth being born and expanding from the Light of Consciousness." In this moment, he realized there are no specific goals and no limitation in life.

Maybe this is what John meant when he wrote, "You will know the truth and the truth will make you free" (John 8:32). We are free to just be. This is why Holmes taught it is not necessary when we die that anyone ever know we lived…but while we live, we live!

9/1/15

DEAR REV. MARY,

The days and nights within this land have been trying and very chaotic. There has been severe tension and a campaign of harassment, provocation, and violence implemented by the powers that be. During this campaign, many inmates, as well as guards, have been hurt and considered collateral damage, for it is said the ends justify the means. They now can justify new rules and regulations that violate policies and procedures.

Prison politics always reveal themselves to also be moral problems that embody human dilemmas. Their solutions to the problems, which they themselves create, are primitive and cruel. The ideology that somehow misery and suffering are ordained conditions haunts the prison system. The scourge within this land is the insincerity between men, the pestilential Judas Iscariot spirit that poisons human interaction.

I've been listening to men unburdening themselves while I've been here in the hole. They think that for the time being, things are bad; that for the time being, they must make the best of it and adapt or humiliate themselves; and that one day, real life will begin. They prepare for death, complaining that they have never lived, or wait in vain for the day when real life will begin, and so life passes by. For the majority of prisoners I have come across within this realm, not one lives in the present. No one gets any benefit from what he does every day. No one is in a mindset or condition to say, "On this or that day, at that moment, my life began!"

There has been one situation after another after another that has been used in every attempt to provoke me into lashing out, yet I refrain. I ended up in the hole anyway because they were determined to put me in here. I'm intentionally downplaying the events that have been happening in recent months, but through it all I've created a mantra that brings me peace: "God doesn't think frustration, so I shall not."

For now, my Sri Aurobindo study workbook is on hold, as are some other things I intend to send to you. The article that was in the *Science of Mind* magazine was impressive. I was surprised and somewhat flattered. I enjoyed the wonderful energy that was put into the conversation, my imagined conversation with Dr. Ernest. I even made several photocopies of the article and sent them out to friends and family. I will also have a photocopy for the clemency package I've been putting together to send out. I thank you for even considering to put forth a format like that from excerpts of my letters.

When you receive this letter, it is because I've been waiting for a letter from you because I was denied my address book. The majority of us in the hole have been denied numerous items and have had items taken that we are allowed. For instance, they took my writing paper, left me with five stamps and five envelopes. Some inmates had their toothbrush and sheets taken; others, their religious books and family pictures.

I know that a new being is necessary in order to survive within a foul atmosphere that smothers the consciousness of the masses. Yet how can a decent person act within a world as debased and corrupt as this one and during such turbulent times? Perhaps one must find a way to live, even if he cannot act, and perhaps with the hope that thinking and living right may finally come to be a mode of action.

I've never seen such bold gestapo tactics used on a mass scale without guards reporting this behavior to their superiors and to those who run the Department of Corrections. Within this land, men must be healed. Most people understand truths well enough. It is courage and energy they lack, a readiness to sacrifice themselves. The prime need is for one man to speak the truth without regard to convenience or fear.

The gestapo has taken my reading books along with religious books. A lawsuit is the wisest course of action for prisoners to fight for their religious liberties. I don't know what staff expect prisoners to do from morning to night. They spend the best part of their time telling each other stories, many fake and some true. The stories are not entertaining or enlightening, but they tell them anyway.

I know I will be in here for another five to six months, but during my isolated stay, I ask if you could please send me photocopies of tomes to study and photocopies of any literature you deem necessary for my advancement.

I know this condition is temporary and not permanent. They can only do so much for so long. I remain optimistic and positive regardless of the unseemly conditions. The growth of my consciousness has been revealed through a series of illuminating encounters with other people and experiences that have pertained to crucial information or were a time and space where a difficult mental exercise awaited.

Note: In late September 2015, Michael filed a grievance with the Department of Corrections that he was being deprived of his religious liberties in restrictive housing by not having his religious holy book, The Science of Mind.

Response from the DOC:

10/13/15
A REVIEW OF THE EVIDENCE SHOWS OFFENDERS ASSIGNED TO RESTRICTIVE HOUSING UNIT ARE ALLOWED TO HAVE ONE SOFT-BOUND SACRED WRITING. UPON REVIEW, THE ABOVE-MENTIONED BOOK IS NOT CONSIDERED A SACRED WRITING. YOUR COMPLAINT IS DENIED.

10/13/15

A Grievance Response filed with the DOC on 11/13/15 by Michael, complaining he was not being allowed the opportunity to study his religious beliefs while assigned to restrictive housing. He requested to receive The Science of Mind.

Note: Michael finally got a response to his appeal and it read:

12/11/15
UPON RESFARCHING SCIENCEOFMIND.COM, THERE IS NO INDICATION THE MOVEMENT CONSIDERS THE BOOK TITLED, "THE SCIENCE OF MIND" AS A SACRED TEXT. TT IS DEEMED ONLY AS A PRIMARY SOURCE, OUTLINING FUNDAMENTALS OF THE BELIEF SYSTEM, MUCH LIKE A CATECHISM OR DOCTRINAL STATEMENT OF ANY FAITH. THE DOC ADMINISTRATIVE SEGREGATION STATES, "SACRED WRITINGS (BIBLE, KORAN, QURAN, SCROLL, ETC.) RESTRICTIVE HOUSING OFFENDERS MAY BE IN POSSESSION OF ONE SACRED WRITING-SOFT BOUND TEXT." YOU FAILED TO PROVIDE ANY ADDITIONAL EVIDENCE TO SUPPORT YOUR CLAIM. YOUR APPEAL IS DENIED.

CHAPTER 8

2016

Twenty-five Years in Prison, Searching for Truth

Adapting to a primitive and backward environment, like being surrounded by psychic vampires — 2016 is the year I turn forty-four and marks my twenty-fifth year of incarceration — Making this a year of celebration and achievement, overcoming all illusions of obstacles — What began as an academic interest has become a quest for personal and spiritual growth — Right thinking increases and strengthens my faith and puts me in a continuous peaceful state of mind — I feel compelled to search out the vast wisdom and institute every grain of truth so I can continue to evolve and grow — Hopefully the opportunity for freedom will manifest itself — I understand myself as a thought-evolved being — I have ceased to fuss and fume and worry. I remain poised, steadfast, and serene — Knowledge has been my greatest treasure since all else has been taken from me.

1/1/16

DEAR REV. MARY,

A believer, a mind whose faith is consciousness, is never disturbed because other persons do not yet see the fact which he sees.

— RALPH WALDO EMERSON

Pertaining to Chong Ran mindfulness meditation, I did think that it was a true mental discipline. I've read several books that would combine nonfiction with fiction in an effort to enhance the story being told. I appreciate that you were able to find out the truth. I admit I was intrigued by how it was described as a mental discipline, for the knowledge of Mind has formed the spine of my studies for decades.

Well, 2015 was one of those years in which adapting to a primitive and backward environment was very demanding of my energy. It is like I was surrounded by psychic vampires. It had to dawn on me that life in all its forms desires to express itself, yet there also must be a means of articulation, a chosen means. The means intimately controls the nature of what may be expressed. It supports the law by its very nature and, within this land, the inhabitants become that articulation.

They have lived in darkness for far too long and their years of deceptive ideology has worked an evil alchemy upon them, so that their combined thoughts have become an entity of sorts. There is no life without structure. I had forgotten that one must respect the workings of that structure in every guise, for it can only be what it is. Any might is defined and limited by its very nature, for no power can transcend the structures that made its existence possible.

I engage with what is before me and adapt. It is a constant struggle, but it is a positive struggle. Every day I build constructive energy so that I am ensured that I succeed as a creative force.

2016 is the year I turn forty-four. Also, it will mark my twenty-fifth year of incarceration. So, this New Year, I plan on making this a year of celebration, achievement, and

overcoming all illusions of obstacles as well. This year I am also determined to complete my book. I've been working on it for about eighteen years. It has taken a long time to accumulate the information needed to put this type of tome together. I have about 3,000 handwritten pages. I've entitled it *The Grimoire of an African Genius*. I used the word *grimoire* because it indicates a book of magic, but as I explain in the book about magic, a magic trick done by a magician always provokes the question, "How did he do that?" Yet to the magician, who knows exactly what he did, it is not considered in his eyes magic, but sub-rosa knowledge. So, my definition of magic is a person who has mastered the techniques of a specific type of knowledge and has the ability to do something other people do not.

Well, the powers that be have moved me from L2-A to 2-B to 2-D, where I am currently housed for the moment. I will probably be here until March. I've been selected to participate in a correctional science data gathering experiment, called Phase 5 Program Experiment, in which, as always, the majority of the guinea pigs are African males. In the part of the experiment's phase that I am now in, much of what they had taken from us has been given back. Also, we've been given our televisions, but we are not allowed books, which to me is always an indication of foul intentions.

Since I've been in the hole, I've been in a nonstop battle to get my *The Science of Mind* book. Under the law and constitution, this is one thing a prisoner is allowed while in the hole, so I have filed a grievance. Missouri Correctional staff are only familiar with the Holy Bible and the Koran. I've been trying to introduce the people of this land to the twenty-first century, yet it continues to be a battle. I'm sending you a copy of my IRR response. This was the first stage in my grievance process. I am now in the last and final stage. If I am denied, I have an opportunity to file a civil lawsuit against the Missouri Department of Corrections and SECC, so please send the IRR response back to me because, if need be, it will be used as an exhibit and evidence.

I am also sending the fax number to the Deputy Division Director of Adult Institutions in Jefferson City, Missouri, who will decide if I will be allowed to receive my *The Science of Mind* book or not. I gave them pictures of the book and the website, which they blatantly disregarded. If you can possibly fax the Deputy Division Director photos of the book and information that this is a religious book and is considered sacred writings to the practitioners of Science of Mind, you will be like my "Sergeant at Arms" in this battle for religious liberty—and thank you.

William J.H. Boetcker said, "The individual activity of one man with backbone will do more than a thousand men with a mere wishbone." Well, once again, I thank you for your assistance, and the blessing of knowing you has made a profound difference in my life as well as the lives of those whom I interact with.

2/14/16

DEAR REV. MARY,

What began as an academic interest has become a quest for personal and spiritual growth, as well as a search for fundamental universal and human truths. Since I began my studies of Science of Mind, one of my greatest challenges has been to accurately reflect the nature and techniques of the knowledge I've acquired, while at the same time disentangling the practices from the free-world platform in which they are practiced more regularly to fit the 9th Dominion in which I dwell.

Like many others, I was the embodiment of a discordant life script threatened by unregulated evil spirits, anxieties, and negative energies. I vented my anger and rage in explosions of violence, unfocused energy, and illogical actions that had depressing and damaging effects on myself and on others.

Rev. Mary, when you began to teach me about the ways of Science of Mind, I began a healing process within and, also, I began to create a healthier environment to gain mastery of my passions and create more positive experiences in my life and take control of my destiny.

Some people look at the errors in man, the problems of man, the lack of skills on the part of man, the ignorance of man. They look at all the shortcomings and not what he was created for. Rev. Mary, you took a leap of faith in me. You were able to recognize the inherent soul that has been given an excellence. You understood that the limitation put on man does not mean he is imperfect. You've instilled in me a very simple understanding that spiritual development and training is centered on the reprogramming of the mind so that my reasoning has taken as its premise the Divine Laws.

Within this realm, I've missed the kindness of good people who are compassionate when so many are pitiless. There are those people who make their way through this world without corruption, who eschew envy and greed, and who value love and truth and cannot be drowned in a sea of lies. You are one of those people. You are a person who shines—and by the light you cast, you have warmed me. Without your guidance, I do not believe I would have been able to make this leap in evolution so quickly.

Directing my mind toward the Divine, by attuning my emotions and feelings toward expressing love, I have been able to attain mental peace within the maelstrom of this realm. I thank you for everything.

2/20/16

DEAR MICHAEL,

Thank you for your latest letter and IRR Response. I have put together some information that may help you in obtaining *The Science of Mind* text. In addition, I have sent this information to the Deputy Director IRR in order to help them understand the value of the text from a minister's perspective.

Each day I know that your time at Southeast is getting shorter and shorter and pray that your next location is a big improvement so you may have all of your books and writings. If you need a place to keep your writings safe, feel free to send me any for safekeeping. With your brilliant mind at work on the issues of spirit and seeing prison from your enlightened perspective, each writing is precious.

How interesting that you are included in a data-gathering experiment. I don't understand why taking books away is helping anything, but it again deprives people of some ability to escape the present moment or, for spiritual books, to find peace in the present moment. It seems unusually harsh. I applaud your continual focus on staying present to what is, which in itself contributes in positive ways to energize forces around you and the system and the planet.

I just finished a conversation on the phone with a lady who calls me periodically for spiritual coaching. At sixty-eight years old, she finds it extremely difficult to hold on to any positive feelings in her life, so she has a lot of health issues, relationship issues, and a lot of regret. I hope you don't mind, but I read her part of your letter about your twenty-fifth year milestone and your plan to make 2016 a year of celebration, achievement, and to overcome all illusions of obstacles as well. It took her breath away for a second. The rest of our conversation was so much more positive on what she could do to stop her habitual defensiveness and resistance. Once again, your wisdom reaches out in powerful ways.

4/4/16

DEAR REV. MARY,

Let us move on and step out boldly though it be into the night and we can scarcely see the way. A Higher Intelligence than the mortal sees the road before us.

— CHARLES B. NEWCOMB

Thank you for helping me in my endeavor to awaken the gatekeepers of this realm to the reality of the many varieties of systems of belief that they are unaware of. I have not received a decision from the Deputy Division Director as of yet, but I am still waiting.

On April 1, I was released and considered a graduate of the Phase 5 program experiment. I've been put on bed space, so I'm still waiting for a cell in the general population to come open before they actually physically release me from the hole.

They are giving us some of the liberties of the general population while we wait, by allowing us to walk to the chow hall (kitchen) for breakfast, lunch, and dinner, giving us recreation, allowing us to take showers every day and get on the phone. They allow us to go to the canteen once a week and get $5 worth of snacks. I will not be able to go to the property room until my actual release to get the books you sent to me, including *Seven Thousand Ways to Listen* by Mark Nepo.

You mentioned in your letter that you had a conversation with a sixty-eight-year-old woman who found it difficult to hold on to positive feelings in her life. I am glad that portions of my letter that you shared with her were able to have a positive effect on her. This reminded me of the knowledge I gained from the book you sent me called *Power vs. Force* by David Hawkins.

A friend here asked me my opinion of whether there is a Divine Plan. The thought of a Divine Plan does not make me feel manipulated. I personally believe that those who may say this, for them it may be a familiar cliché that they are accustomed to saying, because they may not know how to articulate what they feel, which I believe is one's sacred purpose, known as kismet or fate.

Under the Law of Omnipresence, I believe a Divine Plan and a Divine Pattern are both exactly that: Divine. It is an innate self-actualization in which one unfolds their full potential of mind, body, and emotions in developing the whole organism to fulfill one's inner capabilities, motivated from within, that results in higher fulfillment of life experiences.

I am somewhat familiar with the existence of patterns in nature. I am aware of a science known as teleology, which is the explanation of phenomena in terms of their goals and purpose. The view is that the universe exists and events occur to become what they were intended to be according to their inherent natures. Teleological proof of God's existence concludes that such a complex and intricately designed universe must have a designer manifesting a Divine purpose. It is the study of a final end from the perspective that there is a purpose to life and the universe has created a sort of blueprint or overall design that makes all things meaningful.

The ordering of events happens in accordance with the Laws of the Creator, an energy and principle that determines the course of events, which humanity influences by their thoughts and actions. Then events correlate with mankind's past and present activities, whether recognized or not, for the Laws prevail throughout all eternity regardless of mankind's interest in or knowledge of them. Patterns throughout the universe repeat themselves as though a template were being used over again and in different scale sizes. The patterns in man's life repeat themselves, but it is man's personal choice and belief that influences their direction.

There is a large number of inmates who believe in the written word in the Bible. I recognize that there are numerous people who have been positively and greatly inspired by it. There have been many people who have not been able to truly understand it or apply what was being taught to their lives, and in the hands of the unctuous malevolent (Jim Jones, David Koresh, etc.), the Bible has been used to manipulate, control, and undermine many.

When I studied the Bible, I studied with great enthusiasm 1 and 2 Corinthians and Proverbs. Yes, I believe that it has relevance to the path I am on. I've had experiences that turned me away from the Bible and religion in general, and I've had experiences that have turned me toward it. I wasn't able to spot the symbolic allegorical level of teaching within it until I started my theological studies. Like many, I would take what was written literally, even though my logical reasoning would disagree with it. I also believe that this is where many people may have problems, for it may be hard for the mind to digest certain things that are written symbolically within the Bible. So things may be taken out of context and understood differently than it would be with someone who was a maven in Bible lore and symbolism.

For me, the twin pillars mentioned in the Bible represent Two Trees, the Arbre-Sec (dry tree, sun or solar principle) and the Arbre-Moville (wet tree, moon or lunar principle). These trees represent portals, sentinels, the Universal Reign of Law. In spiritual and psychological terms, they represent something vast and unknown, both within and outside myself. They are the Soul of the Universe, a sacred doorway to enlightenment and Godhood.

Perhaps one would wonder why trees as pillars? Trees have been a sacred motif in many traditional societies and early religious writings. The tree in general has been connected to the attainment of knowledge through interaction with the gods. Adam and Eve achieved wisdom by eating from the Tree of Knowledge. In India, Yama, the first man, drank with the gods beside the cosmic fig tree, Asvattha, which represents eternal life and the cycle of life and death, while the Buddha achieved enlightenment beneath the magical Bodhi tree. In Druid ceremonies, dancing around the maypole or the Tree of Life was once a real tree used to embrace spring and return of life to the fields. Countless traditional people revere the tree in this way. Among Osmali Turks, the Tree of All Life has a million leaves and on each is written the fate of man. For the Mongols, the World Tree is called Zambey, and the Tengeri (gods) feed from its fruits. These Pillars of Trees represent a system that seeks to elevate man to his Divine essence.

Journal Page:

I have a thirteen-year-old nephew and a seven-year-old niece. I've been part of their lives since they were both the age of three. I have been actively teaching them in small increments much of what I have learned from my studies of Science of Mind, as well as studies from other sources. My intentions are for both of them to be able to tap into the Universal Mind consciously at an early age. At birth, the Divine Nature in man slumbers as a potential in the same manner that the ability to understand quantum physics resides in the psyche of a three-year-old. If I am consistent in nurturing this nature properly with proper attention to their well-being, as well as their minds and souls, they will go beyond identifying colors and shapes to manipulating the psychical forces of nature.

Journal Page:

I have been contemplating how children could avoid many of the negative pitfalls we as adults have experienced and have had to learn to avoid in our adulthood. I believe if there were a written format of the Science of Mind teachings designed specifically for young children and young teens, it would enhance their relationship with Universal Mind in a way many other religious teachings have not been able to.

I personally believe all children are gifted in their own individual way. I've come across literature that has called gifted children "Indigo Children" because of their purportedly colored auras. These children have been described as possessing increased empathy, creativity, curiosity, and will. They are also reported to be spiritually inclined from a young age and to exhibit strong intuitive capacities. There is a complete book called *Beyond the Indigo Children: The New Children and the Coming of the Fifth World* by P. H. Atwater.

Journal Page:

Today for the second time, I watched a movie called *Groundhog's Day,* starring Bill Murray. In the movie, he repeats the same thing over and over because he has a negative belief system and outlook on life. The only way he can break the pattern is to change his belief system, and then the Universe allows him to proceed to the next day. The first time I watched this film, I was more interested in it for its comedy content. Watching for the second time, I was able to recognize the parallels of all that I have been studying and its profound message through comedy.

4/23/16

DEAR REV. MARY,

I was finally released on the fourteenth of April and received a certificate for graduating the Phase 5 experimental data-gathering Criminal Thinking Program. Out of seventy-two of us who were put in the program, so far only three of us have made it out successfully.

I've been very busy since my return to the general population getting my business affairs in order. Within the first couple of days out, I probably shook a hundred hands and received a hundred hugs. To tell you the truth, I had no idea how much my presence was missed and by so many. I've only been here a couple of years, yet nine month's absence had a profound impact and the guards even seemed to take notice.

I also received my final response on my grievance appeal the day before I was released. I have included a copy of it and the other responses also within pertaining to getting my *The Science of Mind* religious book while in restrictive housing. As you will see, the SECC prison chaplain here really didn't do his research properly, and I believe he only read what was in the *Science of Mind* magazine, so I sent him to look at the website. His attitude in what he said reflected his ignorance and his blatant falsehood and the denial of the IRR and grievances violates the Religious Land Use and Institution-alized Persons Act exercising religion (RLUIPA).

I went to the law library, and it seems that this could be a very serious lawsuit. I inquired about the 1983 civil lawsuit forms. It costs $350 to file. This is a very expensive fee, one I cannot afford. I would really like your opinion on this matter. Do you think it is feasible to pursue this matter in the courts? I believe I have all the evidence and grounds to fight against this injustice.

Sometimes I question my way of being and how I now respond and/or react to the guards' malice. There was a time when pretty much everything they did seemed to arouse the hostility and open contempt I held toward them. The ability to actually put this new knowledge into practice I have attained from Science of Mind. It has allowed me to meet them on a higher plane of existence and to see what can truly manifest from positive thought and understanding of the Universal Laws.

Right thinking increases and strengthens my faith and puts me in a continuously peaceful state of mind. The tempering of my Spirit could only be achieved by actually practicing the teachings on a regular basis. A person preoccupied with the mental torture of being offended or angered is in a position of being vulnerable to spiritual, emotional, physical, and mental damage.

> *A man being pursued by a lion has to run. If he wastes time*
> *becoming angry with the lion or feels offended by being attacked,*
> *he will be lost.*
>
> **— SOURCE UNKNOWN**

When I got out of the hole, all the books you sent to me were waiting for me in my property. I have a lot of reading to do, so please do not send any more books for the time being. Thanks so much for your support and supplying me with tomes of great knowledge that will aid me in my evolution and growth. You are forever a beacon of light for those who grope within the darkness.

6/15/16

DEAR REV. MARY,

I've been contemplating writing a few Missouri senators about how inmates are being excluded from practicing and studying their system of belief while in ad-seg. Hopefully, I will meet with support on this issue through this route.

Also, I've completed the book by Mark Nepo, *Seven Thousand Ways to Listen*. I found his journey enlightening, reflective, and arduous. On page 208, he describes ways of listening and he lists statements that begin with knowing others have wanted to move the world and were forced to accept how the world moved them—and so on and so on. These were profound statements that spoke to me on another level of being. Also, on page 210, in the chapter entitled "The Endless Search," Nepo states that at deeper levels of one's search, we are like fish who keep swimming, because if we don't keep water moving through our gills, we will die. I feel like this at times. My search is endless, and I crave to know more and more and want to apply all I can—and teach all whom I can as well.

I feel compelled to search out the vast wisdom and institute every grain of truth so that I can continue to evolve and grow. I have a way of thinking that the human being begins at childhood, then proceeds to adulthood, and our next progression should be godhood, a continual growth after we have shed our human flesh beyond this plane of existence.

6/23/16

DEAR REV. MARY,

I have always known there is something in the universe that was vast and more real than the world in which I live—and my Spirit has always inevitably been drawn to it. Prison has the tendency to make one lost, and the prisoner becomes no longer amazed, delighted, or involved in their surroundings. Life for the prisoner becomes lifeless and worthless. Our hunger for love and involvement is replaced with an institutionalized reverence for the vicariousness television entertains, which usually results in a form of trancelike madness.

Not being able to reflect the Divine laws in a positive way, I manifested directives that were at odds with the world, and whenever I vented my frustrations, I sent more negativity out into the world. My consciousness has been raised by controlling and harnessing the energies within. I've been able to destroy the ignorance and other human faults that obstruct the soul from full expression in an individual.

Once the Science of Mind teachings are properly practiced, the internal life force is automatically balanced and raised. I continue to move forward toward my destined goal, and I thank you for showing me the way.

8/31/16

DEAR MICHAEL,

With instant news from around the world and political process for president this year, there seems to be a high level of anxiety and pent-up anger in society. Anxiety seems to be like a virus that has taken a lot of people over the top, doing and saying things they would not normally do. So, my task is to help those who are using Science of Mind in their life to gently remind them that all of these things we see and hear are effects—and every effect has a cause. And the root cause is a separation from our relationship with the Infinite Intelligence that created it all. As more people understand it's all one, we're all brothers and sisters, we're all created as unique beings, created with intense love, we would not do those things that we see, hear, and read about being done to each other.

The principle of Oneness is defined as: There is One Infinite Intelligence, One Source, and One Being, which creates everything out of Itself. We call It many names, including, but not limited to God, Universal Spirit, Universal Intelligence, First Cause, or The Thing Itself. Universal Spirit is undivided, complete, and whole within Itself.

Reflecting on this principle and understanding the creative process helps me stay grounded when things in the world seem a bit out of control. And as you know, it is a daily practice and sometimes several times a day.

11/2/16

DEAR REV. MARY,

Since I've been applying the Science of Mind teachings, I haven't had a physical confrontation with a guard in about seven years. I am amazed at my change, because there was a time when I felt offended, I would nurture my rancor in silence and dissembling guise conceal my enmity until the opportunity presented itself to revenge myself. Yet offense doesn't register any more like it once did.

> *Do not conform any longer to the pattern of this world,*
> *but be transformed by the renewing of your mind.*

— ROMANS 12:2

I must admit that this realm in which I dwell, life can sometimes seem unbearable. Physical and mental pain, difficult decisions, financial hardships, oppression, the death and loss of loved ones, shattered dreams, all these things can engulf you if you let it. But with time and effort, calmness of mind becomes one of the gemstones of wisdom.

I've become calm in the measure that I understand myself as a thought-evolved being. And even though there are many things that happen in this land that I do not agree with, I have ceased to fuss and fume and worry. I remain poised, steadfast, and serene. Those who are screne live a life that dwells in the ocean of Truth, beneath the waves, beyond the reach of the tempest in the eternal calm.

I knew that if I continued to accept only those limited thoughts that had been recycled numerous times, I would never activate greater portions of my brain to receive and experience any thought other than what I had already experienced. Every time I accepted a thought that was greater than what I had accepted as my standard, the greater thought offered itself as a carrier to expand my reasoning from that point onward.

Knowledge has been my greatest treasure since all else has been taken from me. With knowledge, I can create. I can build kingdoms with unlimited vistas. Knowledge urges me to expand, to seek even greater knowledge and to seek an ever-broadening identity of being. I came from the boundaries of a limited way of thinking into a more unlimited expanse. I've become invigorated with simplicity and, in that simplicity, I've found peace of mind and the joy of life.

With this letter, I'm sending you a more recent picture of me with my mother and my baby sister, who is twenty-three. She is a college student in Jonesborough, Arkansas, which is only an hour and forty-five minutes from this prison. She came to visit me by herself on Father's Day this year, and we had an opportunity to converse about her academics and courses that she plans to excel in. She reads a lot of the Science of Mind literature that I have received from you. I make copies and send them to her. I believe it has opened her mind up to more greater possibilities of dealing with the issues that life will present to her.

When she was born, I was given the privilege to give her a middle name, which is Michelle. I've been in prison her whole life, but we are close even under the circumstances of my incarceration. She relies a lot on my wisdom and she is more comfortable speaking to me about things than she would be with our mother.

CHAPTER 9

2017

Understanding the Criminal Mind and How My Behavior Hurts Others

Working toward the possibility of greater wholeness, of positive thought, as well as a consistency of right thinking — Since studying Science of Mind, I haven't had an assault in almost ten years — Realizing my behavior hurt others left me crushed, knowing my choices produced lasting harm in the world — Coming into accountability, I realized how demented and domineering I had become, all derived from fear — As a criminal thinker, my excessive reactions to small events often reveal a negative sociopathic issue — Letting go of old ideas, old habits, and even old lives allows for a new one to grow — I am dedicated to work for the good of others, to eliminate my destructive habits and weaknesses — Divinity has brought me to this point, to be who I truly am.

2/17/17

DEAR MICHAEL,

Last Sunday I was the speaker at our center and the topic I was given was "God Comes Through the Wound." I didn't particularly like the topic, but when I reread your last letter it became very clear that sharing your evolution would be a perfect way to frame that message. Along with it, I added some of Bo Lozoff's writings from his book *We're All Doing Time: A Guide to Emotional Freedom*. It ended up being one of the best talks I've given, if I judge it by the responses I received. And the admiration for your awakening on the spiritual path was supported by audible gasps and "wow" moments throughout the talk. Many said they were so glad to hear we were still communicating and remembered the last time I shared some of your wisdom. I thought you would like to know how many people think about you and really admire your writing.

5/13/17

DEAR REV. MARY,

Just a short note to let you know I'm receiving *Science of Mind* magazine again. Thank you for renewing the subscription for me.

In your book *32 Easy Lessons in Metaphysics and the Science of Mind,* you mention an author named Eckhart Tolle. I just recently read his book, *A New Earth,* a very enlightening book, especially dealing with the destruction of the ego. In this environment, I've witnessed how the ego can lead one into madness. This is a particular subject I will study more about, as well as experiment with to collect data.

I'm going through some chapters within *The Life Divine* to see what I want to put together for you. I am grateful that Science of Mind has been more like a discipline, as well as knowledge, a path, and wisdom.

6/26/17

DEAR REV. MARY,

I received both books you sent by Janet Connor. I've already finished reading *Writing Down Your Soul.* I haven't started the writing process in the companion book as of yet. Connor brings up a lot of valid points in her book. I know personally that writing has been a successful meditative discipline for me, especially when I was going through a time of spiritual limbo.

Her book is akin to what I call "mind alchemy," a process that includes a writing thesis on life, which stimulates the creative process and allows for spiritual growth and also allows one to be receptive to that which corresponds to one's own understanding, changing thoughts of God into thoughts of gold. Writing also has a calming effect, for it allows one to channel their energy in a way that can eventually become beneficial and lift one's spirits.

I received the July 2017 issue of *Science of Mind* magazine with author Mitch Horowitz on the cover. I've read his book *Occult America.* This book was pretty informative on a lot of subject matter I have already studied, yet it brought enlightenment into subjects I am currently studying as well.

8/10/17

DEAR MICHAEL,

I was so glad to hear that you are enjoying Janet Connor's books! My summer class using *Writing Down the Soul* had nineteen students, and by the end many felt it was the best therapy they could have received. So, it did reach deep into their souls' experiences and desires.

Recently there have been two instances where friends were having traumatic experiences. Recognizing that there are no accidents, I went into meditation and began writing about why these incidents were occurring from a soul's perspective. It was an interesting experience for me, and when I sent both letters to my friends, they had amazing realizations that put it all into a perspective since they had not thought about before. Both the family and the parents are examples of pure love and compassion.

8/30/17

DEAR REV. MARY,

I completed the Criminal Thinking class back in July. I'm currently on the waiting list for two more classes, Anger Management and Pathways to Change. I've also just recently finished celebrating the month of Black August. I've mentioned this to you before. It is paying homage to the many monumental events that happened pertaining to African people all over the world during the month of August.

The Criminal Thinking class was perhaps one of the most illuminating classes I've taken pertaining to self. I was able to understand how I think like a criminal and why. To understand my arrested development, I had to accept a profound truth: that all of my adult life thus far has been lived in an environment created to demoralize, to cause abjection, and to deprave all those who inhabit this realm.

I learned much about myself during this six-week program, all of which has been helpful in that I reinforced my applications of positive thought. I didn't know who I truly was until I was obliged to reach deep within to draw upon the resources that nature has given me.

Arranging my life according to the positive principles that counsel me also meant holding on to the difficult. For in moments of recognition and self-acceptance, I've integrated the richer aspects of my negative self so that I am able to gain some small purchase on the immensity of my soul.

Living within the 9th Dominion has taken much courage and endurance—courage to face what must be faced and the endurance to stick it out until I finally arrived at the destination intended for me from the beginning. So much of my life has been lived through reflexive adaptations, so knowing how I really wanted to live was often difficult and scary. Yet everything felt peaceful and right when I decided to live in truth and live as I was meant to live.

In the Science of Mind teaching, it is written that the only way God can evolve as a spontaneous individual is to let him alone and allow him to awaken himself. It is also written that on the road to self-discovery, he must be subject to the Law of Reality and if, in ignorance, he violates this law, he must thereby suffer.

The life I have conducted from the narrow, biased lens of consciousness has been a mistake, yet a necessary mistake for my growth. In my adaption, I would diverge from the path that my nature desires. In my quisling collaboration with fear, I would settle for something lower in importance. Yet and still, I am bound to and through my errors, and my most profound human struggle is found standing at the meeting point, the spiritual nexus, between my individualized assignment in this existence and my human frailties.

I cannot imitate Gandhi, Dr. Martin Luther King Jr., or Jesus. Those lives have already been lived and much better than I could ever attempt to manage. Yet I can meet my summons on this road of personal growth and in my travels. When I come across doubt, despair, defeat, I offer them luminosity and faith, and I chose to live life more fully.

I discovered a truth while working with the Criminal Thinking class. Working with it is working toward the possibility of greater wholeness. By definition, wholeness cannot be partial, so my theology, philosophy, psychology cannot remain partial either. My soul demands wholeness, a work that requires me to enter into a discipline of positive thought as well as a consistency of right thinking. I could not avoid the spiritual discipline this rigorous task demanded and that is necessary, for it allowed me to know that the simplest, most functional definition of "negative" is that which renders me uncomfortable with myself.

I am one who dared to be myself in the face of adversity. Choosing right over wrong, ethics over convenience, and truth over falsehood. These are the choices that measure my life. I want to travel the path of integrity without looking back, for there is never a wrong time to do the right thing.

The word "prison" is being replaced by the words "correctional institution," a veneer that proclaims its aim is to provide rehabilitative programs that impose behavior modification techniques that reduce recidivism. These programs are rarely successful in this effect because there exists the goblin social/psychopath who is unmoved by programs that try to get them to be accountable for the harm they do. Yet this type of prisoner knows that if he plays the game that the prison higher ups want him to play, he will have his time reduced and be released to continue his criminal activities. Therefore, he is willing to go through the prison programs and say things that prison authorities want to hear. These authorities deem him as being "rehabilitated" and ready for free society. The goblin prisoner pretends to accept the idea of the prison programs as a part of the game he has always played, all out of sheer self-interest.

The huge number of lives lost to the prison graveyards shows what can happen when energy and dedication are applied to flawed beliefs and philosophies. These beliefs are rooted in a lack of knowledge of self and of the world today. Much of the prisoner's cherished beliefs, ideas, and theories are predicated on a flawed premise or are just outdated. What we think and believe determines what we perceive and experience. A preponderance of flawed beliefs seems to pervade and permeate lives of the less educated, who do not have a strong mental barometer to filter unsound beliefs from sound ones.

Unfortunately, a lot of good people subscribe to bad philosophies, whereupon what constitutes a good or bad philosophy is not only in the truth of them, because truth is relative, but in the results they produce. The cumulative evidence, the overflow of prisons with the people who live by such beliefs, is the point of reference that something is wrong and needs to be changed.

This is something I can attest to. It was 2009 when I began writing to you, Rev. Mary, and was introduced into the Science of Mind teachings. At that time, I was in the hole for an assault on an inmate. Before that, in 2006, I was in the hole for an assault on a staff member. Since I began my studies in Science of Mind and actually applied the knowledge, I haven't had an assault in almost ten years. This is because I meet confrontation, anger, spontaneous violence, malice, and hatred with a different mind state, a different spirit, and a humane smile.

It takes a strong sense of self to be able to examine and take responsibility for the negative self when it shows up and rears its ugly head. It is much easier to deny, blame others, project violence, or bury it and just keep moving. It is at those moments of human frailty when the criminal thinker is most dangerous to himself, his family, and society. Even if the criminal thinker were to begin to tumble to the fact that he was in the grip of motives and agendas contrary to his professed values, he would more than likely offer a justification for why he thought like he did or did what he did. Indeed, one of the surest signs of our defense against our negative dark self is our ready rationalizations that surface to justify our position on any action or subject.

Is it hubris, the frequent inflation of the ego, to believe that it—the ego—knows enough about the complex consequences of our choices? In my youth, my mind would override my family's and friends' warnings against a particular event into which I would cast myself. Choices were made and the piper paid in the end, for my friends and loved ones were able to see what I apparently could not see.

When I became conscious that my values and my choices and their unforeseen consequences were quite divergent, when I realized that my behavior hurt others, especially those whom I loved, I was crushed. Realizing that my choices, conscious and unconscious, produced lasting harm in the world, the weight of this posed a difficult task of self-acceptance and self-forgiveness. While the capacity to accept responsibility for the consequences of my choices is the measure of a moral being, for me not to acknowledge moral complicity in the world's woe is itself a sociopathic issue.

I am able to see, perhaps from the perspective of decades, that even the good I intended was not without its problematic consequences, because the good I did was often tinged with the hidden agenda, the complicit collusion, the manipulative motive. These energies can operate unconsciously because it has become normal for the criminal thinker. At the time, I believed I knew myself and that I was choosing wisely, prudently, and with the best intention. Coming into accountability for my own past is the first step in recognizing what has hitherto been unconscious, namely the presence and activity of my darkest negative self.

In criminal thinking class, we discussed the five universal fears. The fear of losing myself was one that was always in the back of my mind. The one that was most dominant was the fear of being physically hurt. This is a natural fear for all humans, yet in the mind of a criminal thinker it grows into what is known in the occult as an egregore, a thought form that becomes more cohesive with time and, empowered by one's imagination, takes on an existence of its own and can draw energy from fear and other sources. For me, it grew into what I learned was an "ownership attitude."

For two decades, I have had a permanent table in the chow hall that I considered mine. The table sits in a corner with a wall and a rail to the right of it, a wall with a window right behind the seat in which I sat, and another half wall to the left of it. With this placement of the table, I can see every inmate who enters and exits, and I am protected from any sneak attack from behind.

I have been in an "instant ready-to-resort-to-violence" mode when someone was sitting at "my" table. For two and a half decades, my dwelling has been within a criminal environment and I've always taken my own security measures to preserve my life. This became my normal. I didn't recognize the criminal thinking that came with my fear.

I decided to experiment and trust in Spirit for my safekeeping. I tried not sitting at the table. Inmates would come into the kitchen and see that no one was at this table, but they still wouldn't sit there. This is when I realized how demented and domineering I had become about an inanimate object—all derived from fear. I put out so much negative energy over this table that others would fear to sit at it, even though it was empty. So I began to invite guys to sit with me who normally wouldn't ever sit at this table. Those who I invited were in a state of trepidation, thinking something was amiss. I had put out an energy that made people feel as if they were trespassing, which made them feel uncomfortable.

For the last few weeks, I've been rotating my sitting arrangement, sitting at different tables and with different people, not for the other inmates but for myself, so I can release this unnecessary *ad nauseam* energy of possessiveness and ownership. In doing this, I felt lighter. Being territorial was a burden I carried that now is no longer mine to carry. It took this criminal thinking class for me to even realize that I was in this frame of mind. Selfish thoughts translate into selfish behaviors.

I once saw a cartoon that depicted two people walking down a sidewalk, about to collide. One was a priest grinning because he was walking his little devil on a leash, and the other was a devil grinning because he was walking his little priest on a leash. They were brothers, though they knew it not. How many men like me have been carried along on the leash of such energies and how many men know the harm they bring with them into the world?

After reexamining and reanalyzing my life, I've come to understand that all issues have more than one facet to consider. One facet is that my capacity for self-delusion could be very strong and that I am always at least part of the problem. I learned as a criminal thinker, however, ruefully, my excessive reactions to small events reveal not only a complex hiding beneath, but quite often a negative sociopathic issue as well.

For a man to truly live, a part of him has to die. As one grows, life follows the same process at every stage. There are points where one must let go of old ideas, old habits, and even old lives. When one sheds his skin, he allows for a new one to grow. If the caterpillar is not ready to lose her old self, she never becomes a butterfly.

Having balance is an important thing, but one day the good must dominate the bad for one's life to mean anything. To become strong, meaningful, and a worthy human being, one has to eliminate that which is weak within him. Often this process is hell, but any metal only becomes strong once it has been through fire. The fire purifies and strengthens the metal, as struggle, sacrifice, and strife have done for me. After growing from weak to strong, I am dedicated to work for the good of others. I am strong enough to continue to eliminate my destructive habits and weaknesses, for to stay in my weakness would only destroy me.

Simply driven by events to an accounting, I've come to terms with my negative patterns. I understand my past is contaminated with negative choices, and I understand how aspects of my true self have been inconsistent with how I wished to view myself. Finding one's own truth is a task that is never too late to take on, because where I now stand in my life is a constant reminder that Divinity brought me to this point to be who I truly am. And it is good to become good, because it feels good and I feel God.

CHAPTER 10

2018

Helping Others
Works to Erase the Mental
Mechanism of Anger

Adversity teaches patience, compassion, and tolerance, bringing a new perception of the world — Overcoming ignorance, anger, and greed and turning toward happiness and good fortune stems from our own positive actions and thoughts — Working as a Daily Living Assistant, helping handicapped inmates — Many staff members believe a lifer doesn't need to be rehabilitated, which is erroneous thinking — I've encountered another world within this one, a world of illness, dementia, paranoia, illogical fears, chronic maladies, and blatant madness — None of these patients has any religious services, which saddened my heart — How does one introduce spirituality to the refused? — Science of Mind teaches that anger and malice cannot breathe the same atmosphere as goodness and purity — Within this realm, pretty much everyone is angry about something — I gave up the last remaining vestiges of anger a couple of years ago — Intelligence is the power of choice, while anger cripples rational thought.

1/15/18

DEAR REV. MARY,

> *As the inner light dawns,*
> *it delivers the outer life from bondage.*

— SOURCE UNKNOWN

A short note to let you know that I'm now in a different house. The honor houses are 3 house to 6 house. I now have the privilege to be out all day and, also, I have access to a microwave and a washer and dryer.

Within this realm, it can be very difficult for prisoners to rise above the ugliness of prison life and live their lives with joy and virtue. But it is not impossible. For it is adversity that teaches one to practice patience, compassion, and tolerance, and if a prisoner can learn to incorporate these values into his daily life, he can change his perception of the world around him. By cultivating compassion, empathy, wisdom, and love, he can overcome ignorance, fear, anger, and greed. And whatever happiness and good fortune we experience in our lives stems from our own positive actions and thoughts.

I've recently been moved to the wing next door, into 3-A-204. I'm still on honor status, but 3-A is the ECU (Enhanced Care Unit). I've been assigned as a DLA, which is a daily living assistant. It is somewhat like an orderly you might see at a hospital or in an elder care facility.

We assist handicapped inmates, many of whom are in wheelchairs, on breathing apparatuses, or who suffer other ailments. They are all on the bottom walk and the DLA lives on the top walk. We take them to and from medical, to the chow hall, or we bring food to them. We clean their cells and at times engage with them in activities like card games and board games. I've only been over here for a few days, so I'm still learning all of my duties. I have learned so much on my journey, I don't know what the future holds for me, but I try every day to improve my environment, and I strive to become a better man.

With this missive, I'm sending an article from the *Cure Newsletter* pertaining to lifers and also the next class. I'll be attending this program, designed for prisoners who have short time and will be leaving. I've been consistently requesting that I be allowed to take this class and should not be discriminated against just because of having a life without parole sentence. Many staff members believe that a prisoner who is a lifer doesn't need to be rehabilitated, which to me is erroneous thinking and one of the reasons recidivism is so high.

Note: Included with this letter was notification that Michael was chosen to attend the "Pathways to Change" class and a copy of a page from Missouri CURE, a non-profit all-volunteer criminal justice advocacy organization. Their mission statement is: CURE believes that all prisons should be only for those who MUST be incarcerated and that prisons should only exist for the purpose of education and rehabilitation.

Rev. Mary joined CURE as a member.

4/23/18

DEAR REV. MARY,

My DLA classes and Pathways to Change class have taken more of my free time than I anticipated. I had to rearrange my schedule now as a DLA because of my patient's medical appointments. I am officially a Certified Daily Living Assistant. I've completed all my classes and I'm sending you copies of my certificates.

I'm glad you and Rev. Cath DePalma communicated with one another. She has sent me a lot of writings by Thomas Troward. In your letter, you mentioned a book you were teaching from entitled *The Moral Landscape* by Sam Harris. Reading some of the key concepts you shared, I know this would bring up very interesting conversation and discussion.

There have been so many unethical practices coming to light in the media this year dealing with sport doctors, politicians, newscasters, and Hollywood personalities. Even our governor here in Missouri was exposed for his unethical morality. The abuse of power and manipulative methods toward women and young girls has been a big issue for the year 2018.

I've encountered another world within this one, a world of illness, dementia, paranoia, illogical fears, chronic maladies, and blatant madness. I knew these things were a part of the 9th Dominion, but to experience it in such a concentrated form took me aback. But I realized that I could be of great help to these men, so I've immersed myself within my role as a Daily Living Assistant. I've also stepped up to become a wing worker, cleaning showers, doing the laundry, sweeping, and mopping.

One thing I noticed since I've been in this Enhanced Care Unit wing is that none of the patients have any religious services that they attend, yet they attend bingo or movie nights. This saddened my heart because I believed that those who would be in such states of being—some with cancer, others who have HIV—would be trying to reconcile with their Creator.

How does one introduce spirituality to the refused?

7/7/18

DEAR MICHAEL,

What a wonderful surprise that you are now a Daily Living Assistant! I find it amazing that those people you are helping were not known to you before. I never thought about it actually, whether prisoners are segregated based on health issues but, of course, dementia and mental health issues would be a challenge in the mainstream population. In the outside world it is difficult, since about 30 percent of those who are homeless have mental problems and there is very little help for them. That those in your institution can be cared for by someone like you is a blessing. Your certificates are super cool!

Regarding introducing spirituality to those you care for, perhaps there may be an opportunity to read to those you serve, perhaps something you could write, like an uplifting paragraph each week. There are some great quotes and ideas in Bo Lozoff's books.

10/10/18

DEAR REV. MARY,

I just completed an eight-week class in anger management and I've included a copy of the certificate with this letter. I've read that Science of Mind teaches that anger and malice, revenge and animosity cannot breathe the same atmosphere as goodness and purity. They will fall away as we climb to those heights where the indwelling Spirit lives. Proverbs 16:32 says, "He that is slow to anger is better than the mighty, and he that ruleth his Spirit, than he that taketh a city."

Within this realm, pretty much everyone is angry about something. This is just an abnormal attitude that has become a normal fixture in the 9th Dominion and its canaille. I gave up the last remaining vestiges of anger within me, perhaps a couple of years ago, because intelligence is the power of choice while anger cripples rational thought and therefore limited my choices. By using the full power of my intellect and choosing not to act out of anger and habit, I was able to increase my odds that the events of the future would be more beneficial and positive and more to my liking.

Understanding the mental mechanics of anger, I understand that it finds power in the mental discomfort of the unwanted happening and the blocking of the wanted happening. Anger arises when one has an unmet demand. The demand may be tangible, like the expectation to be paid after one has completed a job, or intangible, where one may want a complete stranger to respect them. Whether an event is trivial or significant, the cause of anger is always the same: underlying emotional tumult when there is a need that is not being met and one expects it to be met. The word "demand" is used because it is an internal demand that one makes on the world and the people who dwell in it and it includes needs, desires, and expectations.

I have learned that there are four types of demands:

1. The *important and reasonable* demand, such as you want your spouse to love you. This type is entirely justifiable and feasible.

2. The *reasonable but unimportant* demand, such as you want to be seated by the window in a restaurant. Although reasonable, this demand may really not be so important.

3. The *irrational* demand, such as you don't want to put up with traffic annoyances or you want respect from a stranger. This demand is asinine and unreasonable.

4. The *impossible* demand, such as you want everyone to fear or love you. Demands like these are usually ongoing and are expressed in terms of generalities. This type of expectation is impossible and thus provides the justification for ongoing anger that is the basis for a chronic renunciation of happiness. Retaining anger caused by the this demand is uncomfortable and, when repressed, one will carry it with continuing damage to one's psyche and physical being.

When one's aversions become fixed, they become hatreds. And hatreds are ossified angers. Albert Einstein said, "Insanity is doing the same thing over and over and expecting different results." To know truth, one must live it. The mind is always looking for an excuse to avoid discipline.

12/14/18

DEAR MICHAEL,

So sorry for the delay in writing. I'm not sure if you have heard of the major wildfires we've experienced in northern California. At our church, we've been working hard to help those who have lost everything. In July/August the Carr Fire in Redding destroyed more than 1,000 homes and kept our whole area locked in smoke for two months.

This past month, the Camp Fire just south of us burned 150,000 acres and destroyed more than 6,000 homes, displacing more than 55,000 people. Due to the wind from the south, that fire kept us again in smoke for about a month. More than eighty people died in that fire, as it ravaged the town in a matter of hours. Anyway, we have been collecting gift cards and money for those at our sister church in Paradise, including the minister and most of the congregation. Right now, we are enjoying five days of rain, and all fires have been put out.

By now, your sister's twin boys are hopefully thriving. What a special gift to a family. Now you have a new name, probably Uncle Mike. It sounds nice!

CHAPTER 11

2019

Reaching
Outward, Thoughts
of Parole

Appearing in *Open Doors,* a youth intervention video, speaking on the pitfalls of living and glorifying the gangster lifestyle — As a DLA, witnessing an overwhelming excess of elder abuse — In the hole for a dangerous contraband infraction, keeping a weapon close at hand — Before a dream is realized, I have to purge a habit born out of fear, preparing my Spirit and my will — For the first time in two decades, I really want to be a free man again — When a person really desires something, all the Universe conspires to help him to realize his dream — You took my thoughts out of the grave and gave me a chance to breathe and think in a brighter way.

3/21/19

DEAR REV. MARY,

A lot of activities have kept me from concentrating on things. Back in December, I and a few other comrades from Kansas City were in an *Open Doors* youth intervention video. We spoke on the pitfalls and the negative results that come from living and glorifying the gangster lifestyle and the illusions and self-deception that come along with it. The officer in charge of this program said it was one of the best videos to date. He said that he received a lot more feedback from this video than from others he previously made.

If there exists any type of youth outreach program that Science of Mind operates or is affiliated with that would like to use this video as an eye opener for troubled youth, let me know and I will figure out how to get a copy of the video to you.

As a DLA, I've witnessed an overwhelming excess of elder abuse from correctional officials and medical staff. I had no idea this type of problem existed until I became a DLA, with the help of another DLA inmate who has been here since the Enhanced Care Unit's (ECU's) inception. I've been able to convince the caseworker and the Function Unit Manager to implement some commonsensical, little, or no-cost changes, such as housing unit adjustments for the extremely older inmates and the severely handicapped; modifying shower times so the water will be warm enough for those who always seem to be cold; and providing additional blankets and cold weather clothing, like gloves and long johns. I and another inmate take a cart up to the canteen and put all the ECU patients' canteens on the cart, bring it back to the unit, and pass them out. This is done every Tuesday. It keeps the handicapped from having to go out in bad weather and wait in line.

The consequences of lack of adequate health care for any and all prisoners is exacerbated when it comes to elderly prisoners. The leading causes of death in the state prisons include heart disease, cancer, and liver disease. Contributors are years of prison life, including non-nutritional food and poor-quality water. The DOC is starting to recognize that in the prison system, a fifty-year-old is considered elderly.

There is really no one who oversees this ECU program, so the DLAs really do not have support on how to run the program. It has been haphazardly run since I've been part

of it, but hopefully with the help of others, we will try to solve some of the issues that now exist.

Included with this letter is a news article dealing with lifers and an opportunity for a parole hearing. The article is entitled "Bill Could Let Mo. Inmates Serving Life Get Hearing." It says that some Missouri inmates sentenced to life without parole who've served at least twenty-five years in prison could get a shot at a parole hearing under a criminal justice reform bill being considered by state lawmakers. A bill sponsored by Republican Rep. Jim Neely of Cameron would create three standards for an offender to meet before a parole board would hear his or her case, such as the rule to serve a minimum twenty-five years of a sentence. The proposed legislation also would require inmates to accept accountability for crimes and make reasonable efforts toward rehabilitation. Neely's bill joins a handful of others moving through the Missouri General Assembly this year aimed at reforming the state's criminal justice system and reducing the prison population. There are voices concerned about the implications, but Rep. Neely trusts the eyes and ears of the parole board.

4/13/19

DEAR MICHAEL,

You can't imagine how I almost jumped out of my skin when I read the article that a bill could let Missouri inmates serving life get a hearing. Hope you don't mind, but I sent a letter to Rep. Jim Neely about you and that you would be the perfect role model for his bill. A copy of what I emailed to him and also sent snail mail is enclosed. I'm praying for a response. Should you be released, you would be a great prisoner advocate and role model in helping teens avoid prison life. I will search the internet to see if I can find the video you were in, *Open Doors*. It sounds really great. I would love to show it at church and around the community.

I'm rereading your letter as I write this and I can feel how frustrating it is to see where things can be improved for the elderly and infirm. Know you are doing work that is greatly needed, yet be patient since changing a system so ingrained in processes is difficult. Love is important in changing hearts. If you would like to write an article about your experiences with your work in the ECU, I would love to get it published somewhere, perhaps *Sun* magazine.

4/13/19

REP. JIM NEELY
MISSOURI HOUSE OF REPRESENTATIVES
201 W. CAPITOL AVENUE
ROOM 110B
JEFFERSON CITY, MO 65101

RE: POTENTIAL BILL FOR THOSE WHO SERVED TWENTY-FIVE YEARS TO GET A PAROLE HEARING

DEAR REPRESENTATIVE NEELY,

AS A MINISTER, I HAVE CORRESPONDED WITH A PRISONER IN CHARLESTON, MISSOURI, SINCE 2009. MICHAEL NICHOLS (#180862) IS IN FOR LIFE. HE SOUGHT ME OUT THROUGH A SPIRITUAL MAGAZINE WHERE I HAD WRITTEN A MONTHLY COLUMN FOR MANY YEARS.

DURING OUR CORRESPONDENCE, MR. NICHOLS HAS TAKEN SEVERAL OF MY COURSES BY MAIL ON PERSONAL AND SPIRITUAL DEVELOPMENT—COURSES THAT INCLUDE THINGS LIKE THE ESSAYS OF RALPH WALDO EMERSON AND THE WRITINGS OF MYSTICS AND GREAT SPIRITUAL LEADERS. THROUGH THESE HE HAS GROWN FROM A VERY ANGRY AND HATEFUL YOUNG MAN TO ONE WHOM I AND OTHERS CONSIDER A PRISON MONK WHO HELPS OTHERS ADAPT TO PRISON LIFE. HE CURRENTLY SERVES IN THE ENHANCED CARE UNIT OF THE PRISON, HELPING THE ELDERLY AND INFIRM. RECENTLY HE WAS THE PRIMARY PERSON IN A FILM CALLED *OPEN DOORS*, A YOUTH INTERVENTION VIDEO. OVER THE YEARS HE HAS TAKEN MANY OF THE COURSES OFFERED IN THE PRISON, SUCH AS THE CRIMINAL MIND, A COURSE THAT I WISH WERE OFFERED IN CALIFORNIA PRISONS!

I AM ALSO A WRITER WHO IS IN AWE OF MICHAEL NICHOLS'S USE OF THE ENGLISH LANGUAGE AND HIS DEEP THOUGHT INTO EVERY AREA OF LIFE. ONE YEAR HE WROTE A SHORT STORY THAT I SUBMITTED TO *WRITER'S DIGEST* MAGAZINE. OF COURSE, IT DIDN'T WIN, BUT THE REPORT BACK FROM THOSE WHO REVIEWED THE ARTICLE WAS IMPRESSIVE.

IF YOU WOULD BE INTERESTED IN A FULL RESUME OF WHAT MR. NICHOLS HAS ACCOMPLISHED IN PRISON, I WOULD BE HONORED TO PUT THIS TOGETHER FOR YOU. HIS TURNAROUND HAS BEEN MORE THAN AMAZING. HE WOULD BE AN EXCELLENT ROLE MODEL FOR THE BILL THAT YOU ARE INTERESTED IN GETTING PASSED. THANK YOU FOR YOUR CONSIDERATION.

SINCERELY,
REV. MARY MITCHELL

4/21/19

DEAR REV. MARY,

I'm sending you a rough draft of a letter that I will include in an entire portfolio along with my application for clemency. Included in the portfolio will be all of my certificates that I've earned since I've been in prison and other accomplishments outside of prison walls, a letter of appreciation, plans for reintegration, an employment plan and work history, a budget plan for one year, and a three-year plan for reintegration, including community service goals. I will send you a rough draft of the entire portfolio I'm putting together.

I really appreciate the letter you wrote to Rep. Jim Neely. I agree with you that this is now the time. There have been so many Missouri prisoners released whom I never thought would be. Some have been trying to come back to prison after their release, which I find so bizarre. I'm sending you the news articles in a separate letter about those issues. I will be sending you the rough drafts of all that I will be including in the portfolio. Also, I would like to include copies of letters from you and any other supporters of my release.

Note: Within a week, Rev. Mary wrote to Rep. Neely with information about Michael Nichols, reflecting what progress he has made during his incarceration and requesting further information about the potential bill and when it might be passed. Rev. Neely's office responded that they hoped to have a bill passed within a year and requested additional information about Michael, which she provided.

MAY 5, 2019

REP. JIM NEELY
MISSOURI HOUSE OF REPRESENTATIVES
201 W. CAPITOL AVENUE, ROOM 110B
JEFFERSON CITY, MO 65101

RE: FURTHER INFORMATION YOU REQUESTED ON INMATE MICHAEL NICHOLS FOR THE POTENTIAL
    BILL H.B. 95 FOR THOSE WHO SERVED TWENTY-FIVE YEARS TO GET A PAROLE HEARING

DEAR REPRESENTATIVE NEELY,

THANK YOU FOR REQUESTING ADDITIONAL INFORMATION ON INMATE MICHAEL NICHOLS, AN INMATE
WHO HAS SERVED MORE THAN TWENTY-FIVE YEARS WITH THE POTENTIAL FOR A PAROLE HEARING.

HE SENT ME THE NEWSPAPER ARTICLE ABOUT THE BILL AND I IMMEDIATELY WROTE TO YOU.

IT IS INTERESTING THAT WITHIN DAYS WHEN I SENT HIM A COPY OF MY LETTER TO YOU, HE HAD ALREADY BEGUN PREPARING A PORTFOLIO THAT HE WROTE TO ME WILL INCLUDE ALL OF HIS CERTIFICATES HE HAS EARNED SINCE HE HAS BEEN IN PRISON, OTHER ACCOMPLISHMENTS OUTSIDE OF PRISON WALLS, A LETTER OF APPRECIATION, PLANS FOR REINTEGRATION, AN EMPLOYMENT PLAN AND WORK HISTORY, A BUDGET PLAN FOR ONE YEAR, AND A THREE-YEAR PLAN FOR REINTEGRATION, INCLUDING COMMUNITY SERVICE GOALS. I WAS IMPRESSED!

OVER THE TEN YEARS I HAVE BEEN CORRESPONDING WITH MR. NICHOLS ON HIS REQUEST FOR SPIRITUAL GUIDANCE, HIS LETTERS BEGAN WITH SUCH HATE AND VILE FEELINGS ABOUT THE PRISON SYSTEM AND EVERYONE IN IT. IT SLOWLY CHANGED WITH SPIRITUAL PRACTICES TO SEE THAT WE ARE ALL CREATIONS OF GOD, INFINITE INTELLIGENCE, AND WE ARE ALL ON OUR INDIVIDUAL PATHS. HE BEGAN TO SEE THAT HIS REACTIONS TO ANY EVENT COULD BE POSITIVE AND UPLIFTING

ONE OF MY FAVORITE STORIES IS ONE HE SHARED IN MAY 2012:

I've been in solitary confinement for a minor infraction with a guard who believed his clothes gave him superhuman powers. During that time, I read the last book you sent, *This Thing Called You,* and learned much about the world in which I dwell. I have been made ready for the part I must play in discovering my purpose of existence. I have accepted the calling.

Recently, a guard verbally attacked me for having blue shoelaces on my shoes and was shocked when I found the inner strength to take the shoelaces out and give them to him. Now, because of my action, mystery has been added to my reputation, and I'm even more frightful by virtue of my new unpredictability. It has taken courage, faith, and flexibility to grow in this labyrinth of steel, yet I have come to terms with who I am. The power of a positively committed mind exceeds any other force that I have come across in these lands.

AND RECENTLY IN MARCH 2019, HE WROTE:

In December, I and a few other comrades from Kansas City did an *Open Doors* youth intervention video. We spoke on the pitfalls and the negative results that come from living and glorifying the gangster lifestyle and the illusions and self-deception that come along with it. The official in charge of this program said it was one of the best videos to date and that he received a lot more feedback on this video than on his previous ones.

HOPEFULLY YOU OR YOUR STAFF WILL HAVE TIME TO READ THE ATTACHED, WHICH I TYPED FROM MICHAEL'S RECENT TWENTY-PAGE HANDWRITTEN HISTORY. HE CONTINUES TO PREPARE HIS PORT-FOLIO, WHICH WE WILL GET TO YOU WHEN IT IS READY.

SENT IN GRATITUDE FOR YOUR CONSIDERATION AND COMPASSION FOR THOSE LIKE MICHAEL WHO HAVE MADE SUCH AN INCREDIBLE TURNAROUND AND ARE NOW HELPING OTHERS IN SO MANY WAYS.

SINCERELY,

REV. MARY MITCHELL

ENCLOSED:
MICHAEL NICHOLS #180862, A HANDWRITTEN HISTORY, APRIL 30, 2019

Editor's Note:
Michael's handwritten history appears at the end of this book as his author's bio.

6/1/19

DEAR REV. MARY,

I'm teaching myself how to put together a portfolio. I want those who receive it to understand the nature of the being that has replaced the ignorant asinine being I once was.

I've been researching (in a book dedicated to helping those who are older than fifty) to find a job without a four-year degree. I have another book entitled *Best Resumes and Letters for Ex-Offenders*. There is some knowledge I must attain before I can send this application off to its beautiful destination.

I received the *Conversations with Ernest* book that includes the piece you submitted to *Science of Mind* magazine, which was published there. I've been showing it off to my friends, who have become curious now about the Science of Mind teachings.

I no longer work as a DLA. It was becoming unwieldy, unhealthy, and I was able to smoothly leave without upheaval or upsetting the natural order of the canaille. This allows me the freedom to spend quality time working on my avenues for exodus.

Included in this letter is a rough draft of my three-year reintegration plan. I will also be sending you a budget plan, as well as job arenas I might prove to excel in.

6/6/19

DEAR REV. MARY,

PLAN FOR SUCCESSFUL REENTRY

Prepared for the Missouri Board of Parole
Presented by Michael J. Nichols
SECC, 300 East Pedro Simmons Drive, Charleston, MO 63834

THREE-YEAR PLAN FOR REINTEGRATION:

FIRST YEAR –
Follow all the directions of the Missouri Board of Probation and Parole:

- Inquire into a ninety-day period in a transitional living center;

- Secure all proper and valid state identifications and Social Security card;

- Begin searching for employment and volunteering two to four hours weekly toward community services, making social amends;

- Open savings and checking accounts;

- Contact organizations to apply for benefits, including health and counseling;

- Join a local Center for Spiritual Living for Science of Mind teachings and that has active assistance in mentoring;

- Rely on public transportation;

- Establish, reestablish, and strengthen meaningful family and community ties;

- After establishing solid employment, negotiate the down payment for the purchase of an apartment; and

- Work diligently to further develop a strong bond with a spiritual mentor of the Science of Mind community.

SECOND YEAR —
Continue following all of the directions issued by Missouri Board of Probation and Parole:

- Continue employment, volunteering for community service, frequenting local Centers for Spiritual Living for counseling and guidance;

- Continue strengthening family and community ties;

- Continue regular contributions to financial accounts, including saving for a down payment on a good reliable used car; and

- Until then, acquire driver's license, car insurance, and proper vehicle registration, as required.

THIRD YEAR —
Continue following all of the directions issued by Missouri Board of Probation and Parole:

- Continue employment; alternative options for employment are temporary service jobs provided by the unemployment office;

- Continue to save money, look for health benefits that are affordable; and

- Officially petition for final discharge for parole going into the fourth year.

DURING MY INCARCERATION:

During my incarceration, I have maintained consistent employment. Positions I have held are: tutor, cook, dorm maintenance, medical porter, ad-seg lawn maintenance, laundry worker, recreational worker, dishwasher, and Daily Living Assistant for the elderly and handicapped.

My leisure time has been used for weight lifting, bodybuilding, and the study of educational spiritual materials and reading Dean Koontz novels, as well as helping out with the dogs of the MO DOC Puppies for Parole Program.

7/29/19

DEAR REV. MARY,

I'm just now having the opportunity to write. I've been in the hole for almost two months for a dangerous contraband infraction. I'm just now getting the utensils necessary to write a letter.

I greatly appreciate your willingness to assist me with my portfolio. The only things I have left to do for its completion is add to it photocopies of all my certificates, letters from people I've been communicating with, along with those from family members, a letter of apology to my victims that I'm working on as I sit here in the hole, and also a budget plan that I was going to create based on the salary of a Correctional Officer of about $22,000 a year.

It sometimes seems to me that as soon as I start making great strides and focus on liberation from these dungeons of doom, I end up in the hole for a habit that I've had since coming into this realm.

Carrying a weapon or keeping a weapon close at hand is something I've been doing since my prison sentence began. So, getting caught with one, I asked myself, is this a negative? I thought that even though it appears to be negative, in fact it is not. I've dreamed every day of somehow or someway attaining freedom. Before a dream is realized, the Universe must test everything I have learned along the way. I believe it does this so that I can, in addition to realizing my dream, master the lessons I've learned as I move toward that dream.

I have to purge a habit born out of fear, to choose between something I have been accustomed to and something that I really need and want. Being in the hole at this time is preparing my Spirit and my will, because for the first time in two decades I really want to be a free man again. When I made that decision and started working toward that, I dove into a strong current that can carry me to my realized destiny.

I pay attention to omens and the present, if I can improve upon my present, I know that what comes later will be better. I realize and understand how the Universe is the river and I am the bank. The river is more powerful than the bank, yet the bank contains it and guides it.

I am confident that God loves His children, and when a person really desires something, all the Universe conspires to help that person realize his dream.

I will probably be in the hole for about six months. I've received all of your sermons and I've been sharing them with guys in the hole.

8/17/19

DEAR MICHAEL,

My heart aches over what happened that has put you in the hole. How sad this must have felt. I had to put your letter aside for a few days before I could read it all. But like so many things in life, we deal with it.

Just this week, a woman came to visit me to show me a couple of letters from her son in a California prison in Tracy, just south of Sacramento, named the Deuel Vocational Institution (strange name!). He wrote about the numerous gangs and that the guards set up fights between gangs just for sport. Her son is only twenty-two and is in one of the scariest prisons in the state. I looked it up on the internet and it has a history of being violent and dangerous and is known as the "gladiator school." He is petrified and doing all he can to stay safe. This includes joining one of the gangs and getting heavily tattooed.

In the last letter, guards caught him with a weapon and have him in the hole and moved his release time out a few years to 2028. His mother is heartsick. I'm helping her get addresses for the legislators so she can write letters about the conditions there. Not sure it will help, but she has to try. If he could even get transferred, it would help.

And for you, perhaps our communication about a pardon was read by those who go through your mail and extra care was taken looking through your things. We'll never know. All of this has had me leaning on my beliefs that everything happens for a purpose. It's the law. And I trust the soul's journey implicitly.

10/1/19

DEAR REV. MARY,

I write to you again from the wasteland (the hole). I've been moved from Housing Unit 1 to Housing Unit 2. I am scheduled to see the Administrative Segregation Committee on October 30. I've been programing and taking a Bible correspondence course, so I should be released.

Replying to your letter, I really appreciate the Plan for Successful Reintegration you typed up. I believe it is the same as the Transition Accountability Plan. I have the Blue

Book for parole on my tablet, yet I haven't had the opportunity to go through it, but I'm glad you sent a copy of it to me.

I will not be able to receive any of the books you sent to me until I'm released from the wastelands. I thank you for sending me these books. The book entitled *Writing Down the Soul* by Janet Conner is a blue book with an owl on the cover. You sent this to me a couple years back, but no matter, I will read it again and send it and the companion book to my niece. I've been sharing literature with her for the last few years as she has gotten older. She is twelve going on thirteen.

In your letter dated August 17, you mentioned that a woman showed you a couple of letters from her son who was incarcerated. Hopefully I can be an agent of transformation through the circulation of my consciousness and bring awareness to the mother and her son and quiet their natural fears with my words of healing. So, I ask that you please share the following with the woman and her son:

> I have spent the lion's share of my life doing time under the state's (Superman logo) supervision. For twenty-eight years, my life has been governed by prison ideology and survival methods and tactics that have kept me out of harm's way for almost three decades.
>
> There exist within the 9th Dominion (prison) written laws that are odd as well as complex and cannot truly be understood or grasped by those with a healthy, normal mentality.
>
> For the prisoner, there are virtues that must be developed, passions that must be curbed, fears that must be eliminated, evil (negative) mind states to be transcended, and education and love to be cultivated and refined.
>
> One of the realities of prison life is that mostly everything one does is under constant observation by guards, cameras, and other prisoners. The other reality is that safety (self-preservation) is the driving force of the majority of prisoners. When one becomes "active" in a gang, he is in effect telling everyone around him that he is now identifying himself with a particular image. The culture within the 9th Dominion has forced him to draw a line in the sand. This realm will quickly force one to identify himself as Alpha, Beta, Sigma,

or Delta, and once one has identified himself with a "show of colors," it will make it easier for one to continue to operate under that banner.

Although the 9th Dominion is often crude and unforgiving, there is a positive aspect of this culture. It tends to respect "authenticity," which is actually the illusion that one portrays, yet if one is consistent about what he claims to be, the "authentic" others will tend to respect that position over time—and even though the others may claim something different themselves, they will eventually come to admit that one at least seems to be genuine in the path on which he is walking.

One must try and understand that this realm is an environment surrounded by a dark, unseen miasma of negativity and illusions. I know that it may be somewhat difficult for you to truly comprehend the choices your son is making, but at this time he has been (according to the Thirteenth Amendment) enclaved and put into a very foreign environment. Yet living in this environment tends to strengthen our individual natures at certain points. Every man in the 9th Dominion is trying hard to survive. Every man feels alone in his individual fight to make it through, so he goes along to get along.

Being tough is the desired image that many feel they must project. It is a common survival tactic that many project into this world. This reality affects everyone, so one has to stay spiritually guarded because in a spiritually unguarded moment an angry response for the smallest insult can escalate into a major negative confrontation and it is easy to get swept up in it. The pressure to conform to the environment is ever present. It can be courageous and dangerous to go against the prevailing attitudes, mindsets, and sub-rosa codes that plague this evil empire.

In the martial art of judo, momentum is the key to victory, not going up against it, but using the momentum to overcome the adversary.

In this case, the adversary is not a single individual or a particular gang; it is his environment. So far, your son has made intuitively sound survival moves that will keep him from becoming prey to an alpha predator. When I came to prison at nineteen, I did the very same thing your son did. I was part of a gang. I have more than fifteen types of guns tattooed over my arms, back, stomach, chest, shoulders, and neck. My nickname is Trigger Mike. I've changed my life and I'm in the hole right now for a weapon as well. The tough veneer, the general mistrust, the tendency to strike out in response to minimal provocations, the carrying of weapons are all highly functional traits in prison. They are also hard habits to break because they can be problematic in the free world.

Do not be vexed. There are ways your son will be able to navigate within his domain, but first he must be armed with knowledge. So, erase the morbid emotion of fear and doubt and rejoice in the positive knowing that the spirit in your son is trying to awaken from being dormant for so long and it is using what is around him to do it. Life is a blessing or a curse, according to the use we make of it. If we continue to make mistakes, we will continue to suffer the consequences. We punish ourselves or we correct ourselves and our mistakes so we no longer suffer from them. God often changes us within our circumstances, instead of changing our circumstances.

Think of the dangers Jesus faced: Herod was out to kill him. The people he grew up with in Nazareth tried to push him off a cliff. The religious leaders wanted him taken out. Judas was waiting for an opportunity to snake (betray) him. His family tried to discourage him. His disciples misunderstood him. And while he hung on the cross, God forsook him. Yet Jesus did not fear. It is natural for men and women to fear. In Proverbs it mentions nearly twenty times that humans are to fear God. The Hebrew word that is translated as fear is *yirah* and fearing is *yare*. These words mean "to reverence." It means to give God the highest respect, honor, love, and loyalty. By contrast, when Proverbs 29:25 speaks of fearing man, an entirely different word, *charadah,* is used. It means to tremble or to be terrified.

Inmates fear their enemies, and people within the free world fear for their loved ones. Jesus showed amazing skills in dealing with various types of people from many different backgrounds and different types of situations. He knew how to lead a diverse group of men, one of whom was a killer of Christians. He was sought out by mothers and young children. He appealed to all sorts of outcasts and misfits, to sick people as well as working people and ordinary fishermen.

Being teachable means being someone who will embrace knowledge. If your son is teachable, his mind will become his most powerful tool when cultivated. Yet it can be hindered when one lives the distortions that arise from filters through which one perceives reality.

I don't know how the California penal institutions scrutinize and/or censor different types of books. Some they may allow, some they may not. Try to find out before you send any books. I recommend that you send him or photocopy and send to him a printout of the following:

- First photocopy all the book of Proverbs from the Bible and send it to him, then send:

- *The Book of Five Rings*

- *As a Man Thinketh*

- Robert Greens's books, *The 48 Laws of Power* and *Mastery*

These books will give him a different perception of what he is truly around. Proverbs can keep him grounded so he will not lose himself and begin a spiritual discipline that he may be unlikely to rebel against.

The knowledge in these books will give him an advantage over his peers, because most gang members do not use their thinking facilities in the correct way. The one who does is highly respected, idolized, recognized for brains over brawn. He is sought after for advice and help.

The next thing I recommend is that he gets a job. Since it is a vocational institute, there should be many jobs available. If he cannot get one of those real good jobs, he can always get a job in the kitchen. It will keep him away from a lot of the negative activities that his peers are indulging in, yet he will still be in good standing with his gang. Many jobs have perks that he may be able to utilize if he is able to perceive accurately.

Knowledge and how we choose to use it can overcome our weaknesses so that when trouble comes, we will be prepared. I leave you in God's Hands.

11/17/19

DEAR MICHAEL,

Your letter of 10/1 brought tears to my eyes as you wrote about the advice you shared with my friend, the mother of the son now in Deuel Vocational Rehab, a prison full of gangs and gang wars. I can't begin to tell you how grateful I am for your wisdom that I will share with my friend and her son. Your insights are so powerful. I will type up your letter and send it to them both. I'll check into the books you recommended also. You are a powerful Buddha to so many in your realm.

What is on my mind right now is if you might be interested in writing a book that would help those new to the prison system. Perhaps varying chapters for the various types of incarceration, the benefit of studying spirituality, how to see life in the picture of Oneness, then how to prepare for what they will experience, and then later live in public. Your letter is a great start to this idea, and I would be happy to type it all up and pay for the publishing costs. And in case you don't know, I have saved every letter you have written to me—and your spiritual and personal growth is astounding, which could be another aspect of the book, your own spiritual path and growth.

11/10/19

DEAR REV. MARY,

This is just a quick letter to let you know that I've been released from the hole for about a week now. I usually would have been in the hole for a year, but I did a lot of programming in the hole and was able to produce about five certificates when I went to go see the committee, which they did not anticipate. So there was no longer any reason to continue to hold me in the hole, so I was released immediately.

12/7/19

DEAR MICHAEL,

It was so wonderful to hear you are out of the hole due to your continuing participation in education programs. I've tried so many ways to access the video on street life and can't seem to find it anywhere. Frustrating! Enclosed is your original and a copy of your certificate. Keep up the good work! Also, I'm sending my letter of recommendation. I will be happy to make any changes you think might strengthen it.

12/7/19

TO WHOM IT MAY CONCERN:

RE: LETTER OF RECOMMENDATION FOR A PARDON FOR MICHAEL NICHOLS #180862

I AM AN ORDAINED MINISTER, LICENSED BY THE CENTERS FOR SPIRITUAL LIVING, HEADQUAR-
TERED IN GOLDEN, COLORADO. I AM CO-SENIOR MINISTER AT THE CENTER FOR SPIRITUAL LIVING
IN REDDING, CALIFORNIA. OUR METAPHYSICAL PHILOSOPHY TEACHES PERSONAL RESPONSIBILITY,
THE POWER OF OUR MINDS IN CREATING OUR LIFE EXPERIENCES, AND THE POWER OF LOVE AND
TRUTH FOR HEALING.

MORE THAN TEN YEARS AGO, MICHAEL NICHOLS FOUND MY NAME IN A SPIRITUAL MAGAZINE AND
WROTE TO ME ASKING IF I WOULD ASSIST HIM IN LEARNING ABOUT LIFE ON THE SPIRITUAL
PATH. OUR PHILOSOPHY IS CALLED SCIENCE OF MIND (ALSO KNOWN AS RELIGIOUS SCIENCE),
A METAPHYSICAL PHILOSOPHY STEEPED IN PERSONAL RESPONSIBILITY AND THE POWER OF POS-

ITIVE THINKING. SINCE THEN, I HAVE BEEN CORRESPONDING WITH HIM ON HIS REQUEST FOR SPIRITUAL GUIDANCE.

HIS INITIAL LETTERS WERE FILLED WITH HATE AND VILE FEELINGS ABOUT THE PRISON SYSTEM AND EVERYONE IN IT. HIS ATTITUDE SLOWLY CHANGED AS HE TOOK CORRESPONDENCE CLASSES WITH ME AND BY LEARNING SPIRITUAL PRACTICES, SUCH AS MEDITATION, TO SEE THAT WE ARE ALL CREATIONS OF GOD, INFINITE INTELLIGENCE, AND WE ARE ALL ON OUR INDIVIDUAL PATHS. HE BEGAN TO UNDERSTAND AND PRACTICE THE PRINCIPLES OF ONENESS, GOODNESS, LOVE, ETC. HE BEGAN TO SEE THAT HIS REACTIONS TO ANY EVENT COULD BE POSITIVE AND UP LIFTING.

IN THE PAST FEW YEARS OF HIS TWENTY-EIGHT YEARS OF INCARCERATION, HE HAS EVOLVED INTO WHAT I CALL A PRISON MONK, HELPING OTHER PRISONERS ADAPT TO THEIR NEW LIFE IN SOUTHEAST BY FINDING A SENSE OF INNER PEACE IN THAT WORLD. OVER THE YEARS, HE HAS TAKEN MANY OF THE CLASSES OFFERED THERE AND HELD A VARIETY OF JOBS.

IN A LETTER DATED OCTOBER 1, 2019, HE DESCRIBED A RECENT COMMUNICATION HE RECEIVED FROM A MAN HE HAD BEEN MENTORING WHO HAD BEEN RELEASED. THE MAN WAS FEARFUL OF DOING SOMETHING THAT COULD GET HIM REARRESTED. MICHAEL SHARED HIS RESPONSE WITH ME:

Maintain your spiritual discipline and apply all that you have learned. Sometimes impatience reinforces greed, and greed can become so intense that patience begins to feel like an unnecessary obstacle on the path to achieving one's goals and/or desires. When one lacks patience, then he tends to be hypersensitive to frustrations and this makes it easier than one thinks to become persuaded by illegitimate or illegal influences toward the expediency of achieving what is desired or hoped for.

MICHAEL WRITES THAT, SO FAR, THE FRIEND HAS HEEDED HIS ADVICE.
IN MARCH 2019, HE WROTE TO ME:

In December, I and a few other comrades from Kansas City did an *Open Doors* youth intervention video. We spoke on the pitfalls and the negative results that come from living and glorifying the gangster lifestyle and the illusions and self-deception that come along with it. The official in charge of this program said it was one of the best videos to date and received a lot of feedback on this video, more than his previous videos.

ONE OF MY FAVORITE STORIES IS ONE HE SHARED WITH ME IN MAY 2012:

I've been in solitary confinement for a minor infraction with a guard who believed his clothes gave him superhuman powers. During that time, I read the last book you sent,

This Thing Called You, and learned much about the world in which I dwell. I have been made ready for the part I must play in discovering my purpose of existence. I have accepted the calling.

Recently, a guard verbally attacked me for having blue shoelaces on my shoes and was shocked when I found the inner strength to take the shoelaces out and give them to him. Now, because of my action, mystery has been added to my reputation, and I'm even more frightful by virtue of my new unpredictability. It has taken courage, faith, and flexibility to grow in this labyrinth of steel, yet I have come to terms with who I am. The power of a positively committed mind exceeds any other force that I have come across in these lands.

ATTACHED IS MICHAEL'S RECENT TWENTY-PAGE HANDWRITTEN HISTORY, WHICH I TYPED FOR HIM. HE CONTINUES TO PREPARE HIS PORTFOLIO TO SHOW THE TREMENDOUS PROGRESS HE HAS MADE ON HIS SPIRITUAL PATH, GROUNDED IN LOVE AND KINDNESS.

SENT IN GRATITUDE FOR YOUR CONSIDERATION AND COMPASSION FOR THOSE LIKE MICHAEL WHO HAVE MADE SUCH AN INCREDIBLE TURNAROUND AND ARE NOW HELPING OTHERS IN SO MANY WAYS.

SINCERELY,

REV. MARY MITCHELL

CHAPTER 12

2020

Focusing on My African Roots to Counter the Social Laboratory That Is the 9ᵗʰ Dominion

Pressed by poverty and corruption, I dream of better things, of retirement, of grace, of beauty — This 9ᵗʰ Dominion can no longer hold me — Years from now I am a successful author, film maker, spiritual speaker, a master of certain forces of the mind — Arrested development has limited my ability. I have never paid a utility bill or owned a car or gone grocery shopping — I now prepare for this major transition — No situation is hopeless — *Regarding COVID-19:* The world has been given an opportunity for great reflection, a chance to change course for the betterment of all beings — I refrain from violence — The prison system evolved to create a realm of absolute compliance — The number one enemy of progress is questions — In the past, I relied on violence — I cannot return to the free world with this type of mind state — I keep myself humble and continue in my studies — I continue my pursuit of liberation.

1/1/20

DEAR REV. MARY,

For years, I've been pressed by poverty and corruption, confined for long hours in an unhealthy dominion lacking all the arts of refinement. But I dream of better things: retirement, grace, beauty. I conceive of and mentally build up an ideal condition of life, the vision of a wider liberty, and a larger scope takes possession of me. Unrest urges me to action. I use all my spare time and means, small though they may be, to the development of my latent powers and resources.

So altered has my mind become that this 9th Dominion can no longer hold me. It has become so out of harmony with my mentality that it falls out of my life just as a garment is cast aside; and with the growth of opportunities, which fit the scope of my expanding powers, I pass out of this realm forever. Years from now I am a successful author, filmmaker, spiritual speaker, a master of certain forces of the mind, which I wield with world-wide influence in my hands. I hold the cords of gigantic responsibilities. I speak, and lives are changed. Men and women hear my words and it remolds their character, for I have realized my vision and become one with my idea.

All major undertakings have their monotonous aspects, and skipping steps does not work when my goals are complex and the stakes are high. I've learned throughout the many, many moons that a man should not necessarily always stay on a single path. I have evolved in my pursuit of attaining liberation from this realm. I have reached a point at which my progress requires that I must raise the bar and make a more serious commitment in my movement forward.

Prior to getting released from prison and surviving independently without any erroneous decision-making, I have to reach a level of maturity and become an apprentice of how the free world truly works and acquire the skills necessary to operate within it. The average person acquires these skills by trial and error, learning from mistakes, modeling, imitating, taking direct instructions, and practicing. Arrested development has limited my ability to truly comprehend the free world's business savvy, yet I have been able to tune into only a minuscule portion of the multitude of the ins and outs of liberated living. In an effort to learn, I've focused and shifted my attention repeatedly, looking for similar things to happen in this circumstance that will help me once I am free.

As I prepare my mind, spirit, and body to make the transition from prisoner to liberty, my picture of the world and my place in it is fluid. Most of what I have learned about the world that now exists has come from television, music, magazines, and books, not from firsthand experiences. I have never paid an electric, gas, or telephone bill. I've never been grocery shopping. I've never owned a car or had insurance. The most money I've had in my hands at one time was no more than $200. The world inevitably changes, so all the information I had accumulated before my incarceration can only take me so far.

I am at the point in my life where I feel the call to extend myself in new ways. Doing well in one state of life does not guarantee doing well in the next. So, I now prepare for this major transition. For me, this is a crucial life-defining moment that carries overtones of a nervous fear of momentous decision-making pertaining to employment, career, finances, relationships, as well as leisure pursuits.

It is said by Émile-Auguste Chartier that, "We must stand firm between two kinds of madness: the belief that we can do anything and the belief that we can do nothing." I've come to learn and understand more about myself since you have been my mentor and friend. I know no situation is hopeless. Even in my growth and positive change, I lack only familiarity with certain knowledge and skills and gaining an aspect of familiarity.

In Matthew 25, Jesus tells the parable about the three stewards left in charge of varying portions of their master's assets. Before traveling, the master of the estate entrusted one steward with five talents, another steward with two, and yet another with one. The first two stewards invested their master's funds and, upon his return, each had doubled the amount left to him to oversee. The master lauded their efforts and rewarded them handsomely. The third steward, fearful of making an investment mistake, buried the talent given to him in the ground. The master's response was swift. He rebuked the third steward for cowardice and unfaithfulness and fired him on the spot.

Failing to try is already failing myself. I can only succeed by trying. Apparently, Jesus took a dim view of sitting on talents and non-productivity. I am not and will not be unfaithful to myself or those who assist me. I am learning that in paving the way to success sometimes one has to bring in outside help, if necessary. I believe it is now necessary for me to acquire a skill of financial development. I welcome any advice with open arms pertaining to making sound investments and how to go about achieving it. If you are willing to share with me anything you believe, it will expand my progress in the financial arena.

I am now in the preparation stages of living a free life. I'm gathering information about colleges that offer free college courses to prisoners in business, with enough hours so I can get an associate's degree in business. I'm getting myself internally accustomed to a new change. I let myself imagine what life would be like when I've been liberated. In this way, I'm mentally trying things on for size to help me ready my being to deal with higher expectations and new demands.

3/6/20

DEAR MICHAEL,

Over the past couple of months, I took a class in "The Metaphysics of Addiction and Recovery," presented by a minister who also works full time as a program manager for a rehab center. In the first class, he quoted from a book by don Jose Ruiz, the son of don Miguel Ruiz: "Awareness is such an important practice that all other spiritual and psychological tools are contingent upon it. One cannot not investigate their domestications, self-judgments, resentments, or all the other beliefs that keep one from living one's truth until one becomes aware of them."

Awareness is so important in our everyday life. What are we choosing to feel, see, think? Is it helping us feel happy, content, kind? What is our intent for the day?

In your 2/9 letter, I'm so excited about your application for clemency. I went back to the website and enclosed is the form and information. Hope you are still working on your portfolio.

Note: In mid-March 2020, the world was in the midst of dealing with the COVID-19 pandemic. Much of the world was in "shutdown mode," with stay-at-home orders and most businesses closed.

4/11/20

DEAR MICHAEL,

How fast the world has changed this past month. Everything in California is shut down, except essential businesses as determined by the governor. Ministers are considered essential services, thank goodness. Most businesses are closed, and I feel for their employees and how the owners will be able to pay everyone. Restaurants only offer take out or have drive-through windows.

Our church is closed, but I go in Monday through Thursday from about 9 a.m. to 3 p.m. to answer the phone, get mail, and get things on my to-do list done. I'm the only one there, but I have a friend, a beautiful songbird right outside my window. I can't see him/her, but the song just opens my heart. When the day comes that we open back up, I hope one of our bird lovers can identify the melody.

5/27/20

DEAR REV. MARY,

I pray that you and your loved ones are well and enduring this time now that the world has been given an opportunity for great reflection and a chance to change course for the betterment of all beings on this planet.

Within this realm, there has been a change, but the magnitude of seriousness pertaining to the infection has not sunk into the minds of the inhabitants or those who work here. There have been several guards who were infected who came to work to spread this COVID-19 plague to more than forty prisoners so far. There has been no professionalism involved with a protocol to stop the infected from entering prison grounds, yet visitations from family members have been stopped.

As I write this letter, prisoners have been given notice that starting May 26, all Missouri DOC adult institutions will participate in sentinel testing, a process of testing most or all members of a large group of people living or working together in close contact.

Well, on March 13, I was targeted to go to the hole, the same day I was to graduate from a program I was taking called Transition Training. I won't go into the details, but it seems the more I'm focused on getting out of prison, the more the egregore of this realm is intent on provoking me into an old, outdated behavior. I do not rise to the bait, but injustices have always irritated me to be proactive. Still, I refrain from violence and will continue to do so unless absolutely necessary.

There is so much going on in these lands. Had I not signed up to take a particular program, I wouldn't have realized how much the prison system has evolved in its methods to co-opt and create a realm of absolute compliance. Prisoners are being put under hypnosis to consume, confirm, and obey. They are being programmed to believe that to think will bring on depression, that the number one enemy of progress is questions.

When taking Transition Training classes, I realized they were using a type of psychology I studied in my early years in prison. It incorporates hypnosis. I didn't even think it was legal to introduce this in the prison system. Evidently it is being implemented with no regard to the side effects it may have on the prisoner. Perhaps this is another reason why I was locked up the night of my graduation. I planned on exposing what it was, yet I wasn't given the opportunity.

When I get out of the hole, I will gather all my notes and the information I have pertaining to the class and send you more detailed insights into the bold experiments they are engaging in. The majority of the inhabitants couldn't conceive of and certainly wouldn't believe in mass hypnosis. I was asked to come aboard, but I refused. I couldn't morally become a facilitator to create docile and nonthinking puppets.

Dealing with human experiences behind layers of concrete and steel requires a working central nervous system and a healthy mental state of being. The regular attitude of the mannequins (staff) toward the inhabitants is both defensive and hostile. Until the inhabitant gives in completely, it will continue to be so. By giving in, I mean prostrating oneself at their feet as you would your God. Only then does the attitude alter itself. Most convicts don't dig this kind of relationship, yet there are many inmates who do love it.

Obsequiousness is rewarded under the mannequins where there were certain emoluments to be earned. Resistance wasn't a problem. Sex, like the allowance of a fish trainer to well-behaved dolphins, was regularly doled out to the co-opted as a premium commensurate with the adequate performance of the obsequious prisoner's dirty duties. This is on the understanding that anyone who availed himself of this privilege would receive an effeminate male to satisfy their desires.

My enemies are many, and they don't always come as flesh and blood. They come as a mentality or ideology that I do not advocate or adhere to. I know that God has approved my purpose. I just must use different methods against those who would see me not reach my Godhood.

In the past, I always relied on violence to stomp out any problem I came against within this realm. I know I cannot return to the free world with this type of mind state, so

I believe I've been given tests to see for myself how I will approach and handle any situation that I do not agree with without resorting to violent measures.

I keep myself humble and continue in my studies, regardless of the illusions going on around me. I continue my pursuit of liberation and my other positive endeavors.

6/28/20

DEAR REV. MARY,

The events taking place out in the free world have been a constant topic of conversation and opinions between many men within this realm. I've read your Sunday talk, "Mindful Speech." In ancient Kemet (Egypt), what you wrote about was and is called "maat," which means to speak truth and do truth. In your Sunday talk entitled, "Just Breathe," this was very touching, as well as poetic.

I want to share with you my view about what is going on out in the free world. I truly believe that rebellion is a necessary response to the continuous and unrelenting violence inflicted on the physical and spiritual being. The intention to engage in rebellion does not form overnight. Instead, it builds over time as a response to the evils of police brutality, poverty, enslavement (mass incarceration), violence, food and medical insecurity, lack of housing, and chronic disease.

Rebellion isn't irrational, unnecessary, confused, sporadic, or thuggish. Rebellion is the concentrated application of energy and thought toward the resistance against a system intent on destroying one's God-given right to life. Rebellion is not a riot. It is an integral part of a movement for systemic and structural change. What is happening in America and across the globe is a rebellion. African people in America are subjected constantly to unspeakable violence with no end or justice. The violence of slavery was translated into a system of mass incarceration.

If you remember studying the Civil War, the Confederate South wanted to keep the institution of slavery alive and well, yet the Union had other intentions. A war commenced, but the war did not end. It is still going on today. The Confederates won the judicial system, the police system, the justice system, and the prison system, along with every luxury and all the riches produced by these institutions.

Despite doing everything right, African people can have their entire future destroyed by racists who weaponize the police to defend European fragility. Police have always defended property and capital. They have always protected the interest of those who choose to benefit from the enslavement of African people. The slave patrols, aka police, were always and still are a danger to Africans. What is happening now is nothing new. So African people, in the spirit of people from Nat Turner to Harriet Tubman, must rebel and shine in the glory of rebellion.

The ignited fires are warranted when one comes to understand that this burning is both cathartic and symbolic of a need to resist and dismantle the oppressive confederate system that oversees the hiring of bloodthirsty KKK types who are drawn to gunslinger jobs.

Government cannot be held accountable for every racist individual who decides, "Here's an opportunity to finally kill an African and make my ancestors proud." Yet when things fall along racial lines, when the killer can be seen so clearly in the act of killing and still be rewarded and not held accountable, there is something more sinister involved. George Floyd's murder set off the unaddressed inequities and structural injustices, legal terrorism, and historic violence against African people in America. If laws are only enforced against men like me and others are above the law, such injustices and rebellion continue and continue and continue and continue.

7/19/20

DEAR REV. MARY,

May you be in positive spirits and may the spirit of joy and laughter be upon you this day! I received your letters with the cover, title, and table of contents design. I've been out of the hole for fourteen days now. I had to reorganize all my notes, writings, etc., and am now in a new housing unit.

Since I've been out of the hole, I've had the chance to continue my reading. I'm a couple of chapters from finishing the book you sent entitled *Becoming Supernatural* by Dr. Joe Dispenza. I incorporated his meditation technique to achieve gamma brain wave states. I will do this until the end of the year to see how effective this method truly is and what beneficial gifts I attain from it.

I also picked up another book from the property room that you sent, *Moving Mountains* by Rev. Dr. Raymont L. Anderson. I will be reading this as soon as I'm finished with Dr. Joe. I see that he is in the August *Science of Mind* magazine as well, and you mentioned him in your letter. I will be reaching out to him.

The 9th Dominion has allowed me to understand the dynamics of mind control and how it is implemented to probe the staff and prisoners for weaknesses and destabilize personalities to see if the subjects can be programmed for mind control. If these elements exist, and they usually do, they will be brainwashed into becoming operatives, puppets, trained and unable to think or act independently of the master's interest or outside the enslaving doctrine.

In the Bible, Colossians 2:8 reads, "See to it that no one takes you captive through hollow and deceptive philosophy, which depends on human tradition and the basic principles of this world." In the Koran, Sirah 3:139 reads, "So lose not heart nor fall into despair, for you gain mastery if you are true in faith." In *The Life Divine* by Sri Aurobindo, in Chapter 27 he quotes the Yajur Veda, which reads, "I have arisen from earth to the mid-world. I have arisen from the mid-world to heaven, from the level of the firmament of heaven, I have gone to the sun-world, the Light!"

There exist master manipulators within these lands who use techniques to conform and sway the weak minded toward their concepts of domination, power, and control. My transition to develop a greater self, as I live in the now of this life, has taken me beyond all of this. I continue to express my truth, for it is always stranger than fiction.

8/9/20

DEAR REV. MARY,

Greetings to you on this beautiful day during this beautiful month, Black August. May the Divine Creator of and in all and beloved ancients and ancestors from yesteryears and yesterday find you and your loved one thriving in healing Spirit.

Rev. Mary, I want you to understand one important thing about the 9th Dominion. This is a place where very elaborate experiments are carried out. It is a social laboratory and, just like everyone else, I am a thing to be tested, poked, and provoked. In their gathering of information, to them I am no more than a thing and a number, even though I am that and more. I do not lose sight of their truth about me. Man's deeds do not lie.

Along with this letter, I'm sending you my Transition Training Certificate. Please make about four copies for me and keep one for yourself and send me the original back. Thank you.

In your letter of July 6, you asked what else you could do to help me. Well, there is a book entitled *The Way of the Superior Man* by David Deida. I believe this book will improve my mastery over my masculinity and enforce confidence with the opposite sex. Could you please order this book for me?

The inhabitants of this land lose the art of interacting with females. We are unorthodox, brash, and unpolished. I want and need to change that, and I believe this book will help me in this area.

When you receive this letter, I will probably be moving into another cell as well as writing my rough drafts to send to you. I will be writing again soon. There is much to discuss.

2021

Practicing Revolutionary Spirituality, Transforming from Struggle to Clear Purpose

The riot, the whole, the situation — Understanding and surviving in ad-seg — Scarecrows, straw men without vision, living lives filled with fear — Moving forward in expression to help others — The Creator is the author — Maintaining a peaceful state of mind — Living by God's mercy and grace — Decades spent searching for Ancient Wisdom.

4/28/21

DEAR REV. MARY,

You asked me to write to you about this recent experience. First, I want you to know that I am humble for everything God has brought into my life and allowed me to accomplish. I know Science of Mind teaches that evil is that which seems destructive and that evil is an experience of the soul on its journey toward the realization of reality. Also, it teaches that evil will remain a problem as long as we believe in it, for of itself it is neither person, place, nor thing and will disappear in the exact proportion that we cease using destructive methods.

For an African man in prison, this was one of the hardest teachings for me to digest and actually let go of. It has taken me many moons to accept this as truth because what I see seems to contradict this teaching. I have not yet had the chance to read the book *Egregores* by Mark Stavish, but I will. Perhaps along with the information I gain from this book and the teachings of SOM, I'll have a clearer understanding of these entities I deal with within the 9th Dominion that are not "evil."

On January 3, 2021, thirteen days before my forty-ninth birthday, I was attacked by malevolent forces in the guise of correctional officers. I defended myself. During this ordeal, my right forearm was broken and my left wrist was broken. Both are now healed because of my faith and understanding of the Creator's ability to allow me to heal. I received no medical treatment. I was prescribed some ibuprofen and told to drink more water.

I've filed a grievance, and I'll pursue a lawsuit. I had to put a sock on my forearm as a cast and make a sling with my socks. I do physical therapy every day. It's been almost four months now and I'm back up to 1,000 push-ups a day and 3,000 sit-ups and crunches a day. I do 500 push-ups on my fist to strengthen my wrist, forearm, and hands. My recovery has been very successful. My elbow bone pops a lot and I cannot yet stretch my right arm all the way out. I believe a ligament was also torn, but I have healed pretty well, considering the circumstances.

Because of the attack on me, a few days later several guards were attacked, which led to a full-scale riot. (Google "Modoc SECC Riot January 3-13.") Many officers and inmates were hurt. They have closed down Housing Unit 5 and intend to close down Housing Unit 6.

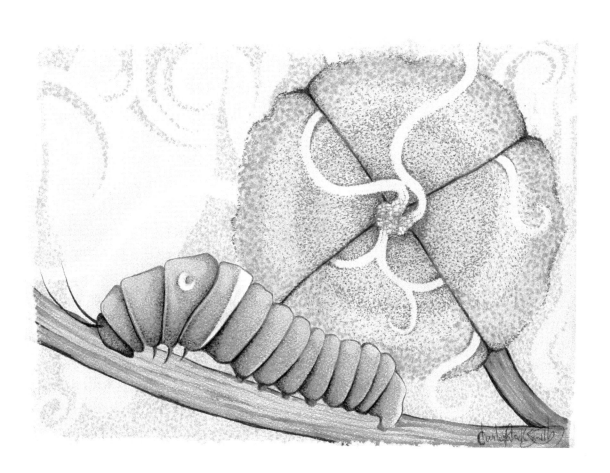

More than 400 prisoners have been transferred out of this land in the last ninety days, and they are sending out at least forty to fifty a week as I write this. The guards have gone from three eight-hour shifts to two twelve-hour shifts. Many guards quit because of what happened. They are now hiring more.

They may transfer me to another land or they may not. Yet instead of worrying about how long I'll be here, I focus on accepting the fact that the time frame doesn't matter. It's not in my control. Accepting my situation and not fighting against it and not letting it frustrate me signals to my brain that I am not under threat. So, I surrender resistance to this circumstance. This is one of the reasons I was able to heal quickly.

The hole is the most unique part of the prison system. It is designed to torture and break men. It has devastating effects on the weak minded. You have those who suffer from depression, anxiety, and other complexes, and they cannot adjust to this environment. The darkness of their crimes makes them cringe inside their minds, making them more susceptible to the hole's madness.

In the hole, one's madness is amplified, as are one's fears. The inhabitant goes through mental upheavals or breakdowns, and these can be episodic, coming in alternating waves of intense emotional outbursts.

Those in the hole do not have access to materials such as books or study materials. Some may have subscriptions to magazines or newspapers, so this alleviates boredom for some, yet most inhabitants in the hole stay in a toxic mind-state of racism, negativity, and boredom. What I and others may speak about doesn't resonate with them, but I create a gateway to allow the maniac entrance. I notice what's important. I notice who is doing what. I listen to conversations and because I know others are noticing me, I speak wisely at all times so what they hear just might pique their interest.

Many times, I tune into what type of conversations are being held. I listen for a while, then I ask questions. This is a great way to enter a conversation. Interjecting with a statement is risky, especially when they contrast with the participants' stance. It can lead to arguments and accusations of not minding one's own business. But when I ask questions, especially those requesting more information or clarification, I allow an inhabitant to be heard and to express his views.

It seems that within this realm everyone wants to tell others what to do and think, but who is listening to these desolate minds? I am. And because I do, they listen to me.

Being open to feedback and criticism is important. I try not to come off as a know-it-all, even if I do. This way I stay human.

What makes connections with prisoners in the hole harder than average is that you become conditioned and encouraged to separate, isolate, and differentiate. In these catacombs, there is a saying: "Believe nothing you hear and half of what you see." So the prisoner is looking and they are not seeing if you are really about what you say. So I must at all times practice what I preach. Doing this, I have more sway. I gain their respect and attention. They believe the things I say—and the staff hates this. They like the prisoners to argue through the cell doors from morning to night and keep chaotic nothingness within the atmosphere.

I know that most need psychological help and healing, so getting them involved with positive thought is how I plant seeds and tend them while I can, because my time in the hole is temporary.

6/1/21

DEAR REV. MARY,

I wanted to elaborate somewhat on how Science of Mind teachings literally saved my life. I was led to this system of thought and practice by the Higher Power. I've been using this particular way of thought my whole life, and I've been aware that I've used it, but I really didn't understand its true workings. Because I didn't, I misused it, which led to detrimental conditions that caused harm to me and to others.

I have always manifested or demonstrated objectively that which I have thought about. A couple of years ago, I contemplated everything I did in the free world. I thought it was a supernatural or psychic gift or talent that I alone possessed, and in a way it was. It was only natural that I would come across the teachings that would elaborate more of what I was actually doing.

Vodun is a syncretic merging of African, European, Asiatic, and Native American beliefs, philosophies, and practices. Vodun is always evolving and has a voracious appetite when it comes to other religions.

Much like its sacred snakes, Dambellah Wedo and Ayida Wedo, it swallows other systems of religious thought and practice whole. The use of Roman Catholic imagery and ritual is well known, but this is only one example of the ability of Vodun to enhance its liturgy through contact with other systems.

I have always compared myself to the honeybee, which flies to many different types of flowers to collect nectar for its honey. It doesn't discriminate against any type of flower. It is rewarded by them all, even as it learns about a particular type of flower that doesn't yield what the bee may need.

I've studied many beliefs and philosophies, and I've kept the truth that existed in all of them that would benefit me throughout life. In the old Kung Fu theater flicks, a master was the one who expressed and embodied the highest qualities of an individual. He was expert in all techniques and combined them all to create one.

Science of Mind teachings embody ancient and powerful knowledge, and for me to use it correctly in all its applications, I must be able to transform myself into a fit vessel. I must reflect the sacred framework that I represent so I can have a spiritual influence on everyone I come into contact with. But there exist the pessimists I come into contact with, those immersed in the pool of gloom, despair, negativity, and hopelessness. They do not embrace Truth. They despise it, and it affects them as salt does a snail.

Futility means empty and without any purpose. Many times, the minds of men invent plausible ideas that are empty of Truth and are thus dangerous. Moral judgments start in their mind, and because the mind is depraved in its conclusions and does not take God into account, they are intellectually futile.

Romans 1:21–28 says in part, "For although they knew God, they neither glorified him as God nor gave thanks to him, but their thinking became futile and their foolish hearts were darkened. Although they claimed to be wise, they became fools and exchanged the glory of the immortal God for images made to look like a mortal human being and birds and animals and reptiles. … Furthermore, just as they did not think it worthwhile to retain the knowledge of God, so God gave them over to a depraved mind, so that they do what ought not to be done."

Futile thinking is by definition pointless. It accomplishes nothing of any lasting value. Unbelievers are said to be blinded by Satan, becoming increasingly ignorant of God. He gives them over to their chosen pathway. They no longer have any sense of the consequences of sin. They live ungodly lifestyles. Those who are futile thinkers within the 9th Dominion, who constantly hunger and lust for forms of immorality, are scarecrows. These are straw men.

In *The Wizard of Oz,* the scarecrow didn't have a brain and wanted to be given one by the wizard. In the adaptation movie entitled *The Wiz,* the scarecrow, played by a young Michael Jackson, was brainless as well and wanted to be given a brain by the Wiz, played by my unsung hero Richard Pryor.

Straw men are the majority within the 9th Dominion. They are those who, like me, have been sentenced to calendars without end. But unlike me, they stay in a state of perpetual suspended animation. A straw man does not think for himself or anyone else. If you were to ask a scarecrow what his goals are, he would stammer or quickly try to invent some fantasy on the spot.

A goal is an intention to accomplish something. An intention is a purpose. Scarecrows have no purpose and, therefore, they have no voice because only worms come out of their mouths. Their eyes are sewn shut so they cannot see. They form unorthodox communities that congregate in the illusion of a gang or religious organization, yet the one thing they have in common with is hate groups in the free world, the underlying cause of their embarkation, is the drive to defend themselves against any form of threat.

Of course, one cannot fight what one cannot see; therefore, they have to be given vision. The enemies have to be identifiable as combatants. If one is a fly, then a spider is the enemy. If you are human, anything that encroaches on your freedom or quality of life is your enemy. Ask a scarecrow who his enemy is and nine times out of ten, he will point out another prisoner in the same prison garb being held captive just as he is, versus a state-paid miscreant whose livelihood is to enforce the Thirteenth Amendment.

And if you are an intelligent African warrior who isn't asleep within the 9th Dominion, you have collectively more enemies than any other: white supremacy, health issues, economic woes, social inadequacies, brainwashing, and oppression, all of which derive from a type of prejudiced belief based in religious ideology. This ideology is enforced by Confederate-enacted laws reinforced by slave catchers and patrollers, who patrol through the urban jungles to mine for human resources to be warehoused, experimented on, exploited for labor, and monetized for the coffers of the confederation land barons.

A young African looks up and finds him or herself held captive within one of the most complex slave infrastructures designed to this day. In this new and unfamiliar condition, the new captive will be exposed to contagion, for the more one socializes or rotates with the brainwashed scarecrows, the more abnormal and functionless he or she will become, thereby becoming susceptible to the disease all straw men suffer from: indifference. This is a disease that indicates the growth of tumors. Since I recognize this illness, I write, speak, and advocate against a mentality and ideology that causes harm to millions and many come against me in my expression, because they do not like nor do they agree with what it is I do. Yet regardless of another person's dislikes, I continue to move forward in expression and endeavors that will help me and others, either younger or of my age.

I have learned much in these thirty years of incarceration that can benefit many. As long as a person is walking in the Truth of God, no power on earth can hinder him. We are immortal until our work is done. The debased do not want me to believe in God. Those who do not want God in their lives do everything in their power to prevent me from having God in my life, but this is futile thinking.

God didn't want me to waste away within this world. I could have easily, but I didn't. I was guided to a place that saved my life and you as my mentor, Rev. Mary, will always be a great blessing.

6/7/21

DEAR REV. MARY,

I was reflecting on my youth, when my mother would take me to the children's library and leave me there for hours. In one of the book aisles, I came across a series of books that allowed me to pick at least five or six different endings to a story. I thought at the time that these were the most unique books ever created. I would check different ones out every time I came to the library. Those books allowed the reader to go back to a certain point in the book and decide to go left instead of right—and the outcome of the story would be totally different.

I often think about this COVID-19 pandemic and wonder: What if there had not been a pandemic at all? Would there have been a mass movement for Black Lives Matter? Would Michael Jordan have donated $100 million dollars toward it? Would there really be an African-Asian American female as vice president? Would there have been the loss of life at the U.S. Capitol building? Would Tampa Bay Buccaneers really have been able to defeat my Kansas City Chiefs at the Super Bowl?!?

If I were the author of this story, perhaps none of these things would have happened. But I am not the author. The Creator is the author, and it is His creation of Universal Laws that has directed events and outcomes that now manifest themselves.

Daily, I maintain a peaceful state of mind. Sometimes events tempt me to fight against, stand up against, rebel against—always the temptation to be against. But I have learned that I do not have to do this anymore. *The Kybalion* teaches about Universal Laws, and if my memory serves me correctly, it mentions in the Laws of Rhythm, how emotions can be like ocean tides, going back and forth, forth and back, according to situations and events. One has to rise above this pendulum state and move to a position where one does not easily fluctuate and remain there without being tempted to feel this way or that way or a certain way according to the events that are taking place.

I perhaps will have to finish the rest of this year in the hole, but regardless, this too is only temporary and will pass. I will, nonetheless, be out of the hole by January 2023 and I will take off as fast as a cheetah toward my goals, endeavors, and other projects. I will get all the things done that are necessary for me to obtain my freedom.

This time in the hole prepared me for my fiftieth year of life. In January, I turn the big five-oh. I've come a long way in a world in which, according to statistics, I should have succumbed to and should be broken by now. But by God's mercy and grace, I was introduced to concepts and beliefs that wouldn't allow me to wallow in misery, self-pity, hatred, or any negative handicaps that disable the spirit of men within this realm.

Physically, I don't feel that fifty is an age that indicates "old." I still can outrun, out sit-up, out push-up, out lift the average twenty-year-old. I don't think that "old," if that is a thing, but rather prison kept me in a state of mind that initially attributed to arrested development. Now it keeps me thinking youthfully and, therefore, I behave and engage in activities that inspire vitality.

In Vodun, there is the Master of the Agad. It is the Self, known in other schools of thought as the Hierophant. The Master of the Head is the Self on an exalted plane. It expresses the highest qualities of an individual. To know and be aligned with the Master of One's Head is to function according to one's own unique place in the universe and to have realization of one's purpose and acknowledge assistance from forces perceived as highly placed.

With all of the knowledge I have had the luxury to gain in thirty years in this realm, I would really love to pass this knowledge on so others may pass it on, so that the gift I was given can change the lives of many. For me, this is magic. I feel it is Divine Wisdom being used correctly and for great purposes. All that I have learned I realize is nothing but an element, and positive results can come from it to enable so many people to lift themselves out of the bogs of their own creation.

7/12/21

DEAR REV. MARY,

May the day you receive this missive find you in uplifted spirits, in a beautiful space mentally, and in a clear state of receptive understanding.

There is much I want to write, but first and foremost, I must apologize to you for one of my earlier letters in which I wrote and vented about historical negatives and my continued encounters with these negative elements. It was not my intention to cause discomfort and/or ill ease. I ask for forgiveness if this was the impression invoked. Healing for me will manifest itself. I continue to apply treatment methods upon myself until my healing has been completed.

I feel the need to clarify myself so that you can have a more in-depth vision and so that you can see and perceive a clearer, brighter, and much broader picture of how all my studies, beliefs, ideologies, disciplines, practices, experiences, hobbies, etc., have molded me into this being that now writes to you in this moment in time. I previously wrote in one of my letters, "I could not be a conscious moral person if I ignore Truth." I include in this letter several of the truths I have shared previously, such as:

> *That which has been decreed for me has allowed me to retrospectively examine my travels through different stages in my life, which have prepared me for the next stage, until I finally reach my assigned destination.*
>
> *— MJN*

Dr. Mary, please try to understand some realities that most people gloss over as insignificant. First, at nineteen, close to a year after graduating high school, my thought processes were still functioning on the same level they were when I was seventeen. I ended up in the "school-to-prison pipeline." I don't know what it is like to be an adult civilian in the free world, to have major responsibilities, to raise children, to maintain a career, to have a wife, to have dental and medical and car insurance, to own a house or a car or property, to pay bills. I was forty-eight years old when I filed my first income tax form.

The being is hurled into a vortex of virtual reality and dehumanized to the point that its name becomes interchangeable with a number. And that number is grouped with other numbers to form statistics.

— MJN

All of my adult life has thus far been in a cage, on a plantation designed to annihilate me, to destroy every fiber of my being, my soul, my spirit, my mind, and my physical form. Technically, according to scientific prison statistics, I should already be dead by now or on death row, awaiting execution. I am an anomaly and the reason being is more profound than these petty tyrants' minds can grasp, but I will share with you a beautiful but uncanny view of why my survival within the 9th Dominion is successful and why it does not conform with the average "if you can't beat them, join them" survival methods, which have been used for centuries and are predictable and controllable, because they are outdated and useless to me. Everything I did pertaining to my survival within this realm would seem unorthodox to a seasoned career convict, yet it was these unpredictable unorthodox, spiritually influenced methods that gave me a quantum leap and advanced me thirty-three steps ahead of every other being within this realm.

When I write these things to you, I must be blunt. I must be raw and truthful, yet I will tread lightly. I've done what "Prison Advocates" think cannot be done because of their non-belief. *I woke up!* I was awakened by my ancestors (remember the story about the live bird that came out of my toilet?), and because of my ancestors' faith and beliefs, I was encouraged to emulate their sophistication and was provided with Ancient African knowledge to combat those who are also knowledgeable but put their knowledge in use to destroy those gifted, like me.

At various points, whether by apparent whim or Divine Design, I've made course corrections. Whether I received navigational aid from someone else, some event, or my own inner compass, I can look back and see vividly when these moments occurred.

— MJN

Metaphysical authors write about how time and space are really not that distinct. Metaphysical teachings imply that thought, intention, and prayer all have the uncanny ability to transcend time and space. Ancient African science also teaches this, yet it takes the concept thirty-three steps further. For instance, my great-great-great-great grandmother, at the age of twelve, was stabbed in her head with a fork and sexually assaulted by a Southern Baptist Christian European slaveowner. She prayed to her God that her great-great-great-great grandchildren would not have to go through what she and her siblings were going through. And if they were ever enslaved, "Please God, provide them with the strength and power to overcome!" In 1868, my ancient grandmother's prayer was answered because of her faith, intention, and emotion.

That same year, in the Kingdom of Dahomey in West Africa, a Yoraban Shaman Priest, my great-great-great-great grandfather was witnessing his people being slaughtered by Muslim invaders and being captured and sold to European slave traders, so he invoked his God, prayed, and asked in one of the many Bantu dialects "that my descendants be given the power, knowledge, and strength to overcome" the conditions that we were going to be under and were going to be placed upon us.

And before I was born, every prayer for me that existed in my ancestors' hearts manifested itself and allowed me to overcome, as well as my prayers for all those in my family, all those of my bloodline who now exist in this plane of life, as well as for those who have yet to be born. Eternity must be made up of different times.

My prayer for them is to be given the inherited gifts of their ancient mothers' and fathers' strength and power to overcome every devilish negative psychological, emotional, magical, spiritual, and physical attack. This prayer, too, has already been answered.

By any logical and apparent reason, I should be anything but what I am today, but sometimes the Spirit is stronger than the circumstances.
— MJN

Sometimes the choices we make provide us with guidance and a way to grow from the experience.
— MJN

In order to become strong, meaningful, and a worthy human being, one has to eliminate that which is weak within him. Often this process is hell, but any metal only becomes strong once it has been through fire. The fire purifies and strengthens the metal, just as struggle, sacrifice, and strife have done for me; for it is adversity that teaches one to practice patience, compassion, and tolerance, and if a prisoner can learn to incorporate these values into his daily life, he can change his perception of the world around him.
— MJN

The Science of Mind philosophy teaches that a habit is formed first by desire, then comes the expression of this desire. The desire becomes subjective and the subconscious action of thought causes it to be performed automatically. First, we control thought, then thought controls us. The teachings continue into mania and how a person creates such a strong desire that it compels him to put it into execution. Mania is a desire too strong to be controlled, and the person becomes controlled by the very power he has set in motion. This teaching continues into obsession. The obsession of desire produces a mania to express that desire, for thought demands an outlet. Some are obsessed by the suggestion of their environment, such as in the 9th Dominion, for the mental atmosphere of places often obsesses people, compelling them to do certain things and without any apparent reason.

Rev. Mary, I was bearing witness to all of these things Dr. Holmes is teaching, yet I could not quite comprehend what I was perceiving. But I knew the root lay in weakness, so I called it "the Siccness," a saying coined by an underground rapper named Brotha Lynch Hung. He used it when referring to maniacs and perversions. In order for my survival within the 9th Dominion to be successful, I had to know the truth, all the truths about who I am, and my truths lay in the heart of Momma Africa, and thus my Warrior Spirit was forged.

> *It wasn't until I let go of what I thought I was and embraced what I truly am that things began to change in my life.*
> — *MJN*

> *Man is confronted everywhere with alternative routes, some true, others false, and the eye of reason must choose between them. Those who chose well or in error will incur that which serves as a base of their beliefs.*
> — *MJN*

Rev. Mary, you are already familiar with many of my metaphysical studies and those books, but I need to shed some illumination on my studies before I found the Science of Mind teaching. Let me broaden the picture somewhat of my decades of study and application of that which I have learned.

In my youth, there was nothing I put my mind to that I couldn't accomplish. There were hundreds of incidents that showed me the gifts I had inherited and boosted my confidence in my truth.

The Orisha Yemaya bestowed upon me many of my gifts, as did the Loa Ogun. These gifts continue to protect and teach me to this very day and have aided me in my battle for survival, for it is my battles that gave away any distinction of my uniqueness.

Just like in the U.S. military, the uniforms and emblems that each branch wears are what distinguish one from another. And so it is with modern-day tribalism. Certain colors represent a symbol of indomitable strength and fortitude. For me this color is blue, and for others it is red.

Each man within this realm has the potential to be a master of balanced change. We have the means to transform from struggle and survival to enlightenment and clear purpose.
— MJN

One thing a prisoner has that the ordinary free-world civilian does not is hours of leisure time. Not all of us use it wisely or constructively, but we all have it. It is this time that I dedicated to study, experimentation, application, and writing.

Entering these death-lands run by self-ascribed Ku Klux Klansmen, Christian identity adherents, and White Nationalists, I came into contact with self-hate gangs—like the Gangster Disciples, Bloods, Moorish Science Temple of America adherents, and the African Militant organizations, the Crips, the Nation of Islam, the Five Percent Nation of Gods and Earths—and the pseudo-religious gangs—the Al Islamic Muslims, Wiccans, Auster adherents, the Odinists, and Satanists.

I realized a mythical truth that I had now entered the kingdom of predatory demons that have committed every sin imaginable and unimaginable. How could I, Michael, named after an archangel (Revelations 12:7–9), navigate the 9th Dominion of Hell without the demons knowing an angel was in their very midst? How could I live in this realm without becoming a demon myself? This realization immediately transformed my educational quest.

I asked myself a series of questions: How do you see yourself? How do you see others? How do you want others to see you? Then I asked myself a most serious question based on the knowledge that leadership positions demand of one: What image must I create to invoke a sinister vision of fierceness and intelligence that will activate the notion of fear within the inhabitants of this realm?

I have accepted the casting, complete with my own ominous stage name. Coming into this prison environment, I created a persona that would enable me to navigate this labyrinth of madness.

— MJN

When man is confronted with his destiny, he must choose the decision of meeting it with courage, honor, and pride, or succumbing to the demons, stripped of morality, principles, and dignity, to become molded into the form of the typical prison inhabitant.

— MJN

There is something greater than me at work and it takes incredible faith to see the spiritual perspective of a challenge.

— MJN

My studies began with nothing but the underworld—the criminal lifestyle—the gangsters, the Italian mob, the Irish mob, the street gangsters, the Crips, the Bloods, the Vice Lords, the Disciples, the crime families, the kingpins, the drug lords, the drug dealers, the drug users, the pimps, the prostitutes, the johns. I studied serial killers, murderers, kidnappers, and rapists. I studied white collar criminals, hustlers, conmen, scam artists, jewelry thieves, art thieves, bank robbers, burglars, loan sharks, pool sharks, card sharks, gamblers, cheaters, and everything else that exists within the underworld.

I have always been one with the courage to go outside the box in my thinking and actions.

— MJN

An African shaman is like a Roman Catholic priest. To exorcise a demon, he must first have knowledge of it and therefore know what type of demon he is actually dealing with.

— MJN

To seek wisdom, prisoners realize the seriousness of their situation and apply themselves with the necessary vigilance, willpower, discipline, and patience to ensure their success in prison and in life.

— MJN

I've studied different genres of music, musical works by Mozart and Beethoven as well as underground gangster rap, rock, death metal, black metal, and reggae.

I've studied Hindu mythology, Greek mythology, African mythology, Japanese mythology. My studies have included numerous volumes of work dedicated to the art of warfare: Sun Tzu's *The Art of War,* Miyamoto Musashi's *The Book of Five Rings,* books by Bruce Lee, several books by Robert Green, including *Mastery, The 33 Strategies of War, The 48 Laws of Power,* and many others.

I've learned and practiced hand-to-hand combat, African martial arts, and Judo. I've learned where to strike a man to cause the most damage. I've learned how to make shanks, which are homemade weapons made from different types of metal. I've learned how to make blowguns, tattoo guns, tattoo ink, invisible ink, slingshots, hooch or pruno (homemade wine made from fermented fruit, sugar, water, and yeast). It's pretty good, too!

I know twelve ways to produce a fire, but I only use seven or eight. I've learned how to make poisonous drugs by catching black widow and brown recluse spiders.

I've studied the teachings of so-called secret societies, like the Illuminati and the Prince Hall Masons. My studies have included books by Albert Churchward, Alfred Metraux, Milo Rigaud, Ross Heaven, and Aleister Crowley. I've learned and studied books about black magic, white magic, Italian witchcraft, European witchcraft (Druids), sympathetic magic, Wicca, hypnosis, mental telepathy, ESP, mesmerism, theosophy (the teachings by Madame Blavatsky), psychology, filmmaking, political science, geometry, script writing, book writing, American history, and African History.

I've studied the religious beliefs of the Rosicrucians, Christian Science, Christian identity ministries, Aryan Nation philosophy, Skinhead ideology. I've studied the religious texts: The Circle 7, Holy Quran, Holy Koran, Holy Bible, Book of Yahweh, Book of Nicodemus, Necronomicon, Holy Tablets, Ancient Future, Destruction of a Black Civilization and many, many others.

I've studied books by Elijah Muhammed, founder of the Nation of Islam, teachings by Louis Farrakhan, teachings of Malcom X and Marcus Garvey. I've studied books by Donald Goines, Ice T, Iceberg Slim, Pimpin' Ken, and Michelle Alexander, author of *The New Jim Crow.* I've studied and read biographies and autobiographies about Redd Foxx, Richard Pryor, Jimmie Walker, Nelson Mandela, Muhammed Ali, and Don King. I've studied volumes of literature written by freedom fighters like the Black Liberation Army, the Deacons of Defense, and the Black Panther Party for Self Defense. I've studied books written by Bobby Seale, Huey Newton, George Jackson, Eldridge Cleaver, Russell Maroon Shoatz, Angela Davis, and thousands of others.

I've studied the books written by ex-slaves, books written from the perspective of the enslaved, books about those who escaped slavery, and books pertaining to those who shocked slavery systems, like Nat Turner. I've read about slave ships, like *Dreams of Africa in Alabama: The Slave Ship Clotilda and the Story of the Last Africans Brought to America.* I've read and studied thousands of books and subjects that you probably won't find at your local bookstore. I acknowledge this period of my life as essential to my growth and now current persona.

> *In seeking wisdom, there are days filled with productive activity, such as reading, studying, exercising, and introspection of self and life.*
> — MJN

I write all this to provide you with a much broader view of my extensive studies before Science of Mind. What knowledge I've gained from my studies allowed me to create an ultimate shield of protection that infused me with a standard and measurement of absolute Truth. Do you recall the picture I drew with the Adinkra symbol of measurement in the shield? This shield created by accumulated knowledge and various teachings has kept my mind intact when all around me were losing theirs in one form or another. In practicing revolutionary spirituality, it was important to resolve within myself to not let anyone, any oppressive idea, or oppressive system, regardless of how ruthless or cunning it is, leave me in a broken state. I resolved in my spirituality to not let anyone, any ideology, belief, or circumstance break me. This was my most intimate vow to God and my ancestors.

> *One should involve himself in something that is of greater importance in the larger scheme of things.*
> — MJN

In 2008, I was ordained a minister by the Universal Life Church. I earned a doctorate in Ancient African Science. I am the founder of the Kiwa Thinking Network. I represent no more than 10 percent (that's right, only 10 percent) within the 9th Dominion in Missouri Province who still have sound structural minds and can actually see every Truth that I'm allowed to see within this world. Those who can see are my students.

> *Growing up, the one thing I did not receive was the one thing I truly needed: the knowledge of my rich African heritage and culture.*
> — MJN

Until the lion learns to write, every story will glorify the hunter.

— AFRICAN PROVERB

Throughout my decades of incarceration, what struck me as odd was the fact that there are thousands of African men in prison, yet I've only come across two who could tell me the name of the three indigenous African belief systems. All of these incarcerated African men, but no one knew anything about Africa, as if Africa were a thing of the past and no longer exists. This actually amazed me. All of these religious paths that exist and none of these thousands of African descendants have traveled one that they actually inherited. For me, this was a very sad realization. Africa has been stripped of her bountiful and beautiful knowledge because of the negative stigma placed upon her.

When I began to study the ancient African sciences, it all started to resonate with my inner being. Intuition revealed to me that you don't choose Vodun, Vodun chooses you. I first became aware of the philosophy of Science of Mind from a book called *The Mark of Voodoo* before I knew anything about the Science of Mind as an organized system.

One's true self does not speak in words or banal phrases. Its voice comes from deep within, from the substrate of one's psyche, from something embedded within.

— MJN

Application of my knowledge gained from the Medu Neter, Vodun, Santeria, da Regla de Ocha, Macumba, Candomble, Obeah, Palo, the Seven Principles of the Kybalion, Ancient-Future Faith, and Science of Mind have been a magnificent blessing from Universal Mind. I was given a great opportunity to do something worthy. I was kept from self-destructing and from succumbing to the hypnosis.

There are many who have not been strong enough to resist and have become cemented into a demented artifice, yet there has been a small percentage who have undergone various schools of thought and attained enlightenment. These few have shed the debilitating characteristics of the parasite and established themselves on the royal throne of a self-governing mind, reclaiming their right to its scat. Self-rule is practically unheard of for those locked in the vices of disempowerment.

Intuition is an important quality to develop and, if tapped into today, it will serve in providing a sound structural mind that will provide protection against gullibility, against being misled and manipulated. Infusing all my knowledge with Universal Laws, I become a new element within nature. My innate nature has been to rebel against all forms of imbalance. To not revolt against a life of imbalance is actually unnatural.

To stay in harmony, I brought into balance my thinking with my actions. This profound and simple secret allows me access at all times to weapons that can be gripped with my hands, as well as weapons that can be firmly grasped with my mind.

> *There have been many religious disciplines and organized schools of thought rooted in the belief of God in one form or another. I can now say that after the experience of studying many different religious systems that the knowledge that I have attained from the metaphysical Science of Mind teachings has helped me to step into my true Spirit of an ever-evolving consciousness and break away from a society of customs designed to hamper the Divine Guidance that now offers me a way into a much more positive world of thought.*
>
> — MJN

> *Without the knowledge of my ancestors, historical truths, and European historical truths, I would not have come to understand who I really and truly am. I wouldn't have come to understand that only individual opinions are fixed, and dogmatic. Truth is more dynamic than that.*
>
> — MJN

The 9th Dominion can destroy any man, woman, or child without them ever realizing what happened. It is a killer. Sometimes very loud, but for the majority of the time it is silent, because its negative sorcery attacks the quiet recesses of the mind.

African people in North America and the diaspora are a nation of people who still carry the effects of chattel slavery in our collective psyche. There is fear, hatred, dislike, distrust, suspicion, envy, and confusion. When 100 percent control is given to a certain group of people over another group of people, they will abuse that control.

I don't know if you have ever heard of *The Willie Lynch Letter: The Making of a Slave.* I don't recommend you read it, since the letters were supposedly sent to Southern plantation owners and were also preached about and taught by Lynch. I am going to quote a small part of it to stress a particular point pertaining to trauma:

I have a fool-proof method for controlling your black slaves. I guarantee every one of you that, if installed correctly, it will control the slaves for at least 300 years. My method is simple. Any member of your family or your overseer can use it. I have outlined a number of differences and made them bigger. I use fear, distrust, and envy for control purposes. If used intensely for one year, the slaves themselves will remain perpetually in fear and distrust.

— THE WILLIE LYNCH LETTER

Willie Lynch is speaking on enhancing fear, enhancing distrust, enhancing prejudices, enhancing fear of change and of differences through psychological trauma, emotional trauma, and physical trauma. This is a security tactic used during the epoch of plantation slavery to ensure the social norms and status quo go unchallenged.

The methods described in the entirety of these letters are still being used today. This is not a thing that is extinct. When dozens of American white killers in the disguise and uniforms of police shoot and kill, choke and kill unarmed African men, women, and children as an initiation rite to join the Cross and Fear Club, what happens? Does fear increase? Does distrust increase? Are the families of the deceased traumatized? Is a sixteen-year-old African teenager who just earned their driver's license now in a state of perpetual fear when the police pull them over? Do the police officers' actions display trust to the African populace in America? Does the justice system really do justice when an African civilian is murdered in front of dozens of witnesses with video footage?

Do police officers, because of their bold behavior, now go unchallenged by African citizens even though they are in the right? Are African civilians becoming more submissive to police officers because they are afraid that they will be murdered in cold blood as others have been? What if it were American Black gang members in the disguise and uniforms of police killing innocent white men, women, and children as part of an initiation rite? Would the books written and conversation and justice meted out differ?

I know the answers to these questions, because I know the truth.

I recognize that while growing up, a social disorder infused fear, doubt, confusion, and self-loathing into myself and others. I accept the reality that I myself was shaped and formed by social disorder that preferred I remain afraid, confused, self-loathing, and unhappy.

— MJN

I write this to point out how trauma has affected me and how trauma is more than an event at one point in time, but has been used as a purposefully designed system for control.

I believe in the cause of justice and freedom, in principles of love, truth, and peace. But how can one combat injustice with those who only believe in hate and more hate? I have been awakened by the grace of God's gifts. My Spirit has found both wings and light.

— *MJN*

Sankofa is an African philosophy symbolized by a bird looking behind itself. It is also an Adinkra symbol that represents the ideology that African people will learn much about our present if we return to the past to retrieve the information.

Just like the still-existing KKK, as long as the slavery clause in the Thirteenth Amendment exists, slavery exists, which means confederates still exist, plantation owners still exist, slave catchers still exist, and public lynching still exists right before our eyes. All that many believe is in the distant past is alive and thriving. It is in the present, here and now—and it is dangerous. Yet many have not realized these truths because so much has been altered.

The Wretched of the Earth is the title of a book written by Frantz Fanon. He is also the author of *Black Skin, White Masks*. When I used this term in a previous letter, I used it in the way I interpreted from reading this book, which indicates a particular segment of society known as the 9th Dominion. For an example of what I mean, last year U.S. Treasurer Steven Mnuchin received a lawsuit filed against the IRS and Treasury Department by a prisoner who filed his 2019 1040 tax form for his stimulus check, at the time for $1,200. The head of the U.S. Treasury Department said that since he was a prisoner, he could not receive any stimulus money. The court said that yes, he can. The greedy treasurer then filed his own lawsuit and then filed a motion for an injunction to halt and delay the payment to prisoners until after he had "won" his lawsuit. The court said there is no merit in your lawsuit, you will not win.

Many of the prisoners were born in the United States and are therefore U.S. citizens by birth. Under the Cares Act, they are entitled to this stimulus money. The motion for injunction was denied. The judge told Mnuchin that the government had until the end of 2020 to get the money to all U.S. prisoners who filed 2019 1040 tax forms. So, this vindictive treasurer sent out millions of debit cards to prisoners that cannot be used instead of checks in a plot to delay payments. And all prisoners had to send the cards back. I bet this wasn't reported in the news.

The point I'm making is that American society had forgotten about the two million-plus members of this enslaved population, these so-called wretched of the Earth. In the wake of that forgetfulness, millions more dollars had to go to help those very ones they despise. Many like myself are still trying to receive our payments.

The inhabitants within this realm are the ones ostracized economically, socially, and politically, so we were not on the minds of those who decided to put out this money. For the many inhabitants within this realm, for the first time in their lives they now have an opportunity to live just a little bit better because they can now afford to buy vegetables at the canteen or a bottle of generic vitamins or a pair of decent shoes or even a television.

> *These are times when I am urged to see the bigger picture, that God is in everything and everyone, and that something bigger is trying to be birthed through challenge.*
> — MJN

> *The adherents of metaphysics are not guided by a specific doctrine or dogma, but by scientific understanding of the human mind, actions, and man's relationship to God. This is to me what makes the philosophy called Science of Mind a science.*
> — MJN

Mirroring the teachings of Science of Mind, the Metu Neter teaches about Hekua, words of power, which are positive affirmations used as powerful instruments capable of transforming psychological, emotional, and physical states of being. Affirming or reminding myself of my positive qualities and purpose in life is a transformative power that brings my mind into balance. The balanced mind is one that recognizes that the influence of race suggestion is the silver bullet that will get the fangs of those who suffer from this prolific source of disease off of the necks of the downcast of society. And when a balanced mind is used properly, it will protect many by teaching that they do not have to allow this disease to operate through them.

> *Many people in the world of the free believe adversity creates character. However, adversity reveals character as well.*
> — MJN

I see life through a higher vision and I am so grateful to have you in that vision, for without your help, I would not have made it so quickly to this point of being. I am grateful for your years of patience and commitment. Throughout the years of our communication, I have mentioned to you on a few occasions about the Egyptian concept of Maat, which is truth, balance, order, harmony, law, morality, and justice. There is an African proverb that says you go to war for Maat. You don't go to war to take somebody's land. You don't go to war to take someone's property off their land. You don't go to war to take someone. You go to war to protect Maat.

On page 331 in *The Science of Mind* text, Dr. Ernest Holmes asks this: If someone begins a tale of woe about hard times, should we listen to this "tale of the serpent" that might reverse our previous affirmations and make negative ones from their former mental and spiritual concepts? Holmes teaches that we should not refuse to hold conversation with people for fear they will neutralize the position we had taken in our minds. Instead, we can talk with anyone and not be disturbed.

This truth is expressed in the Maat-minded individual. One possesses infinite mental power and the ability to detach or attach to any thought. I, too, exercise mastery over my mind and do not let it exercise mastery over me. I know you also do the same regarding the venting, rants, and ravings in my letters. I do apologize for being uncouth and entering into these mental atmospheres. Sometimes, I become emotionally engaged when I see a supposedly extinct way of life still alive and being justified by so many.

> *When you have good people around you to share real gems of knowledge and truth, then you begin to see things in a whole new light.*
>
> — *MJN*

I thank you for giving me a glimpse into your world and your daily routines. I appreciate you sharing your insight about the world in general. I am also grateful for the exercise you instructed me to follow pertaining to the three pieces of paper and my frustrations. When I did all that you had recommended, as I stood there in that present moment where nothing negative was happening at all, I laughed at myself, because everything I had been thinking about prior to that moment became nonexistent.

As I await my release from the hole, I prepare myself for the holy month of Black August. This holy month will aid in my evolution for my fiftieth year of life on this planet. I want to live a life that is immaculate. I want to be polished, so I use this time in the hole to remove the dust particles that have the tendency to cling onto things.

I must learn how to become a civilian again. I've read how military career men, who constantly engage in warfare for years at a time, must be debriefed and taught how to readjust to civilian norms, because they have spent too many years in survival mode. I believe this is parallel in my living three decades in the 9th Dominion in a constant survival state of mind.

In ways I may never truly understand, my life is connected with many others, even though they seem separate. They both become meaningful as I discover how truly necessary my life and another's life are to each other. — MJN

Peace and blessings.

from Dr. Michael J. Nichols

The Intelligence within all life reroutes us in seemingly unplanned ways. Dr. Ernest Holmes wrote, "Whatever I should know, I will know. Whatever I should do, I will do. Whatever belongs to me must come to me." The forces that move people into alignment are complex so only that which finds a response in us can attach itself to us.

The conscious authority of the higher self transcends any discord of the lower self. Many men in prison behave mechanically without the conscious purpose that gives life its meaning.

The knowledge I gained throughout my spiritual studies showed me a truth that has given me no option but to adhere. I cannot pretend to be ignorant. Science, religion, and my direct experience are all ways to attain knowledge. In fact, all three powerfully contribute to my knowledge. Science objectively confirms the facts that my spiritual teachings, and my direct experience led to my Truth.

This book is a glimpse into my walk into spiritual consciousness with the help and guidance of my mentor, Rev. Dr. Mary E. Mitchell. She taught me that trusting in the Divine will eventually reveal the reality of Love.

from Rev. Dr. Mary E. Mitchell

Since July 2021, the letters between Michael and I focused primarily on how the book was coming along, as we created things like the index and glossary.

After I retired from full-time ministry in August, I was invited to create a weekly radio program on KKRN, 88.5 FM, a community radio station in Round Mountain, California. Because I have so many books in my library, I call it "Off the Shelf with Mary," a half-hour program that airs on Saturday mornings. In each program I highlight two of my favorite books on various subjects, such as science, metaphysics, business, spirituality, or relationships, subjects that might offer the listener just what they are looking for to enhance their life.

I copy and send each manuscript to the four prisoners I correspond with—and they are quick to let me know if they missed one. In September, Michael wrote that even in the hole, he reads the radio programs out loud to the other inmates, and they enjoy discussing the topics.

He recently started an experiment. Every day he writes an affirmation with his dominant right hand, then rewrites it with his non-dominant left hand. He does this every morning after he meditates and writes. This practice starts his day on a positive note, and his left hand has strengthened significantly.

In November 2021, Michael received a "rejection of mail" invoice, which stated that one of my letters was rejected because it included a few postage stamps. He wrote, "There was a time when prisoners could receive stamps from loved ones and friends, but since the riot in January 2021, everything that was allowed to help an indigent prisoner had been stopped for those in ad-seg. My committee hearing is scheduled for November 23, and I am ready with numerous certificates from correspondence programs I completed while in the hole, so there should be no reason for me not to be released but pettiness."

CONTINUED

By the end of November, Michael met with the Administrative Segregation Committee and they gave him sixty more days in the hole, so he will have spent a whole year there. He expects to be released to the general prison population in January, the month of his fiftieth birthday. He requested that he be transferred so he can start anew in a prison that would be more conducive to his endeavors.

He wrote, "This is a time of my endurance, where my strength and patience are being tested. As I prepare for a new year, a new phase of my life, I stay in constant awareness and preparation for my freedom. Things are changing within the realm, and the changes are positive. Several prisoners who were serving life without parole have been released because they were juveniles when they committed their crimes. This was a change many of those prisoners never saw coming, but now they are in the free world. So, I stay patient and do all the things necessary that I can do and I leave the rest to the Universe to do what I know that It will do."

On December 1, he wrote, "I was approved for a transfer and possibly by the time you receive this letter I will be in a new land. There is no place for me to go but up! I have taken all and everything I have from my studies and combined it to aid me from the first day forward. Once again, I am grateful for the opportunity to show how SOM principles and teachings helped me. I pray that those who practice it will take these teachings and applications to higher levels in the new year."

In January 2022, Michael was transferred to another Missouri prison, where he was immediately put into ad-seg for "monitoring" for 30 days. He writes, "I do not plan on being bogged down here as long as I was at Charleston. I only plan on being here six to eight months or twelve months maximum before I am transferred to a prison more conducive to my preparation for freedom. That means job training and intense programming. This will allow me a better opportunity with the parole board.

"I await to see what befalls me, but until then, I continue to exercise doing my physical, my mental, and my spiritual practices to keep my vibrations at their highest levels."

Michael's journey of transformation continues. Our prayer is that his journey uplifts, informs, and, perhaps, transforms the lives of others as well.

Absolute ~ existing independently and not in relation to other things; not relative or comparative; also a description of God.

Absolute moral standards ~ the belief there are universal ethical standards that apply to every situation.

Absolute reality ~ ultimate reality as it is in itself, unaffected by the perception or knowledge of any finite being.

Accredited ~ an officially recognized course of study.

Adinkra Symbols ~ symbols from Ghana that represent concepts or aphorisms.

Administrative Segregation ~ a prison cell where one who is being punished is kept alone; solitary confinement; also referred to as ad-seg or the hole.

Affirmations ~ positive statements that can help challenge and overcome self-sabotaging and negative thoughts.

Affirmative Prayer ~ words that assert positive beliefs about a desired outcome and connect with the spirit of God within.

Amelioration ~ the act of making something better; improvement.

American dream ~ the ideal by which equality of opportunity is available to any American, allowing the highest aspirations and goals to be achieved.

Ancient African System of Initiation ~ initiation rites or ceremonies performed when people take on a new role in life. In various parts of Africa, such rites may usher individuals into adulthood, secret societies, or positions of leadership. During the ceremonies, individuals often receive some secret knowledge or new privileges or power.

Anomaly/anomalies ~ something that deviates from what is standard, normal, or expected.

Arbre-Moville ~ wet tree, moon or lunar principles.

Arbre-Sec ~ dry tree, sun or solar principles.

Artifice ~ a plan or trick to deprive another of the intangible right of honest services.

Ascendancy ~ occupation of a position of dominant power or influence.

Ashe ~ a West African philosophical concept of the breath of life within.

Asvatta ~ eternal life and the cycle of life and death.

Augmented ~ having been made greater in size or value.

Axions ~ a hypothetical boson having no charge or spin and small mass, proposed to explain the existence of certain symmetries of the strong nuclear force.

Bat Ge' ~ Fighting the War.

Bhagavad Gita ~ a portion of the Mahabharata (a Hindu Sanskrit epic), having the form of a dialogue between the hero, Arjuna, and his charioteer, the avatar Krishna, in which a doctrine combining Brahmanical and other elements is evolved.

Black August ~ a month dedicated to paying homage to fallen Black revolutionaries, incarcerated freedom fighters, and Black resistance, historical and ongoing.

Bodi Tree ~ where the Buddha reached enlightenment (bodhi) after meditating beneath one such tree, the fig tree (ficus religiosa), for forty-nine days.

Bosslings ~ little version of a boss, like a mini-boss.

Buddhism ~ a religion of eastern and central Asia growing out of the teaching of Siddhārtha Gautama (Buddha) that suffering is inherent in life and that one can be liberated from it by cultivating wisdom, virtue, and concentration.

Catalyst ~ in chemistry, any substance that increases the rate of a reaction without itself being consumed. It also means a person whose talk, enthusiasm, or energy causes others to be more friendly, enthusiastic, or energetic.

Celli ~ a person sharing a prison cell with another.

Chongg Ran ~ a specific ancient discipline, a secret mystical philosophy practiced by a tiny order of monks in Bhutan and Tibet. This form of concentration "allows the practitioner to unleash the full potential of the human mind."

Christ Consciousness ~ being open to "what is," a pure and true awareness of everything that is, in so much as is possible while in a physical body.

Clairsentience ~ the ability of a person to acquire psychic knowledge by means of feeling.

Clairvoyance ~ the power or faculty of discerning objects not present to the senses.

Co-Creation ~ the collaborative development of new value (concepts, solutions, products, and services). The spiritual understanding is that humans are created in God's image and God is creative, and through the creative power of our mind, we are all called to be co-creators with God.

Collective consciousness ~ the common consciousness of a group within a community, city, state, etc., that can be positive or negative.

Collective insanity ~ a type of dementia that overcomes an entire population leading to massacres and atrocities.

Contemplation ~ thinking profoundly about something. In religious life, contemplation is a kind of inner vision or seeing, transcendent of the intellect, facilitated by means of practices such as prayer or meditation.

Correctional Science ~ a college program that provides the foundational education required for an individual's career entry into the criminal justice field, specifically correctional operations and probation/parole case investigations.

Creative Force ~ that energy in humans to be creative, also called the Divine Urge.

Creative Thinking ~ thinking outside the box. Often, creativity involves lateral thinking, which is the ability to perceive patterns that are not obvious, like devising new ways to carry out tasks, solve problems, and meet challenges, such as bringing a fresh, sometimes unorthodox, perspective to your life and areas of interest.

Criminal Thinking Program ~ describes ten indicators that extreme criminal thinkers rely on to justify their actions in support of a criminal lifestyle.

Criminal Underworld ~ an organized crime network.

Daily Living Assistant (DLA) ~ work that prisoners can do to help handicapped or elderly inmates.

Debilitation ~ to lose or cause to lose strength or vigor.

Dehumanized ~ to deprive someone of human qualities, personality, or dignity.

Demigods ~ a mortal raised to divine rank. In prison, guards who feel they have a high status.

Demogorgons ~ demons associated with the underworld.

Denouement ~ the outcome of a complex sequence of events.

Department of Corrections ~ a governmental agency tasked with overseeing the incarceration of persons convicted of crimes within a particular jurisdiction.

Dhammapada ~ a Buddhist text believed to record the actual words of the founder of Buddhism, Siddhartha Gautama, better known as the Buddha, who lived between 563 and 483 BCE.

Dialectics ~ the art of investigating the truth of opinions.

Divine Design ~ in Christianity, the Lord's hand guiding you. By "divine design," He is in the small details of your life as well as the major milestones.

Divine Plan of Being ~ a belief that God has a divine plan for our lives, something for all of us to do with the talents, gifts, and abilities each has been given to bring glory and honor to God.

Drapetomania ~ a mental disease Dr. Samuel A. Cartwright claimed was peculiar to the "Negro race" in 1851.

Druid ~ a priest, magician, or soothsayer in the ancient Celtic religion.

Duality ~ refers to having two parts, often with opposite qualities, like the duality of good and evil. In theology, a belief in duality is the idea of that there is a God and a devil, each with equal power, which logically would result in the destruction of everything. The opposite belief of duality is Oneness, that there is one God or Universal Intelligence that created the universe and everything and everyone in it.

Dyadic Model of Reality ~ written by Dr. Edgar Mitchell; suggests all of nature is in a sense wavelike, field-like, and mind-like and nature's energy moves forward through an irreversible process on a macro level.

Dysaesthesia Aethiopica ~ a mental disease Dr. Samuel A. Cartwright claimed was peculiar to the "Negro race" in 1851.

Egrams ~ temptations.

Electicism ~ the practice of deriving ideas, style, or taste from a broad and diverse range of sources.

Emnity ~ the state or feeling of being actively opposed or hostile to someone or something.

Enigma ~ a person or thing that is mysterious, puzzling, or difficult to understand.

Ephesians ~ a letter addressed to early Christians and included as a book in the New Testament.

Esoteric ~ intended for or likely to be understood by only a small number of people with a specialized knowledge or interest.

Eugenics ~ the practice or advocacy of improving the human species by selectively mating people with specific desirable hereditary traits, aimed at reducing human suffering by "breeding out" disease, disabilities, and so-called undesirable characteristics from the human population.

Evolution ~ the change in the inherited traits of a population of organisms through successive generations.

Fetters ~ a chain or manacle used to restrain a prisoner, typically placed around the ankles.

Fifth Kingdom ~ Judge Thomas Troward's synonym for death.

First Cause ~ the supposed ultimate cause of all events, which does not itself have a cause but is identified with God/Infinite Intelligence.

Furtive ~ attempting to avoid notice or attention, typically because of guilt or a belief that discovery would lead to trouble; secretive.

Gestapo ~ the secret police force of the German Nazi state notorious for its terrorism and brutality. More currently used to describe any police force or other authority regarded as sinister, ruthless, brutal, etc.

Ginen ~ that aspect of the Vodu religion that establishes a direct link between Haitian Vodu devotees and their African ancestral land.

Gnostics ~ dualists who worship two or more gods; Christians are monists and worship one God.

God ~ the creator and ruler of the universe and source of all moral authority; the supreme being.

Grimoire ~ a book of magic spells and invocations.

Gye Nyame ~ an African symbol meaning "except for God"; symbolizes God's omnipotence through the knowledge that people should not fear anything except God.

Hermetic Philosophy ~ written by the Greek Hermes Trismegistus.

Hole ~ a cell for solitary confinement in a prison.

Ife ~ a town in west central Nigeria.

Impact of Crime on Victims Class (ICVC) ~ a prison program that helps prisoners realize and understand the impact of their crime on their victims.

Impetuous ~ acting or something done quickly without thought.

Indigo Children ~ children with purportedly colored auras, possessing increased empathy, creativity, curiosity, will, and spiritual inclinations.

Invisible Essence ~ the life-giving force in the body.

Ipsissimus ~ the highest level for a psychic to reach, a master of their own power.

Kemet ~ the name Egyptians gave to their country, which literally means the "Black Land" (kem meant "black" in ancient Egyptian). The name derived from the color of the rich and fertile black soil.

Kismet ~ destiny or fate.

Law of Attraction ~ a universal law whereby positive thoughts bring positive results, while negative thoughts bring negative outcomes.

Law of Cause and Effect ~ a universal law specifically dictating that every single action in the universe produces a reaction, no matter what. Every single thing within the universe then is relative and nothing is separate.

Law of Correspondence ~ a universal law that there is harmony, agreement, and correspondence between the physical, mental, and spiritual realms.

Law of Creation ~ a universal law that underscores that life doesn't just happen to us. To make things happen in life, people must take action instead of waiting for something to magically appear.

Law of Existence ~ a universal law whereby all interactions in the Universe are governed by four fundamental forces. On the macro level, the forces of gravitation and electromagnetism rule, while the strong and weak forces dominate the micro level of the atomic nucleus.

Law of Growth ~ a universal law that humans grow from infancy through many levels of intelligence and capacities to eventually reach the elderly stage of growth.

Law of Intent ~ a universal law that if you are intent on doing something and determined to get it done, this motive or purpose is supported by the natural creative process to make it happen.

Law of Logical and Sequential Evolution ~ a universal law on the sequential order of things, a consecutive or logical order, or following a certain prescribed order.

Law of Mental Equivalents ~ a universal law that what you experience in your life is the mental equivalent of what you have created in your mind.

Law of Perfection ~ a universal law that everything is perfect in its divine state. Humans are perfect in the sense that who a person is in the moment is who that person is meant to be, as a result of the individual's previous beliefs and choices.

Law of Prosperity ~ a universal law that states there is an unlimited Source of everything we might want or need, available to all people, all the time. The key to using these limitless resources is in focusing attention on the Divine Energy and making the right steps in focusing both thoughts and feelings toward having and experiencing the possibilities.

Law of Relativity ~ everything in our physical world is made real by its relation to something else.

Laws of the Universe ~ natural laws through which everyone and everything is governed, such as the laws of: Attraction, Polarity, Rhythm, Relativity, Cause and Effect, and Perpetual Transmutation of Energy.

Licensed Practitioners ~ those who are trained by a spiritual organization in the practice of mental and spiritual healing.

Life Without Parole ~ a court-ordered sentence to prison for life without parole, effectively meaning a sentence cannot be suspended, but a prisoner may be released following a pardon.

Mahabharata ~ a Hindu Sanskrit epic, the longest written poem in the world about the idea of sacred duty.

Malevolent ~ having or showing a wish to do evil to others.

Mandated Single Cell Confinement ~ the hole, officially called Administration Sequestration.

Meditation ~ a mental exercise (such as concentration on one's breathing or repetition of a mantra) for the purpose of reaching a heightened level of spiritual awareness.

Miasma ~ a highly unpleasant or unhealthy smell or vapor.

Mind, Conscious ~ all the things a person is are currently aware of and thinking about. It is somewhat akin to short-term memory and is limited in terms of capacity.

Mind, Subconscious ~ the function of a person's subconscious or subjective mind is to store and retrieve data. Its job is to ensure that a person responds exactly as programmed. The subconscious mind makes everything a person focuses on and believes fit a pattern consistent with that self-concept.

Mind Alchemy ~ the process of transmuting thoughts to improve one's life and expand the mind. Mental alchemy involves the replacement of beliefs that are hindering development with positive ones that will be helpful.

Minion ~ a servile dependent, follower, or underling.

Missive ~ a letter, especially a long or official one.

Muscle testing ~ a method of gathering accurate biofeedback on the body's physiological and psychological state by stimulating the muscular system. The body's cells know their entire history and what they require to regain full health. Muscle testing is a way to retrieve the knowledge imbedded into the cellular memory of the muscular system.

Myopic ~ lacking imagination, foresight, or intellectual insight.

Necropolis ~ a large cemetery.

Ninth Dominion, also 9th Dominion ~ what prisoners call prison.

Nonlocal ~ action at a distance; direct interaction of physical objects that are not in proximity. Prayers are nonlocal activities.

N'wari ~ a bird God of the Shangaan tribe of Zimbabwe.

Obfuscation ~ obscuring the intended meaning by intentionally making a message difficult to understand, usually with confusing and ambiguous language.

Objective Consciousness ~ the conscious mind.

Odin or Odinist ~ a reconstructionist religious organization focusing on Germanic paganism, Germanic mythology, Norse paganism, and Anglo-Saxon paganism.

One Mind ~ the premise that all individual minds are part of an infinite, collective dimension of consciousness called the One Mind.

Oneness ~ a spiritual experience best described as unity between the two energies of Self and the Universe, often expressed as recognizing that all of humanity are brothers and sisters to each other.

Ontological ~ a branch of philosophy on the science of what is, of the kinds and structures of objects. Ontology seeks the classification and explanation of entities and claims about the nature of being and existence.

Open Doors ~ a 501(c)3 nonprofit organization whose mission is to strengthen communities by supporting those formerly incarcerated.

Orishas ~ spirits that play a key role in the Yoruba religion of West Africa and several religions of the African diaspora.

Ownership Attitude ~ an attitude of ownership of people, places, or things that arises from fear.

Pact with the Devil ~ a slave revolt against the European French slave owners and Napoleon's armies.

Palingenesis ~ a concept of rebirth or re-creation.

Paranoia ~ a mental condition characterized by delusions of persecution, unwarranted jealousy, or exaggerated self-importance.

Parole Hearing ~ an official hearing within the Department of Corrections to determine whether an inmate should be released from prison to parole supervision in the community for the remainder of their sentence.

Prayer ~ a conversation with our Higher Power (God) offered to develop a personal, meaningful relationship with the One that created the universe. A prayer can express a request, gratitude, or anything that is in our hearts.

Precognition ~ clairvoyance relating to an event or state not yet experienced.

Principles ~ a fundamental truth or proposition that serves as the foundation for a system of belief or behavior or for a chain of reasoning.

Psychic ~ a person who claims to use extrasensory perception (ESP) to identify information hidden from the normal senses.

Psychotic ~ disruptions to a person's thoughts and perceptions that make it difficult for them to recognize what is real and what isn't.

Puritanical ~ practicing or affecting strict religious or moral behavior.

Quiddity ~ whatever makes something the type that it is; an unusual personal opinion or habit; eccentricity.

Race Consciousness ~ beliefs of groups of people in the human race; the race consciousness of a community, state, or country operating through the mentality of the individual and expressed through a larger group of people.

Race Personality ~ the diversity of personality traits in the human race.

Realm ~ the 9th Dominion, prison.

Recidivism ~ the tendency of a convicted criminal to reoffend after being paroled.

Rehabilitation ~ the action of restoring someone to health or normal life through training and therapy after imprisonment, addiction, or illness.

Relative Reality ~ anything that is subject to change.

Sanskrit ~ an ancient Indo-European language of India, in which the Hindu scriptures and classical Indian epic poems are written and from which many northern Indian languages are derived.

Science of Mind ~ a philosophy that brings together spiritual principles from many of the major world theologies in a positive and life-affirming way to form a compendium for personal action.

Scientology ~ a religious system based on the belief that human beings are immortal, that a person's life experience transcends a single lifetime, and that human beings possess infinite capabilities.

Seed of Perfection ~ the idea that each person is a specialized spiritual being and, therefore, perfect.

Seraphs ~ an angelic being, regarded in traditional Christian angelology as belonging to the highest order of the ninefold celestial hierarchy, associated with light, ardor, and purity.

Shank ~ a homemade knife.

Slave Codes in America ~ in U.S. history, any of the set of rules based on the concept that enslaved persons were property, not persons.

Sociopath ~ a person with a personality disorder manifesting itself in extreme antisocial attitudes and behavior and a lack of conscience.

Socrates Solecism ~ a violation of the conventional usage, grammar, etc., of a language; ungrammatical use of words.

Soul ~ the subjective part of mind; the subconscious; the creative medium reflecting the forms of thought given it.

Soul of the Universe ~ the Divine Source, the one that underpins everything in love. Love is the only emotion that trumps all other emotions. It is the answer to every question. Divine Source, creator of all, is pure love and love is what humans spend their entire lives seeking.

Soul's Journey ~ the soul continues into infinity learning throughout its infinite journey.

Spirit ~ the spiritual or immaterial part of a human being regarded as immortal.

Spirit of Ogu ~ warrior god of iron and war that controls much of the material in the earth and represents a primitive force and energy.

Spirit of the Divine ~ in the traditional theistic concept of God as the most perfect being possible, the main divine attributes flowing from this understanding are: personhood, transcendence, immanence, omnipresence, omniscience, omnipotence, perfect goodness, unity, simplicity, and necessity.

Spiritual Amnesia ~ the forgetfulness of God's goodness, which can easily lead to a downward spiral toward spiritual emptiness.

Spiritual Mind Healing ~ healing of the mind that involves the transfer of energy; in other words, it is not from the healer personally, but the healer links with Universal or Divine energy to channel healing for the mind, body, and spirit.

Spiritual Path ~ to embrace the mystical paradox that while we are singular, physical beings on this journey, we are also profoundly connected to one another, animated and sustained by the same vast Spirit that abides everywhere.

Spiritual Reality ~ to recognize everything seen and unseen is animated by a higher power often called God or Infinite Intelligence.

Spiritual Realization ~ when a person knows "who I am" and "who is the real doer" in this world, that individual is able to come out of the suffering and misery of day-to-day life to become happy and peaceful in their worldly life and exhibit more of the nature of the Christ Consciousness.

Spirituality ~ the recognition of a feeling or sense or belief that there is something greater than oneself, something more to being human than just a sensory experience, and that the greater whole of which humanity is a part is cosmic or divine in nature.

Subjective mind ~ subconscious mind, soul.

Sub Rosa ~ in secret.

Surah ~ a chapter in the sacred scripture of Islam, the Qur'an.

Synecological Sibrosa ~ a branch of ecology that studies the relationship between plant and animal communities and their environments.

Synergy Cooperation Theory ~ the unpredictability of behavior or system wherein the separate behaviors of any of the parts is true cooperation.

Taking a Chance on Change ~ a prison anger management class.

Tehuti ~ an Egyptian God, also known as Thoth and to the Greeks as Hermes Trismegistus.

Teleology ~ the philosophical interpretation of natural phenomena as exhibiting purpose or design.

Tengeri ~ a Hungarian word for corn or maize.

Thanatos ~ a death instinct.

Tomes ~ slang for theatre of the mind.

Transition Accountability Plan ~ the plan a prisoner must develop for review by a parole board.

Tree of Knowledge ~ also called the Asvattha tree, Bodhi tree, Tree of Life, Tree of All Life, World Tree, and Pillars of Trees.

Triune Nature of God ~ spoken of as the Father, the Son, and the Holy Ghost.

Truth ~ the spiritual belief that God is all there is, the reason, cause, and power in and through everything. It is birthless, deathless, changeless, complete, perfect, whole, self-existent, causeless, almighty, Spirit, law, mind, intelligence, and anything and everything that implies Reality. The Truth is It must be infinite and all and can have nothing outside Itself or unlike Itself, including humanity.

Unconscious Invitation ~ an idea presented by Dr. Ernest Holmes that simply states that every individual is always creating experiences, consciously or unconsciously, by inviting experiences into their life with persistent thoughts, beliefs, and strong emotions.

Unequivocal ~ leaving no doubt, clear, unambiguous.

Unity ~ the state of being united or joined as a whole; the Oneness of God and humans. Often described as the One Life, of which we are a part; One Intelligence, which we use; One Substance, which is brought into manifold manifestation; One Principle, as Jesus taught: "That they may all be one, even as Thou, Father, art in me and I in Thee, and they also in us."

Universal Laws ~ in law and ethics, Universal Laws refers to principles as concepts of legal legitimate actions that govern the conduct of human beings. Universal Laws include the Law of Vibration, Law of Action, Law of Correspondence, Law of Cause and Effect, Law of Compensation, Law of Attraction, and the Law of Perpetual Transmutation of Energy.

Universal Mind ~ a metaphysical concept suggesting an underlying essence of all, the creative medium of Spirit.

Universal Reign of Law ~ concepts of legal legitimacy, whereby those principles and rules for governing humanity's conduct, which are most universal in their acceptability, their applicability, translation, and philosophical basis, are therefore considered to be most legitimate.

Universal Spirit ~ the conscious mind of God; the Universe of conscious mind and self-determination. The complete nature of God is reflected in humanity and humans use the same law that God uses; for there is but One Law and there is but One Spirit. Both God and humans use the same Creative Medium or Universal Subjectivity.

Upanishad ~Vedic Sanskrit texts of Hindu philosophy that form the foundations of Hinduism.

Vex ~ to cause someone to feel annoyed, frustrated, or worried, especially with trivial matters.

Vodun ~ a synonym for Voodoo, also spelled Voudun

Wicca ~ a predominantly Western movement whose followers practice witchcraft and nature worship and who see it as a religion based on pre-Christian traditions of northern and western Europe.

Witness Consciousness ~ another level of consciousness where the witness coexists alongside the normal consciousness as another layer of awareness. Humans have this unique ability to be in two states of consciousness at once.

Xenophobia ~ fear or hatred of foreigners, people from different cultures, or strangers.

Yajur Veda ~ derived from the Sanskrit roots, *yajus*, meaning "worship" or "sacrifice," and veda, meaning "knowledge." Yajur Veda is sometimes translated as "Knowledge of the Sacrifice."

Yama ~ the first man who drank with the gods beside the cosmic fig tree.

INDEX

Rev. Dr. Mary E. Mitchell

Mary E. Mitchell has had a fascinating career in wood products, environmental restoration, and metaphysical ministry. Her love of forestry and wood products began when she worked for a wholesale lumber company in Ohio, followed by receiving a B.S. in Forest Industries Management from The Ohio State University.

Upon graduation, she was hired by a West Coast corporation, where she was the wood fiber manager, purchasing all of the wood fiber needed to make products at two pulp and paper mills in Puget Sound. A highlight was when one of the mills was sold to a German company and they had to relicense the mill's tugboat. The new company was so impressed that a woman was the wood fiber manager, they renamed the tugboat "Mary S," as her name at that time was Mary Schroeder.

Years later, she accepted the wood fiber manager position at a new fifty-megawatt wood-fired power plant in Anderson, California. Ten years later, she became the manager and grant writer for a Resource Conservation District in Anderson, which was awarded millions in grant funds for stream and fisheries restoration and healthy forest projects.

In the early 1990s, Mitchell found her spiritual home in a metaphysical teaching based on a philosophy called the Science of Mind. She received a practitioner's license, followed by a minister's license and was ordained in 2008. In 2009, she unexpectedly found herself in a correspondence ministry with prisoners who had read her magazine articles and were interested in whether metaphysics was practical enough to help them adjust to the daily challenges of prison life.

For her many years in service to the local Center for Spiritual Living (CSL) as a staff minister, assistant minister, and then co-senior minister, she was honored with a Doctorate of Divinity from CSL in 2020. Over the years of her involvement, she served on many committees for the parent organization, Centers for Spiritual Living in Golden, Colorado.

Dr. Mary's passion is metaphysical studies and teaching Science of Mind classes. This year she will be teaching her ninety-fourth class. Her hobby is writing, and she has

CONTINUED

published several books: *Jump Into Life* with James Golden; *Engaging Grace: How to Use Our Co-Creative Power in Daily Life;* and *The Practitioner Handbook* (first and second editions) — written and published as Mary E. Schroeder—and *History of the Center for Spiritual Living, Redding 1971–2014; 32 Easy Lessons in Metaphysics and the Science of Our Mind; The Practitioner Handbook* (third edition); and this volume, *My Search for Ancient Wisdom, One Prisoner's Journey of Transformation*—written and published as Rev. Dr. Mary E. Mitchell.

Today, Dr. Mary focuses on her ministry, writing, and recording a weekly radio program called "Off the Shelf with Mary," where she reviews her favorite books for KKRN, a community radio station at 88.5 FM. She lives in the community of Lake California in Cottonwood, California, with her husband, Paul, and two tabby cats you would never guess are sisters, Amazing Grace and Mama Mia.

#180862
Southeast Correctional Center
Charleston, Missouri

A HAND-WRITTEN HISTORY, APRIL 2019

I entered prison at 19 years of age, a high school graduate, gifted trombone player and an avid reader. Yet I did what many young African-American males do in an attempt to gain the illusion of success and importance. I strayed off the path of benign endeavors onto the path of malignant deeds and ended up with life without parole in prison. Upon entering into an alien realm, I was hostile toward everyone, for in my mind, survival within this foreign landscape was a top priority.

After graduating high school and in an attempt to find my place within this world, I was tempted by the life of criminal pursuits, for its song had been strong and my mother's values and morals that held me in check since early childhood had become way too weak to hold me any longer. My mind would override my family and friend's warnings against a particular event into which I would cast myself. Choices were made and the piper paid in the end. For my friends and loved ones were able to see what I apparently could not perceive.

Growing up in America as a young influential male, there was always the outlaw seduction, which, like sirens, temps one with its enchanting song, offering me a place to belong; the only place or so I was made to believe, that I could own and the allure was overwhelming. Like a swimmer in the grip of an undercurrent, I had succumbed out of sheer inevitability.

Giving into the stereotype of African men and giving myself over to the criminal underworld meant choosing an inordinately difficult life, one that all too frequently leads to behavior that hurts others and produces lasting harm in society.

CONTINUED

I chose a path, one I believed could find genuine sympathy for my plight and it had been trodden and traversed by the older men who at that time I idolized and wanted to emulate. The street hustlers and gangsters whom in my childish eyes seemed infinitely more successful and attractive than the community social workers, teachers, police officers and priest, whom I had always had an affinity to as well.

Within the criminal domain, I learned that I was taking the path of least resistance and the forces I had unconsciously set in motion, unbeknownst to me, were already setting the stage for me. I had hidden my true self behind a façade of gangsterism and became a co-conspirator in my own imprisonment. And worse, I involved innocent people who became victims due to my own interpersonal conflict, which also produced shadows that projected indirectly upon other innocent people.

Early on in life, I learned that telling the truth wasn't all that bad. It has been something that I continued throughout my life, especially when I ran into trouble of some kind, and this is why even pertaining to this crime that I'm incarcerated for, the morals of my mother's wise words resonated through my soul: "The truth will set you free." And I admitted my guilt for this crime I committed. The capacity to accept responsibility for the consequences of my choices is the measure of a moral being. For me not to acknowledge moral complicity in the world's woe is itself a sociopathic issue.

I write of this to convey to you how very important it is for me to honestly reflect on my harmful and negative behavior as well as my positive redirection to redemption. I am able to see, perhaps from the perspective of decades, that even the good I intended was not without its problematic consequences, because the good that I did was tinged with the hidden agenda, the complicit collusion, the manipulative motive. Energies that can operate unconsciously, because it has become the normal in the mind of the criminal. Coming into accountability for my own past is the first step in recognizing what has hitherto been unconscious, namely the presence and activity of my darkest negative self.

During my now thirty years of incarceration, I cannot lie nor conceal my conduct in prison. I have had antagonistic incidents against co-opted prisoners and overweening correctional officers. I am by no means the cliché "model inmate." Being condemned to a life without a future, with the possibility of freedom diminished, allowed for vindictiveness to become an acceptable end in itself. It was easier for me to accept erroneously the message that life is meant to be lived short and that the only glory I was likely to attain was the glory won by elevating the maladjusted dogma developed within prison that was at the same time debilitating my whole being. The constant pressure of fighting negative engineering had taken a heavy toll on my spirit, sapping energy that could be devoted to more positive endeavors. My life form had become a paradox and self-destructive.

Just when I believed I would be engulfed by the pestilence and negative miasma of this realm, something greater offered me a blank slate and a protective shield to change, study, grow and evolve. As time moved forward, I found the calm place where my mind, soul and body could function as a healthy, healed, enlightened spiritual being began.

A scholar once said, "What I fear is man's ability to adjust." By that he meant that humans inherit an evolutionary capacity to adjust downward, from a higher to a lower primitive place, position, or condition in order to survive a hostile and destructive environment.

The existence I've carved out within this dominion is not unique, yet I began to reform and teach myself, so that I could someday bring my brilliance into manifestation so that it could benefit not only myself, but friends, loved ones, people whom I never met, and the victims of people like myself.

I had a life-changing epiphany when I realized that I had to re-embrace life. With the decision made in embracing life, I had an affirming vision of the future. I knew I needed to make my penance and leave my old negative behavior behind. As I moved forward, I began to shed all negative thoughts and actions. I began to set attainable goals, at the same time slowly but surely avoiding conflict and potentially negative situations. I knew I could only triumph if I found the strength to say, "I denounce the inhumanity that this realm symbolizes." I made myself believe that my worth as a man had nothing to do with the size of a reputation. In the end, my worth can only be determined by what I make of who I am, which required me to reject with every fiber of my being the pitiable figure the prison dominion would make of me and to discover my own true and better self.

The Missouri Department of Corrections offers many types of programs for men to make amends and rehabilitate. I decided to participate in these programs so I could learn and grow from my errors while understanding the impact my crime had on my victims, not because how it would look on paper, for I am without a parole date.

I've taken these programs because I knew that I truly needed them to help me in ways that self-education could not. The chains that were still binding parts of my mind and heart began to yield. I didn't know who I truly was until I was obliged to reach deep within to draw upon the resources that have been provided for me. I needed help in sincerely developing empathy for those to whom I caused harm. Empathy allowed me the full capacity to change for the better for the life of all people. The time that I have dedicated to specific programs has been a process of positive transformation and has been very helpful in that it reinforced my applications of positive thought.

Every obstacle within this realm presented an opportunity for me to improve not only myself but also my condition. I now see every experience as being capable of teaching me something. I've been working non-stop to improve myself, as well as put myself in a better position within this realm.

Over the last few years, I've had numerous jobs. I've worked as a medical porter, housing unit porter, recreational worker, school tutor, canteen worker, laundry worker, washed pots and pans in the kitchen, and as a Daily Living Assistant (DLA) in the Enhanced Care Unit.

I have transformed mentally, spiritually, and improved my ethics and education. I've acquired new friends and mentors in the free world who are a part of the religious community called Centers for Spiritual Living, who teach the text *The Science of Mind,* which is a positive living and thinking philosophy that has helped me immensely in my faith, knowledge, thinking, perception, and cured me of my diagnosed arrested development. I've developed a plan for a life of penance and success according to spiritual guidelines containing steps needed for life in general and also to avoid recidivism, if by grace I am released from prison.

I have evolved on an educational, emotional, and psychological level. Being able to express remorse and empathy for the people I've wronged was one of my greatest challenges, as well as my greatest accomplishments. In order for me to break the cycle of wrong thinking, I had to engage in the religious discipline to forgive myself for causing suffering to others. I had to take an honest, unflinching look at the type of mindset that sent me to prison in the first place, and how I had built my house in the prescription for curing sociopathic thinking. I had to divide the social conditions of my birth and background, which I cannot change, to the things I could change and still had a chance to do so. I went inside my house, took inventory, and started renovating. It is said that change is the end result of all true learning. In order for me to become a strong, meaningful, and worthy human being, I had to eliminate what was weak within.

Now I am required by my own mind to work for the good of others. As a human being, I simply want to be free without any negative faults hindering my movements. I'm thinking about freedom in the purest sense, to love, live, play, laugh, cry, and even die. These many years imprisoned have taught me to rediscover my humanity.

For the first time in my life, I have an optimistic view about the world. I've questioned my doubts and my certainties with a deeper awareness than I felt I had previously. Perhaps it is an expanded intuition and sensitivity that accompanies one's age. Perhaps there is a purpose for me to guide someone who may be on the wrong path, to a better, brighter, and positive one.

I am now in my fifties. I entered prison in my late teens. I've spent more time within this realm than I have the free world. All of my adult life thus far has been lived in confinement. Potted plants grow until they become pot-bound and need to be placed into a bigger container for the next evolution of their life. For me, to be repotted or be transplanted into a bigger container would be the free world, free society.

In the English Standard Version Global Study Bible's glossary, I looked up the word "pardon." It read: "see forgiveness." That definition then reads: "Forgiveness is a release from guilt and the reestablishment of relationships. Forgiveness can be granted by God to human beings and by human beings to those who have wronged them." The wrong that I committed by taking the life of another man was an immoral and an unwonted act of a boy. And for this act, I am remorseful and ashamed.

Michael with his mother Irma and sister Rachel

The first indication of **WISDOM** is the active **PURSUIT** of wisdom.

‒ LEADERSHIP FREAK

Printed in the USA
CPSIA information can be obtained
at www.ICGtesting.com
LVHW010210021123
762859LV00012B/496